D0409463

SOLID JOYS AND LASTING TREASURE:

AN HISTORICAL COMPANION TO MANY FAVOURITE HYMNS

Solid joys and lasting treasure
None but Sion's children know.
John Newton, 1725–1807

SOLID JOYS AND LASTING TREASURE

AN HISTORICAL COMPANION TO MANY FAVOURITE HYMNS

by
Tyler Whittle

ROSS ANDERSON PUBLICATIONS

Published in 1985 by
Ross Anderson Publications Limited
Larkhill House
160 St. Georges Road
Bolton
BL1 2PJ

British Library Cataloguing in Publication Data
Whittle, Tyler
    Solid joys and lasting treasure: an historical
    companion to many favourite hymns.
    1. Hymns, English—History and criticism
    I. Title
    264'.2'0922   BV312

    ISBN 0–86360–022–0

Photoset in Linotron Plantin by
Northern Phototypesetting Co., Bolton
and printed and bound in Great Britain by
Kingprint of Richmond

CONTENTS

LIST OF
ILLUSTRATIONS

ACKNOWLEDGMENTS

For permission to consult and quote from material in the Hatfield House Archives I am indebted to the Marquis of Salisbury, K.G., as I am to Mr Paul Yeates-Edwards, Fellows' Librarian at Winchester College for a sight of his most useful English Church History – a Bibliography.

I also owe thanks to Miss Helen Webb for her help as a librarian, and to Mr Michael Malone, who commissioned the book, edited and published it, and who, together with Mrs Rita Bratt and her team, ensured that the hand-written manuscript so speedily reached the galley-proof stage they have probably set up a record in the now notoriously sluggish business of book publication.

Finally I want to express my gratitude to those who have joined me in my hunt over this rather unusual piece of literary territory; to Mr Mark Bence-Jones of Glenville for his work on Irish families and houses; to the Reverend Canon Alan Coldwells for his usual patient and painstaking proof-reading; to Mr Gore Vidal for information on the nineteenth-century American background; to Mrs Francis Cooper of Markree for copious material on the site which inspired 'All things bright and beautiful'; to Lady Denham, who has a particular interest in the book's title; to the great-nephew of Mrs Alexander, Major Travers King, for valuable information on the family; to Mrs Leslie Mackay for foraying to Hatfield and making digests and copies of letters there; to Mr Michael Maclagan, Richmond Herald, for advice on the Humphreys and Howard families; to Canon Michael and Mrs Rylands for much on Malpas and Bishop Heber; to Brigadier W. M. T. Magan and the Very Reverend Dean Patrick Mitchell for the kind loan of reference books; and, as ever, to Mr Michael Shaw, and to my dear family.

June, 1985   Tyler Whittle

Kennedy's portrait of Mrs. Alexander

dedicated to
GEORGE,
The Right Honourable Viscount Tonypandy, P.C., D.C.L.,
formerly Mr. Speaker Thomas of the House of Commons,
with respect and affection
and in friendship.

CHAPTER ONE

BEGINNINGS: IN EVERY CORNER SING

RIGHT from the beginning Christians honoured God with song. St. Paul urged members of the first church at Ephesus to speak 'one to another in psalms and hymns and spiritual songs, singing and making melody with your heart, to the Lord'. He did the same to the Church at Colossae. And he and St. Silas, wrongly imprisoned at Philippi, spent the night praying and singing hymns to God until an earthquake providentially released them.

From Jewry there was the rich inheritance of the Psalter. Attributed to King David, during whose reign the oldest might have been composed, the psalms were an accumulation of devotion and praise from many, many sources, and over a very long period. They made God alive to his people and explained his law; and, covering almost all man's experience of his maker, they acknowledged the Divine Attributes, God's majesty, loving-kindness, his power and his mercy, his justice, his munificence as a provider. To the psalms were added canticles, or little psalms, and a variety of hymns. Some of the last were in the Syrian mode using metre or chants which were verbally rhythmic, and sung perhaps in one of the two forms of Aramaic, the language used by Christ himself. Others were declaimed in the somewhat formal style of the Greeks. Probably most were in Latin, and not the sinewy, carefully-scanned Latin of the classical poets, but in lines that loosely scanned and which allowed for the introduction of rhyming, an essential aid to those with bad memories.

A first, perhaps the very first, non-Christian reference to such praise of the Christian God was made by Philo (20 BC–AD 40), an inept Jewish ambassador to the Emperor Caligula, but so successful in his writings he was known as the Jewish Plato, and the

Alexandrian Greeks immortalised him with their approbation, quipping 'either Plato Philonizes or Philo Platonizes'. This felicitous writer noted the responsorial chanting of the Christians. Sixty or so years later precisely the same subject was mentioned by Pliny the Younger, a poet and orator, but principally remembered as the writer of masterly letters, who was appointed Governor of Bithynia, a Roman province on the littoral of the Black Sea with a frontier to the south of mountain ranges, a province famous in the Empire for timber and fine cheeses. Pliny was Governor from AD 111 until he died two years afterwards, and he reported back to the Emperor Trajan that followers of the Christian cult rose early on a certain fixed day of every week to greet the dawn with a hymn of praise to their Saviour; all singing *invicem*, following one after another, what we would now call antiphonally.

Our knowledge of such hymns is slight. One of them, a very early Greek hymn of the third-century or earlier, was mentioned by St. Basil in the fourth-century, and evidently was deeply rooted in the ancient Hebrew custom of blessing the evening lamp. Miraculously, it is still used at Vespers by the Greek Church when the lamps are lighted for that evening service. A translation by Robert Bridges is sung in the Western Church as the fine evening hymn:

> 'O gladsome light, O grace
> Of God the Father's face,
> The eternal splendour wearing.'

But few primitive hymns have such a long and distinguished pedigree; most, inevitably, were ephemeral. Those that stood the best chance of survival were repetitious and had more than a mere local appeal. They had the dual purpose to laud God with song and to edify his people. Because heretics cleverly wrote hymns to spread their erroneous doctrine, the Church replied with orthodox hymns. The Council at Laodicea in Phrygia, held at some time between 360 and 381, forbade the use of non-Scriptural texts, but it was a difficult discipline to impose.

Probably St. Ambrose (340–97) had the greatest influence of all on hymnody in the Western Church. Even by the standards of his day he had a conspicuously successful career. Of a noble Roman family, he rose to be governor of Liguria, in which province there fell Milan, a Western Imperial seat. During the conflict between heretics and the orthodox, he showed humanity to the former while clinging to the latter, and had such plain sense that, on the death of the Archbishop, the Milanesi acclaimed him as successor. In the words of Gibbon: 'At the age of 34, and before he had received the Sacrament of Baptism, Ambrose, to his own surprise, and to that of the world, was suddenly transformed from a governor to an archbishop.' Christened, Ordained, and Consecrated all in one day, he firmly led the Church in Cisalpine Gaul for twenty-three years. Many grand hymns are attributed to him; among them 'O splendour of God's glory bright', 'Creator of the earth and sky', and 'O Trinity of blessed light', and he had enormous influence on the writing of hymns. First of all, he declared they should be sung in praise of God. Petition was acceptable; so was the honouring of the saints and the keeping of feasts, fasts, and solemnities; and thus, willy nilly, converts were instructed in the Faith.

The precepts of St. Ambrose were faithfully followed by his contemporaries and successors. There was Prudentius (c. 348–413), like St. Ambrose a lawyer, but Spanish, and a cloistered monk from the age of fifty-seven, who wrote many great hymns, nine still in regular use; the best known, perhaps, his Christmas hymn 'Of the Father's heart begotten' and his hymn for the Epiphany, 'Bethlehem, of noblest cities'. Then there was Venatius Fortunatus (c. 530–609), an Italian who moved north to France and became Bishop of Poitiers in the Gallican Church; author of the office hymns for Passiontide, 'The Royal banners forward go', 'Sing, my tongue, the glorious battle' and 'Thirty years among us dwelling', and the Easter processional 'Hail thee, Festival Day! blest day that art hallowed forever'.

Far to the north, in the rude kingdom of Northumbria, which, by the eighth-century, touched both the Irish and North Seas and stretched south from Edinburgh almost to the High Peak in Derbyshire, there lived St. Bede the Venerable. He was a monk of SS. Peter and Paul, entering the twin monastery of Wearmouth and Jarrow at the age of seven, being made deacon at eighteen, and ordained priest at twenty-nine. Bede seldom travelled far, and never outside the kingdom, yet he exercised enormous influence over his age as a biblical scholar, historian, teacher and writer. He is remembered chiefly as the author of the *Ecclesiastical History of the English Nation*, and called 'the Father of English History'. A later historian described him as 'able to dazzle the whole earth with the brilliance of his learning'; and the Pope wrote to Bede's Abbot to ask if he could be sent to Rome to enlighten the Papal Court. It was not Bede's way. He loved teaching as much as learning, and he loved to quote the great St. Ambrose to his pupils: 'I have not lived so as to be ashamed to live among you, nor am I afraid to die because we have a good God.' He taught to the last, distributing keepsakes to his pupils and to his fellow monks on his deathbed; little gifts of peppercorns and incense and rough handkerchiefs. In the list of his works is a *Book of Hymns*, mostly compiled, but some dozen have been ascribed to his pen. Appropriately he died on the vigil of the Ascension in 735 aged 62, for he is now best remembered for his Ascensiontide hymn, 'Sing we triumphant hymns of praise'.

There was also the Ambrosian feeling for putting praise at the centre of hymns in the Byzantine Church, which emerged as the Church of the Eastern Empire. It differed from the Western Catholic Church in its liturgy and practice, but gave us many notable hymns. There was, for example, 'A great and mighty wonder' by St. Germanus (634–734), patriarch of Constantinople until an Emperor, described by Gibbon as a 'martial peasant with a hatred of images', drove him from office because of his devotion to the sacred Icons. Another hymnwriter, St. John of Damascus, called 'last of the Greek fathers' and victim of yet another eastern imperial iconoclast, Constantine, lived hidden in a monastery between Jerusalem and the Dead Sea to a great old age. By all accounts it was a dreadful place. It still is; a lonely, sunbaked, forbidding building on an eminence above the Kedron Valley, so wild that the jackals at the feet of the gorge scavenge on rubbish hurled out by the monks. It was here, in the terrible wilderness, that St. John enriched the Church by his Easter hymns 'The day of the Resurrection' and 'Come ye faithful, raise the strain'.

The hymns of the first millenium were hymns of stature.

It is as fruitless to speculate on what songs they sang as on the songs sung by the Sirens or to guess at the Music of the Spheres. An ancient roll, dating from the third century, showed the simple melody and tone with Greek characters, but hundreds of years passed before notation, as we know it, was invented. Still further delayed than the modern staff was the discovery of polyphony; that two or more notes of a different pitch might be sounded simultaneously to make music. But tradition has it that hymn tunes were often of secular origin; borrowed from local songs known in the street.*

After the firm rule over Europe by Charlemagne, his empire

---

* The tradition still exists. The most popular musical setting now in England to George Duffield's martial hymn, 'Stand up, stand up for Jesus' was first the melody of a contemporary American ballad ''Tis dawn, the lark is singing'. The well-known French melody *Au Clair de la Lune* was used for the Evangelical hymn 'If I come to Jesus' by Mrs. Van Alstyne. 'Marching through Georgia' is used for the modern hymn of Christopher Idle 'Come and see the shining hope that Christ's apostles saw', and the tunes of *The Londonderry Air* and *Ye banks*

disintegrated into petty kingdoms, duchies, and principalities. The Church suffered schism between East and West, Greek and Latin, but barbarity was stayed and civilisation maintained because it was the power of Christianity to infiltrate peoples and be absorbed by them. Goths, Franks, Saxons, Russians, Norsemen, all came to accept the Creeds. The last case was the most dramatic. The descent by Vikings upon England, Ireland, Iceland, Normandy, Southern Italy and Sicily had a lasting influence upon the lands and peoples they seized but the conquerors were themselves ultimately conquered by their new environment. By the end of the tenth century they had abjured their bloodthirsty pantheon and become Christian. It was far away from Scandinavia that they built the magnificent cathedrals that still stand today. Within two hundred years their own homelands were the scene of inter-tribal wars; then, virtually bled to death, merely the home of an ignorant heathen peasantry.

Those who sang in the great new buildings of the Latin Church were chiefly monks or nuns. They sang the choir offices on feasts and holy days and their vigils, and their worship, called the Monastic Hours, employed the Psalter, antiphons and an increasing number of hymns. Thus it followed that many of the greatest hymns of the Middle Ages were written by Religious in vows.

Peter Abélard (1079–1142) was one, and perhaps the most unfortunate of all. Scion of a noble family in Brittany, he decided to devote his life to the study and teaching of theology and philosophy. Therefore, as all other clerks, he was in minor orders from which as a natural progression he would have proceeded to be ordained priest and most probably consecrated bishop. Events decreed otherwise. Abélard was always at the centre of disputes between scholars. His range of knowledge and enquiry was vast, and he was an inspiring teacher, but at the age of about thirty-five, when lecturing in Paris, he was entrusted by a Canon of Notre Dame with the education of his intellectual and beautiful niece Héloïse, and they fell deeply in love. The history of Abélard and Héloïse holds as sure a place in the mediaeval romances as the legend of Tristan and Iseult. But Héloïse was a real woman; she bore a child; and her enraged uncle arranged for the man who had deceived him to be set upon in the

---

and braes O bonnie Doon are the setting of two more unillustrious modern sacred songs. Moreover special arrangements may be temporarily contrived. For example, in the eighties an artificial marriage of Elgar's *Land of Hope and Glory*, played by a cathedral organ and full brass orchestra to accompany the hymn 'At the Name of Jesus', was the apogee of a farewell service to honour a colourful and controversial Bishop in the Church of England, Mervyn Stockwood.

streets and castrated. It was a triple punishment; causing humiliation, and the certainty that Abélard would father no other children; and effectively preventing him from achieving the eminence his intellect deserved, because, by Church law, only a whole man could be ordained priest or consecrated bishop. Héloïse took the veil as a nun. Abélard the deacon became a laybrother in the Parisian abbey of St. Denis. His fortunes sank lower when a Church Council condemned his first theological work. It was ceremoniously burnt in public. Thereafter Abélard appeared to invite disaster. Instead of getting on with his fellow monks he openly condemned their worldliness. Then he added to their fury by questioning the validity of the Abbey's claim that their beloved patron St. Denis was the same person as Dionysius the Areopagite, first Bishop of Athens. Moreover he proved he was right. This was too much for the community. He was driven out and built himself a hermitage at Nogent, but the life of a recluse was not for him. Students sought him out and found him and they remained. Abélard's hermitage became a noted school of theology, named by him for the Holy Paraclete.

More and more his controversial teaching inspired a following and provoked opposition. He was virtually exiled by being made Abbot of St. Gildas de Ruys in Brittany. His house of the Paraclete was given to Héloïse and her community of sisters. Still he was dogged by misfortune. His own corrupt monks tried to murder him. The Councils of the Church condemned his doctrines. Finally he was found guilty of heresy by a Council and by the Pope. His autobiography in letters is appositely named *Historia Calamitatum*. He was persuaded to appeal against the condemnation and he set out on the long way to Rome, but, worn out with the conflict, and weighed down both by chagrin and by the death of his beloved Héloïse, he died of exhaustion by the wayside. He was at the advanced age of sixty-three. It is said he was buried in the grave of Héloïse. Certainly it is claimed today that their remains lie together in the Père-Lachaise cemetery. As a gift for Héloïse and her nuns Abélard had compiled a hymn book, some of the contents being his own work. Two are still in use: 'Alone thou goest forth, Oh Lord', and the more famous mixture of exuberance and nostalgia:

> 'O what fair joy and their glory must be,
> Those endless Sabbaths the blessed ones see!
> Crown for the valiant; to weary ones rest;
> God shall be all and in all ever blessed. . . .'

The cornerstone of Abélard's thought was to give a logically argued foundation to Christianity and thus refute heresies; but the guardians of the received truths of the fathers saw his teaching as choplogic and casuistry which endangered the faith of less clever souls. His most consistent and bitter opponent was Bernard of Clairvaux, also of noble birth and a monk, and a writer of hymns. Bernard grew from being a reserved lad with a talent for composing ribald verses to be an austere Cistercian Abbot with a following so large and dedicated that he lived to be oracle of the Western world, and founder of 160 Cistercian houses, to see one of his monks ascend the throne of St. Peter as Pope Eugenius III, and to have all Europe as his parish. Never out of pain, racked with an undiagnosed malaise, and apparently torn in two by his desire to lead a solitary, contemplative life, and calls upon his quicksilver mind by princes and pontiffs, Bernard was one of the most outstanding men of the Middle Ages. He remains controversial; seen as either the relentless vilifier of those he considered dangerous to true catholicity and order who 'trembled at the freedom of his apostolic censures', or as the timid, unambitious abbot who gave such shrewd judgments to those who asked for them and so spoke to his monks of the Love of God that within twenty-one years of his death he was canonised. The same pen that wrote the deposition of earthly rulers and ordered the replacement of bishops, also wrote *The Steps of Humility* and this hymn long ascribed to him;

> 'Jesu, the very thought of thee
> With sweetness fills my breast;
> But sweeter far thy face to see
> And in thy presence rest.'

The objects of St. Bernard's disapproval were many and various. One, Peter Abélard, has been spoken of. Another, disliked because he was a monk of Cluny and St. Bernard detested Cluniacs, was also named Bernard and was also canonised, and he must have been an almost exact contemporary. *The Catholic Encyclopedia* reports of St. Bernard of Cluny: 'His parentage, native land, and education are hidden in obscurity.' Nevertheless he obtained a lasting name by a work of some three thousand stately verses entitled *On the Contempt of the World*. They are written in a unique metre of great ingenuity*, which to some is awkward, to others one of the loveliest Mediaeval measures. The work is important because it is a satire against the moral disorders of the latter half of the 12th century. Not even the

---

* A dactylic hexameter in three sections, devoid of caesura, with tailed rhymes between the first two sections.

Papacy is spared by St. Bernard of Cluny as he denounced, in poetic wrath, the moral apostasy of his generation. Admirers rate him as close in genius to that of Dante's pictures of Heaven and Hell, but his chief importance to us is because of the centos in the poem which have become universally admired in translation. One of his hymns, in particular, remains after seven hundred years, a spectacular memorial to an ill-known saint; 'Jerusalem the golden, with milk and honey blest'.

It is not surprising that Jerusalem recaptured, purified and beautified, was used to symbolise Heaven. During the lifetime of Abélard and the two St. Bernards Europe was increasingly menaced by Islam. The Turks had invaded Asia Minor and founded the kingdom of Rum. Moors came to rule from Aragon, in Portugal, to Baska in North Africa, and from Baska ran the Fatimate Caliphate all the way to Jerusalem, a Caliphate to be succeeded by the Empire of Saladin and the Ayubites. As long as and whenever the holy sepulchre was in pagan hands Christians sought to recover it. Right into the thirteenth century there were expeditions large and small, pious and merely adventurous; and, by the end of that time, Europe had changed beyond belief. The spread of monasticism and the coming of the friars, Franciscan and Dominican, Carmelites and Augustinians, vitalised the Church. It was a watershed which marked the intellectual achievements of the Schoolmen and a great upsurge in trade and exploration and the making of colonies. The maritime republics of Italy prospered in an extraordinary fashion. Marco Polo, the Venetian, travelled to the court of the Great Khan and old trading routes were reopened and new ones made. There was also a movement of ideas and the germ was sown of what later became the Renaissance. There was not yet a corresponding outburst of hymns, chiefly because few people were literate, the inscribing of copies was a time- and painstaking labour, and there was a limit to the number of office hymns which, with the Psalter, could be learned by rote.

Nevertheless some good hymns have come down from this era, notably 'At the Cross her station keeping, Stood the mournful Mother weeping', a composite work but generally ascribed to Jacopone da Todi (1230–1304). This is now considered as a hymn for Passiontide and for singing during the devotion called The Stations of the Cross, but originally it was a sacred poem intended for private devotion rather than in the Services of the Church. It achieved great and lasting fame on the revival of the Flagellant movement in the 14th century for it became the popular song of the Battenti, hooded men who moved in procession from place to place in Holy Week,

The hymn 'Jerusalem the golden', written by the severe moralist St. Bernard of Cluny and translated by John Mason Neale (*Church Hymns and Tunes, 1874 Edition*)

beating or affecting to beat each other as a mark of penance. The sorrow of Our Lady witnessing the Passion is, perhaps, so convincing because of the tragic circumstances in Jacopone's own life. Born of the patrician Umbrian family dei Benedetti, he practised law and married a gentlewoman named Vanna whom he dearly loved. Only a few days after the marriage, during a festa and whilst they were at the theatre, Vanna was suddenly and tragically killed before his eyes. He at once put on the simple habit of a Franciscan tertiary, and for ten years attempted to assuage his grief by strict mortification and acts of penitence. At the end of that time he became a Minorite, the group of Franciscans who kept most strictly to the rule of St. Francis. He wrote a good deal in his native tongue, more than one hundred *laudi spirituali*, and some penetrating satires on Church abuses, quarrelling especially with those who made the vow of poverty a laughing-stock. It brought him into direct conflict with Pope Boniface VIII whom he attacked with a remarkable power of invective. Inevitably he was imprisoned, and only released when Boniface died. Three years later, on a Christmas Day, Jacopone himself died in a small conventual house between Perugia and Todi.

Fifty years afterwards a compatriot was born in Upper Valdarno, then and now one of the most beautiful parts of Tuscany. He was named Bianco and of Sienna because it was down in that city that he spent his boyhood learning about the wool trade. At seventeen he entered an order of mystics, and wrote lyrics and hymns which, on the whole, do not match the stature of Jacopone, but he did leave one great hymn invoking the love of God: 'Come down, O Love divine.' Probably he died in the first part of the fifteenth century.

A gifted and far better known contemporary was Thomas à Kempis (1379–1471) author of the ascetical treatise *Imitation of Christ*, many tracts on the monastic life, books on the spiritual life, sermons and hymns – though some of the last were not discovered until the nineteenth century. Born into a German peasant's family in Kempen near Dusseldorf, he had the advantage of a literate mother who sent both her sons John and Thomas to the famous school Deventer in the Netherlands. Thence they both went to the poor Augustinian Priory near Zwolle where they lived out their lives as Canons copying and writing manuscripts. To be the author (inevitably disputed) of a work which has been translated into more languages than any other save the Bible is fame enough; and more than enough for the placid religious who led so uneventful a life. But he wrote for us two hymns, 'Light's abode, celestial Salem' and 'O Love, how deep! how broad! how high!'. He lived to the great age of ninety-one. There is no sign of the Priory today where he did his inspired work. Two hundred years after his death, the Elector of Cologne ordered that Thomas's bones be moved to Zwolle. There they lie now, in a river port with a large fish market and one of the most famous cattle markets in all Holland.

The year 1453 when the Saracens seized Constantinople, St. Sophia became a mosque, and Greek scholars fled to Italy for refuge, is a convenient date to mark the Renaissance. In fact it began long before, and continued long after, because the influence of the new learning was not felt in any one place with any immediacy, nor for any specified length of time. It was likewise with the Reformation. Luther nailing his ninety-five Theses to a church door in Wittenberg in October 1517 is taken as a convenient date of the commencement of the Reformation; that separation in western Christendom graver by far than the thirty-nine years' struggle between rival popes in Avignon and Rome. It was a religious revolution that had moral, social, economic and nationalistic causes as well as doctrinal, and it began long before 1517 and continued long after, even after the Counter Reformation which the Roman Catholic church made to put itself in order. The first use of printing, which coincided with Renaissance and Reformation, had a profound effect upon both, and in Germany especially printed books of hymns in the vernacular helped to spread the new religion. Both Moravians and Lutherans perceived their usefulness. Martin Luther himself, though highly-strung, in morbid dread of concupiscence, given to depression, and allegedly to doubts as to the rightness of replacing 'the teeth and fangs' of one tiger for another; an ex-monk said to beshrewed by the ex-nun he married; and cruelly afflicted by an infection of the lower bowel; yet had a wonderful gift of language, and, rising above his troubles, translated the Scriptures into robust German and wrote some memorable hymns. More than thirty-seven have been ascribed to him, and, being a lover of music and a talented musician, he also composed. His paraphrase of Psalm 46, *Ein' feste Burg* – 'God is a stronghold and a tower' – of 1529 instantly took an unrivalled position in German hymnody; and was first translated into English by Bishop Miles Coverdale in his *Goostly Psalmes* about 1538. It is calculated that between 1524 and 1546 almost one hundred hymnals of translations of Latin hymns as well as fresh ones all put to popular melodies were published in Germany.

In England, Our Lady's Dowry, where the Church had always been a trifle headstrong and never gave total obedience to edicts from

Rome, and where the Reformation took its own quite unique course, hymns were esteemed by the cultured, but the common people preferred their carols. Other nations, of course, had carols, notably the French and Dutch and German, but none is of such rich variety as the English. A jubilant song with the religious impulse, the carol was not quite a hymn, nor yet like a sequence sung at Mass, and it was particularly English. By no means as now confined to the Christmas season, carols answered the ordinary Englishman's need both for something less grand than the Latin office hymns, and for livelier music than plainsong. Quite spontaneously carols rose with ballads in the fifteenth century after the strict regimen of the Dark and early Middle Ages and they were sung until an even grimmer regimen was prescribed in 1647, when Christmas and other jolly festivities were abolished by Act of Parliament and fasts were put in their place.* The carols of these two centuries had catchy melodies and simple, easily learnt lines. They were the songs of the people, almost always in their own language, but sometimes studded with remembered Latin phrases such as 'In dulci jubilo' and 'Gloria in Excelsis'. Some were associated with mime and dance. Some were simple narrations of sacred legends.

The stricter reformers invariably professed exclusive use of the Psalter and paraphrased passages of scripture. Those with the largest influence were Calvin, the most merciless of theocrats, and John Knox, a runty Scot of humble origin who suffered from the twin agonies of the stone and dyspepsia, and yet had a sense of humour, and who survived the irons and the lash of life as a galley-slave to become virtual ruler of Scotland. They too, with Zwingli of Zürich, would accept nothing but versified or metrical canticles and psalms. In 1547 a partial Psalter in French appeared in Geneva. Most of the translations were made years before by the French royal poet Clement Marot, who in his time had been famous for salacious satires at the Court of France. This would scarcely have commended the Psalter to Calvin but for the writer's impeccable protestant credentials. Poor Marot, branded as a Huguenot, fled for his life from France only to die almost at once in the safety of Switzerland. Many of the settings were composed by another Parisian, Louis

---

* This period of puritanism was as severe as the iconoclasm which cursed the Eastern Church nine hundred years before. Works of religious art were defiled or smashed; the savagery of the Old Testament was re-enacted by Parliamentary soldiers who, as 'chasteners of the Lord', slew without quarter, even swording women close to confinement with pitiless zeal, and who had Scriptural Baptismal names ranging from Praise the Lord Barebones, for whom a Parliament was named, to Standfast-on-high Stringer of Crowhurst and Fly-Fornication-Richardson, Christened in the Sussex country church of Waldron.

Bourgois: a talented musician who left home to be an adherent of Calvin; and who, it appeared, received small thanks for his trouble. He acted as cantor, trainer of choristers, and provided music for the psalms as they were paraphrased, but Bourgois enraged his employers by altering some well-known tunes, always a chancy thing to do in every generation, and he was actually thrown into prison. Even when released, he went on attracting disaster, and eventually he was forced to escape back to Paris, where he disappeared, leaving no trace. In 1562, twelve months after Bourgois vanished, the first complete Psalter became available in Geneva. Calvin decreed musical harmony was not far from idolatrous, certainly a dilution of pure worship, but he permitted some form of chanting. But, two years after, exhausted by overwork, he died and, once buried in an unmarked grave in a common cemetery, the rigour of his discipline began at once to diminish.

John Knox his disciple had already returned to Scotland prepared to tolerate godly music though not, probably, *The Gude and Godlie Ballatis* published by three Wedderburn brothers in 1546, which were mostly 'Luther dytements in (to) Scottish meeter'. The first complete Metrical Psalter of the Kirk was composed of eighty-seven psalms of an Anglo-Genevan book written mostly by William Kethe, plus 'borrowings' from England, and twenty-one by native Scots; and it came into general use from 1564 and, with some amendments, was the official Scots' Psalter until 1650 when the present paraphrases were adopted.

In England the first complete edition of the Psalter, the so-called 'Old Version', appeared in 1562. It was principally the work of Thomas Sternhold, a court poet who, for the most part, used the metre of *Chevy Chase*, a ballad long familiar to the ordinary people of England. John Hopkins, a Suffolk country parson, also contributed seven metrical psalms and a number were borrowed from the Anglo-Genevan edition. The whole, set to a mixed bag of tunes, became a standard edition and an appendix was added in 1564. One of the melodies of Louis Bourgois, called 'Old Hundredth', sung to Kethe's paraphrase of Psalm 100,★ has survived for centuries as the hymn 'All people that on earth do dwell', and it is still sung all over the earth. The metrical 'Gloria Patri' or Doxology to the familiar tune has many historical associations. In the first years of the Methodist movement it was promptly sung by the whole assembly on the conversion, or 'turning to Christ', by any member of the

---

★ In the early editions of the Anglo-Genevan Psalter it was set to the paraphrase of Psalm 134.

congregation, and, on one occasion, when Charles Wesley was preaching not far from Haworth where the Brontë sisters later lived, his discourse was interrupted by converts no fewer than eighty-five times, and the Doxology was sung. It has, moreover, long been a custom in the drained fenlands of East Anglia to signal the end of a grave danger by flooding, tempest or, worst of all, a 'stolen Tide' from the Wash. As the waters settle, and the danger passes, the Doxology is started and taken up by those who have struggled successfully with the elements and sung in unison in a huge chorus all over the Fens:

> 'To Father, Son and Holy Ghost,
> The God whom earth and heav'n adore,
> From men and from the Angel-host
> Be praise and glory evermore.'

The 'Old Version' of Sternhold and Hopkins was the predominant singing book in England for 134 years; indeed it was customarily bound in with the Book of Common Prayer and was not superseded until the end of the seventeenth century, a period when people were as absorbed in religious controversy as the Victorians were with death. A fresh version approved by the House of Commons was rejected by the House of Lords. The choice of the peers was thereupon thrown out by the Commons. In 1696 the 'New Version' was published, and 'allowed and permitted' by the King in Council. Its authors were a strange pair of Irish poetasters. The elder, Nicholas Brady, was from a military family in co. Cork who was to hold good preferment in England, marry a daughter of the Archdeacon of Cork, and become Chaplain of a regiment of horse as well as Chaplain to William and Mary and to Queen Anne. Besides his contributions to the 'New Version', he published a translation of Virgil's *Aeneid*, and a high drama about the Goths and Vandals, later recast as Portuguese and Spaniards, named 'The Rape, or the Innocent Imposters', which first appeared on the boards at the Theatre Royal in 1692.

Brady's fellow psalmist, Nahum Tate, was a Dubliner, born the son of an Irish divine named Faithful Teate. He appears to have changed his name to Tate on emigrating to seek his poetical fortune in London. There he translated from French and Latin for publishers; for example, a cautionary treatise named *Syphilis, or a Poetical History of the French Disease*, which, fifteen or so years later, was read by the young John and Charles Wesley for their edification. He also wrote many poems, one, '*Panacea – a poem on Tea*', being still remembered, and turned out original but second-rate dramas, a farce

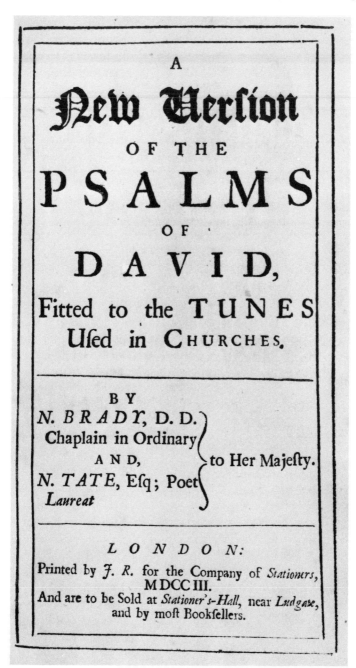

A

New Version

OF THE

PSALMS

OF

DAVID,

Fitted to the TUNES
Ufed in CHURCHES.

BY

N. BRADY, D. D.
Chaplain in Ordinary
AND,
N. TATE, Efq; Poet
Laureat

} to Her Majefty.

LONDON:

Printed by *J. R.* for the Company of *Stationers,*
MDCCIII.
And are to be Sold at *Stationer's-Hall,* near *Ludgate,*
and by moft Bookfellers.

The title page to the *New Version*, 'allowed and permitted' in 1696 and published by
the Irish poetasters, Brady and Tate

45

PSALM xxxiv.

PSALM XXXIV

1. THro' all the changing Scenes of Life,
      in Trouble and in Joy,
   The Praises of my God shall still
      my Heart and Tongue employ.
2. Of his Deliv'rance I will boaft,
      till all that are diftreft,
   From my Example Comfort take,
      and charm their Griefs to reft.
3. O magnifie the Lord with me;
      with me exalt his Name :
4. When in Diftrefs to him I call'd,
      He to my refcue came.
5. Their drooping Hearts were foon refrefh'd,
      who look'd to him for Aid ;
   Defir'd Succefs in ev'ry Face,
      a chearful Air difplaid.
6. " Behold, (fay they) behold the Man
      whom Providence reliev'd ;
   " The Man fo dang'roufly befet,
      " fo wond'roufly retriev'd !
7. The Hofts of God emcamp around
      the Dwellings of the Juft ;
   Deliv'rance he affords to all
      who on his Succour truft.
8. O make but Tryal of his Love,
      experience will decide
   How blefs'd they they are, and only they,
      who in his Truth confide.
9. Fear him, ye Saints, and you will then
      have nothing elfe to fear ;
   Make you his Service your Delight,
      your Wants fhall be his Care.
10. While hungry Lions lack their Prey,
      the Lord will Food provide
   For fuch as put their Truft in him,
      and fee their Needs fupply'd.

PART

Part of one of 'poor' Tate's notable contributions to the *New Version*

entitled 'Cuckold's Haven' which pleased that kindly critic Charles II, and busied himself adding to or imitating or altering existing texts by such well known dramatists as Dryden, Webster, Fletcher and even Shakespeare. His tinkering with 'King Lear', with a happy ending in which the Fool is omitted entirely and Cordelia escapes death to marry Edgar, was played in the theatres until after Queen Victoria's accession to the throne. In 1692 the Poet Laureate and Historiographer Royal, Thomas Shadwell, died of an overdose of opium, having cautiously 'recommended to God by prayer' beforehand, leaving rings to his dearest friends and instructions that he be buried in flannel. That Christmas Eve the sovereigns William and Mary appointed Nahum Tate to the Laureateship. Robert Southey rated Tate 'lowest of the laureates except his predecessor' but, though it is difficult to separate the two authors in the Tate and Brady 'New Version', which was used in an English church as late as 1879, two which stand out above the doggerel are generally attributed to Tate, 'Through all the changing scenes of life' and 'As pants the hart for cooling streams'. He also wrote the world-famous carol 'While shepherds watched their flocks by night'. Poor Tate, as Pope described him, had a sorrowful appearance and was usually in a muddle. He died embarrassingly and unexpectedly whilst hiding from his creditors in the Royal Mint.

The modern hymn in English evolved not only from translation of ancient texts and foreign sacred songs, and metrical psalms written in the vernacular; it was also seeded in the devotional work of cultured English poets, not usually intended for use in church. That many came to be used in the public liturgy was sometimes because of the quality of the tunes composed by musicians of such high order as Orlando Gibbons (1583–1625), Jeremiah Clarke (1669–1707) and William Croft (1677–1727). Gibbons was a genius who, besides composing intricate pieces for the virginals, marvellous madrigals and motets, wrote anthems and hymn-tunes which include settings of 'Forth in thy name, O Lord I go' and 'Peace, perfect peace'. All three were organists and sworn 'gentlemen extraordinary of the Chapel Royal'; and Croft succeeded Clarke when that gentleman, in a state of depression and for hopeless love of an unattainable lady, decided to end it all by drowning or shooting himself. Beside a pond he tossed a coin to decide which it should be, and the coin fell exactly on its side embedded in the mud. Too disgusted to accept this as a providential sign, he returned to his house on the site of the present-day Chapter House of St. Paul's Cathedral, and there he shot himself to death. Clarke composed the tunes for 'The head that once was crowned with thorns' and 'Immortal love for ever full', besides many other fine hymn tunes and anthems. Dr. Croft, related to Judge Jeffreys, the infamous hanger, transporter and whipper of rebels, and himself a suspected Jacobite although in the Royal Household of the Hanoverian George, led a surprisingly urbane existence,* turning out a plethora of choir anthems including *Thirty for State Occasions*, and the tunes of many many hymns, amongst them 'Happy are they, they that love God', 'O worship the King, all glorious above' and, most famous of all, 'O God, our help in ages past'.

Some of the most famous names in literature contributed to English hymnody of the period.† There was John Donne (1573–1631) who gave to the Christian church one of its loveliest mystic hymns. It begins:

> 'Wilt thou forgive that sin, by man begun,
>   Which was my sin though it were done before?
> Wilt though forgive that sin, through which I run,
>   And do run still, though still I do deplore?
> What thou has done, thou hast not done,
>   For I have more.'

The quicksilver, metaphysical poet who wrote these verses had been born a Roman Catholic, related through his mother to St. Thomas More and to two uncles who suffered for the ancient faith. His own brother, too, was imprisoned in the Clink for giving refuge to a Roman Catholic priest. There the brother died of gaol fever; the priest was hanged, drawn and quartered at Tyburn. Despite this sombre backcloth to his life, Donne's youth was giddy. He joined the mad expedition to Cadiz led by the Earl of Essex. He was known at the courts of Queen Elizabeth I and James I as a poet of high intellect, and appointed secretary to the Lord Keeper. But, then, he lost his heart to a sixteen year old girl and married her against her guardian's wish. It cost him his prestigious post. He struggled into middle life, an ornament at Court for his gifts of intellect and his talents, but received no office of profit. James I decided he was to be given Church preferment or none at all, but Donne declined. Finally he agreed to become an Anglican Divine, and almost at once was accepted as the

---

* Articles on Dr. Croft in the *Dictionary of National Biography* and *Grove's Dictionary of Music* state he died childless. Either the writers are ignorant of or have overlooked a previous connection made by him before his second marriage by whom he had a child or children.

---

† Poets also wrote their own 'hymns' which were never sung and never intended to be sung; e.g. Richard Crashaw's *Hymn to the Name and Honour of the Admirable St. Teresa*, Milton's hymns from *The Ode on the Morning of Christ's Nativity* and *Paradise Lost*, and Dryden's *A Song for St. Cecilia's Day*.

The urbane and musical Dr. Croft (*National Portrait Gallery*)

John Donne, the giddy youth turned leading preacher and metaphysical poet (*National Portrait Gallery*)

foremost preacher of his day. His conversion was not so dramatic a reversal as it would have been the century after. It should be remembered that Laud, as Archbishop of Canterbury, was offered a Cardinal's Hat by a Pope hopeful he might quietly bring the English Church back into the Roman fold. And Donne's intellect would not have permitted mere expediency. He was able to reconcile his ordination into the Church of England and his holding of several parochial livings as well as the Deanery of St. Paul's with his theological beliefs. The death of his beloved wife brought from him some of his finest verses. Then he himself contracted a form of typhoid fever which emaciated him, and he wasted away for eight long years until he died, yet, industriously, he wrote his magnificent sermons and used his pen as a poet almost to the last.

George Herbert (1593–1633) was a second contemporary courtier who ultimately became a divine, but his background was grander. The Herberts of the Welsh Marches were a noble family with several branches. George was the fifth son of Richard and Magdalen of Montgomery Castle, but his father died when he was three leaving seven sons and three daughters. Magdalen Herbert was a woman of great spirit. Herbert's biographer, Isaac Walton, tells us she was the happy mother of 'Job's dispensation' of children 'and as often blessed God that they were neither defective in their shapes or in their reason.' Quite soon she dashingly remarried Lord Danvers who was twenty years younger than she. At Westminster, and afterwards at Trinity College, Cambridge, George Herbert was well liked though considered a little conceited and snobbish. He had yet to pupate and produce the imago which all recall.* He was both courtier and scholar; a musician, singing and playing the lute and viol; a favourite of James I who liked intelligence as well as prettyness; a friend of the poets Donne and Wotton; a finished scholar who attracted the notice of Francis Bacon and Lancelot Andrewes; and Fellow of his college. In 1620, the year the Pilgrim Fathers sailed, Herbert was appointed Public Orator of the University. Earlier he had felt a possible vocation to the priesthood, but he became Member of Parliament for Montgomery in 1624, and the Oratorship opened the possibilities of Offices of Profit under the Crown.

But then Herbert came under the influence of Nicholas Ferrar, a

---

* Doubtless Isaac Walton was thinking chiefly of that image when he wrote of Herbert at Westminster 'where the beauties of his pretty behaviour and wit shined and became so eminent and lovely in this his innocent age and that he seemed marked out for piety, and to become the care of Heaven, and of a particular good Angel to guard and guide him.'

luminous, saintly character in the history of the English Church; a layman, never ordained, who strove to return to the best features of the primitive Church and monasticism. He had a profound effect upon Herbert. Coincidentally, King James I died, and illness, possibly the onset of consumption, suggested to Herbert that he should resign his Oratorship. He went to a friend's house in Kent to make a private retreat and consider his position. His hand was rather forced by the gift of a prebendal stall by the Bishop of Lincoln to which was attached the gift of a small estate in Huntingdonshire. Not being ordained, he had to appoint a deputy to perform the priestly duties connected with the offer. Then his mother died, always an emotional time in the life of a sensitive man, and she had wished him to be a clergyman. He fell in love with and married his step-father's cousin, and the new King Charles I presented him with the Rectory of Bemerton at the request of a Herbert cousin, the Earl of Pembroke. It was not great preferment. But Herbert accepted and was made deacon and ordained priest, and proved himself the perfect country parish priest. Twice a week he walked to Salisbury. Daily he said his prayers in his 'pittifull little chappel'. It comes as a surprise to the thousands who know of Herbert's piety and his selfless devotion to the duties of his calling, to discover that he was a country parson for less than three years. In that short time he wrote penetrating and joyous poetry in both Latin and English of the first rank, and proved, by his life, that he was 'a companion to the primitive saints'. All his work was published posthumously, edited by his holy friend Nicholas Ferrar. Amongst his collection of verses intended for private use were some that have been accepted as masterpieces of their kind and are now used as hymns. 'King of Glory, King of Peace' and 'Teach me, my God and King' would alone establish him as a great hymn-writer. But his greatest by far was one from which the title of this chapter is taken. Almost as soon as it was published and came to be used the quatrain was sung by a soloist and the chorus at the beginning and the end of each stanza allowed the congregation to sing with him:

> 'Let all the world in every corner sing,
> My God and King!
> The heavens are not too high,
> His praise may thither fly;
> The earth is not too low,
> His praises there may grow.
> Let all the world in every corner sing,
> My God and King!'

The Effigies of Mr George Herbert: Author of those Sacred Poems called The Temple.

George Herbert, courtier, scholar, musician, perfect parish priest and great hymn-writer (*National Portrait Gallery*)

'Let all the world in every corner sing,
My God and King!
The Church with psalms must shout,
No door can keep them out;
But above all, the heart
Must bear the longest part.
Let all the world in every corner sing,
My God and King!'

The common people lost their carols by order of a bigoted Puritan Parliament. Yet there was a quality about life in seventeenth century England which, despite, or possibly because of, the political and religious earthquakes, allowed some to reflect more deeply upon the mysteries of God and the need to praise Him. George Herbert was its most memorable mystic poet. A far greater poet, second only to Shakespeare, and a totally different man, the humourless, blind Latin Secretary to the Council of State during the Commonwealth, was John Milton (1608–1674). At St. Paul's School at the age of fifteen he wrote two paraphrases of the psalms. One, of Psalm 136, has become a well-known hymn, frequently used at harvest time, 'Let us, with a gladsome mind'. A second, written when he was forty, based on three psalms, is the solemn cento 'The Lord will come and not be slow'.

There were other less inspired poets of the period who left notable hymns. Henry Vaughan (1621–1695), a Welsh physician and minor poet, whose verses were all but forgotten for two hundred years, left 'My soul there is a country'. John Bunyan (1628–1688), was according to one school of thought of an ancient Bedford family occupying the same freehold for centuries; or, according to another, he was a gypsy, a tinker by trade, perforce a soldier in the Civil War, early married, who came to be much influenced by religion. He had command of plain English and knew his Scripture well. He began to write at an early age, his first work having the dismal title 'Sighs from Hell, or the Groans of a Damned Soul', and, as 'Bishop Bunyan', he preached the Gospel with such fervour that he attracted the attention of the authorities. Not being an ordained priest of the Established Church, and as an unlicensed preacher, he was indicted at the assizes for holding 'unlawful meetings and conventicles' and sentenced to imprisonment in Bedford Gaol. There he remained twelve years, enjoying a certain amount of liberty until his gaoler was rebuked and discipline was tightened. There he made long tagged thread laces and wrote four books, one autobiographical. During a second term of imprisonment he wrote the world-famous allegory *Pilgrim's Progress*, the journey of a Christian soul. It was a unique contribution

'Bishop' Bunyan, the most eloquent of prisoners (*National Portrait Gallery*)

to spiritual thinking and to literature, and his characters were
amazingly alive, especially Mr. Valiant-for-the-Truth, Old Honesty
and Mr. Despondency whose daughter was Miss Much-afraid. The
hymn 'He who would valiant be' is the song of Mr. Valiant after his
conversation with Greatheart, and, in slightly modified wording,
remains in every single worthwhile hymn book of the second half of
the twentieth century. It is written in the same metre as many
contemporary ballads and one, 'The Valiant Sailor's Happy return
to his True Love', might well have suggested the song to Bunyan.
Even the familiar tune to which it is set, now called '*Monks Gate*'
because it was 'discovered' by a song collector who lived in the
village of Monks Gate in Sussex, was originally named 'Welcome
Sailor' or 'Valiant' and thus might have been known to Bunyan
himself.

Then there was Bishop Thomas Ken who lived from 1637 to 1711,
at a most momentous time in English history. He was singular in so
many ways. Even his youth was unusual. Losing both parents at a
tender age he was brought up by his sister who was the wife of Isaac
Walton, the biographer and contented author of 'The Compleat
Angler'. Scholarly and of exceptional gifts, Ken was at Winchester
and its sister foundation New College, Oxford, and, as a country
priest, held several livings at which time he wrote most of his
memorable hymns. When preferment came it was as Fellow of
Winchester where he compiled a Manual of Prayers for the scholars,
made a modest Grand Tour with his nephew, and then was
appointed Chaplain to Princess Mary at the Hague. Her stodgy
solemn spouse, the Stadholder William, could not tolerate Ken's
forthrightness and the Chaplain returned to England. Very soon he
was Chaplain to the genial King Charles II and amused rather than
angered that monarch by refusing to let Nell Gwynn the royal
mistress stay at his house at Winchester. King Charles did not forget.
When the See of Bath and Wells fell vacant he declared that no-one
should be Bishop save 'the little black fellow that refused his lodging
to poor Nelly'. Not long after Ken's consecration as Bishop the King
died, and despite the fact that James II was a Roman Catholic, he
accepted him as legitimate sovereign. Nevertheless he was one of the
seven bishops who petitioned the King not to force a repugnant oath
upon the clergy of the Church of England and with them was
imprisoned in the Tower. Eventually they were freed and Ken
returned to his diocese. The flight of the King put the Bishop to the
test. Though there were many parochial clergymen, of the bishops
only Thomas Ken and the Bishop of Norwich refused to swear oaths

Bishop Thomas Ken, Charles II's 'little black fellow', whose conscience led him to defy three very different monarchs (*National Portrait Gallery*)

to the new sovereigns William and Mary. Their king was alive, they said, and they could not swear a second oath. For this they were deprived, and Ken lost his See of Bath and Wells and lived thereafter a life of holy retirement, refusing to continue the Non-Juring Church by saying he would not consecrate new bishops. Thus in the course of time the Non-Juring schism ceased. In his will Ken declared he died in the holy, catholic and apostolic church 'more particularly I die in the communion of the Church of England, as it stands distinguished from all papal and puritan innovations, and as it adheres to the doctrine of the Cross'. Although that Church has no canonising process, the day of Thomas Ken's death is now listed in its calendar of Lesser Festivals and Days of Commemoration. His wider commemoration is in his hymns, 'Awake my soul, and with the sun', 'Glory to thee, my God, this night' and, best of all, perhaps, 'Her Virgin eyes saw God incarnate born', a picture of the exalted place of Our Lady which finished:

> 'Heaven with transcendent joys her entrance graced,
> Next to his throne her Son his Mother placed;
> And here below, now she's of heaven possest,
> All generations are to call her blest.'

CHAPTER TWO

SACRED SONGS

RELIGION was in the doldrums in the eighteenth century. Christianity was virtually denied to the poor and to labourers by an indifferent priesthood, and though of some moment to the mercantile classes and a few eccentric gentlemen, it was a derisory matter to the majority of those of upper rank. Most members of the Established Clergy, or those of their number who could afford it, had a high old time in the hunting field or in the enjoyment of the less robust pursuit of specimens of natural history; ate and drank prodigious quantities; did the minimum duty required by Canon Law; ridiculed piety; and jockeyed for preferment. The poor parsons, and there were 3,528 of them, struggled to keep themselves and their families fed and clothed and warmed; but they were as critical as their more fortunate brethren about the awfulness of Dissent and the awfulness of religious fervour. From Walpole's 'jolly old Archbishop of York, who had all the manners of a man of quality, though he had been a *buccaneer*', and who kept a zenana of harlots at his palace, to the penurious Parson Adamses, their thinking was crystallised in a church bell inscription cast in that century which ran 'Hurrah for the Church of England and down with Enthusiasm'. There was such a crisis in faith and morals after 1730 it seemed as if the only purpose served by religion was to keep the Mob in order.

The scholarly French writer, antiquary and scientist, Charles de Montesquieu, visited London to mix with the best society and study the workings of the Houses of Parliament, the English constitution, and the political works of Locke. He was very much a man of the world, and though from France where irreligion had reached its most profound low since the beginning of Christianity, he confessed himself equally shocked by the religious insincerity of the English. 'If anyone mentions religion,' he wrote in 1730, 'people begin to laugh'. Deism was the vogue, and acceptance of God as an act of reason and rejection of the formal revealed religion of Christianity. Indeed the pagan Neoplatonism which had been carried to Italy by Plethon of Mistra in 1439, and taken up by the Italian Platonists under Marsilio Ficino, interested the enlightened Englishman of the eighteenth century quite as much as the received faiths of early Christianity. This is illustrated by the fact that the Pythagorean-Neoplatonic theory, that stars in their revolutions make a sound, mysteriously finds itself at the centre of Christian hymns.

Joseph Addison (1672–1719), a brilliant essayist, Latin and English versifier, dramatist, painter of life and manners, co-founder of the *Spectator*, which took 'philosophy out of the closets and libraries to tea tables and in coffee-houses', a totally silent Member of Parliament, and unhappy spouse for a short period to a widowed countess, wrote hymns which he contributed to the *Spectator*. These included 'The Lord my pasture shall prepare', a paraphrase of Psalm 23; the beautifully reflective 'When all thy mercies, O my God, My rising soul surveys', which concluded an essay on gratitude; and, best known of all, 'The spacious firmament on high', written in 1712, which restated the pagan conceit of the inaudible music of the spheres:

> 'What though in solemn silence all
> Move round the dark terrestrial ball;
> What though nor real voice nor sound
> Amid their radiant orbs be found;
> In reason's ear they all rejoice,
> And utter forth a glorious voice;
> For ever singing as they shine,
> "The hand that made us is Divine".'*

The passion for reason, deism, the neglect of apostolic teaching, and the embracing of such bizarre Platonic imagery by a hymn-writer of distinction could incline us to the error of believing that the tenets of the Christian creeds totally sank, in this century, like a scuttled fleet. But a few ships of faith were kept afloat by some very remarkable writers of sacred songs. Collections of their hymns were made which enjoyed great popularity in England, if nowhere else,

---

* The Neoplatonic theory was resurrected 152 years afterwards by an American Unitarian, John White Chadwick, at the time of his own ordination when the Federal States were in a painful state of suspense just before Grant's battle with Lee. Concerned, as he wrote, in 'the power that makes thy children free', Chadwick addressed his hymn to the 'Eternal Ruler of the ceaseless round of circling planets singing on their way'.

and the English and English colonials began to treat hymn-singing as a family institution which in some places still survives. The practice of 'lining out' was continued; that is hymns were sung by a knowledgeable precentor with the congregation repeating each line after him until the whole was eventually learnt by rote, but the accomplishments of reading both words and music, which became more common as the century passed, guaranteed firm interest in the work of hymn-writers. The most well-known, and, it is generally considered, the most effective, tended to belong to the strictly severe Protestant schools of thought in the Established Church of England and in Dissent. Of the front-rankers the lives of five are worth examining as representing the developing art of writing sacred poetry; Isaac Watts, Charles Wesley, Augustus Toplady, John Newton and William Cowper. This is not to deny the historic importance and influence of other poets from other schools of thought and from other places as different, and as far apart, as say Thurso and Tullahassee, or Brest and Botany Bay.

The hymn-writers' common background was an age of contradiction. The splendour of Palladian architecture contrasted with the vile condition of the Hogarth slums. Famine slew many, yet those able to eat consumed astonishing quantities of game, poultry, and butcher's flesh. Culture reached an apogee, yet general ignorance was abysmal. In some circles the standard of social behaviour was generally high. But in others manners were odd. Washing was minimal; fleas and bugs abounded; teeth blackened and fell out; powder and wigs and stench-drenching scents were commonly used. Chamber pots were kept in the dining-room sideboard for the convenience of gentlemen port drinkers. Families disposed of their sick and aged pets by hanging them. Men, women, and children were executed in public for petty crimes to the ferocious satisfaction of the onlookers. The practice of medicine was extraordinary; physicians were overcredulous, surgeons savage. The fortitude of their patients was encouraged by much brandy, or a tap on the head, and was usually rewarded by death. Cranks and lunatics were numerous; so, too, were highwaymen, in or out of gibbets, horse-thieves, whores, dead-drunks, press-gangs, duels and the detested window-smashing Mob of this amazing time. Significantly the word 'flabbergast' came into use from about 1760.

★

Isaac Watts was of maritime stock as were many of the inhabitants of Southampton where he was born in 1674. His grandfather commanded a man-of-war under grand old Admiral Blake, but his career was cut short by an explosion in the ship's magazine which blew him to bits. Isaac's father, another Isaac according to some authorities, but named Enoch by others, made no pretensions to gentility and at first carried on the trade of a clothier. He was also a deacon of a local Independent conventicle, which, though made respectable by the Lord Protector Cromwell who was himself an Independent, was anything but respectable after the restoration of the monarchy and the Act of Uniformity. In fact, its adherents could be arrested for objurate nonconformity, and, when Mrs. Watts was brought to bed of her first child, Isaac her husband was half way through a two-year gaol-sentence. Little is known of this lady save that her father was a Southampton alderman with traces of Huguenot blood in his veins, but she must have had intrepidity, looking after the family when her husband was in prison or in hiding in London, and bearing him nine children. We know something of three of Isaac's younger siblings who grew up with him beside the Solent. His brother Enoch followed their grandfather to sea; brother Richard became a physician; and a sister called Sarah married a Southampton draper. When their father ceased to suffer for his religious opinions he founded and kept a boarding-school in Southampton. It flourished, and he proved himself a kindly man who enjoyed writing poems for private devotion.

Nevertheless it was not to his father's Nonconformist school that Isaac went. Instead, after beginning Latin with a tutor at the age of four, he went on with his Latin, to which was added Greek, Hebrew, mathematics, at Southampton Grammar School under the mastership of a pluralist clergyman of the Established Church, John Pinhorne, the holder of three benefices besides his mastership. Watts himself acknowledged the excellence of his teaching in a *Pindaric Ode to Pinhorne*, written at a precocious age. Besides Latin verses, he also showed promise in English poetry, and became such a scholar that a local physician offered to pay for him to attend what *The Book of Common Prayer* called, and still calls, 'the Universities'. However, to enter a college at Oxford or Cambridge it was necessary to accept the Act of Uniformity. The young Isaac Watts was true to the Independent faith he learnt as a child and chose instead instead to attend a Nonconformist academy at Stoke Newington near Aylesbury in Buckinghamshire. He could hardly have done better. The academy was under the superintendence of an Independent Divine and scholar and teacher of great distinction, Thomas Rowe. He was thirty-three and at the height of his powers when the sixteen year old Isaac went to his academy. Rowe needed physical endurance, too, for his chapel at Holborn was almost forty miles, over wretched road, from his academy. It proved too much. He moved the congregation of the chapel to Girdler's Hall and eventually he moved the academy first to Clapham, then outside London, and afterwards to Little Britain in the City. It was convenient to have his two 'kingdoms' within easy reach of each other. Rowe was a superb scholar, the first to teach what was called 'free philosophy' deserting the traditional text-books; and a Cartesian philosopher, unlike those at the universities who were all Aristotelian; and his pupils were so well taught in classics, logic, divinity, and Hebrew, that he attracted a distinguished number.

Amongst Watts's contemporaries at the academy were a number of young men who later became well-known Dissenting Divines. Two of his particular friends had distinctly different careers. John Hughes was a poet and contributor to the *Spectator* whose life was dogged by invalidism, straitened circumstances, and astonishing bad luck. For example, he laboured with the libretto of an opera 'Calypso i Telemachus', which failed because of the vehement opposition of the Italian performers who loathed or were incapable of singing English; then, when he did succeed with a play at Drury Lane, 'The Siege of Damascus', he died of phthisis on the night of the first performance. Josiah Hort, Watts's life-long friend and correspondent, had a better fortune. He gave up Dissent and its pastorate, conformed and was ordained in the Church of England (though later this was questioned). Fortune found him a place as chaplain to the Lord-Lieutenant of Ireland, and as night followed day at that time of pluralism and patronage, he ended with a living, a deanery, and bishoprics successively of Ferns and Leighlin, Kilmore and Ardare. It was said that he was the last great clerical magnate to eat his dinner from a wooden trencher. In 1738 he contracted clergyman's throat and never preached another syllable, though he lived for twenty-three more years, and was actually made Archbishop of Tuam in 1742. It was to this quaint, if chiefly silent, prelate that Watts dedicated his paraphrase from Martial, a youthful *jeu d'esprit* done when they were students together in 1694. In 1693 Watts had Communicated in Rowe's Holborn chapel, thus aligning himself permanently with Dissent. When he left the academy at the end of 1694 he had already established the habit of laborious analysis and accuracy of thought. He was, however, ill. This, at any rate, is the presumption, for he spent the next two and a half years at home, not, so far as we are aware, assisting his father with the boarding-school. Instead he concentrated on the furniture of his mind and attended the Independent Chapel. In this chapel they lined-out hymns of such indifferent quality that the twenty-one year Watts determined to do better. His first hymn, 'Behold the glories of the Lamb', was accepted by the deacons and lined-out in chapel on the Sunday after. Others followed. They began to be circulated in manuscript. It was the beginning of something extremely important in the history of hymn-writing, because Watts chose the simplest metres to fit the tunes best known by the congregation, and his themes were relevant and remain so today.

In 1696 he was offered work, the tutorship of a baronet's son where his academy had formerly been, Stoke Newington. He seized the opportunity, because tutoring one boy would give him plenty of leisure to versify and study. It is said that for five years he devoted his leisure time to the study of Hebrew and theology. During this period he also preached his first sermon, the Independent's answer to the Call and the informal commencement of his pastorate; and he was given permission to accept the assistant pastorate of a chapel in London. This was in 1699, the year Dryden published 'Fables, Ancient and Modern' and George Farquhar staged 'Love in a Bottle'. Watts was still in the employment of Sir John Hartopp and would be for the next two years; but, though frail, he was only twenty-five, and managed the long journeys to and fro between Stoke Newington and the chapel in Mark Lane.

The pastor to whom he was assistant was a polemical divine and physician, Dr. Isaac Chauncy, who had gone as a little boy to New England where his father became President of Harvard. At a tender age he enrolled with his brother Ichabod (there were six sons of President Chauncy altogether) and eventually graduated in both theology and medicine. Dr. Chauncy then returned to England and Oxford, was ordained, obtained a living, was ejected by the Act of Uniformity, and thereupon took charge of an Evangelical chapel in a Hampshire town. There was another Dissenting flock in the same place under the wing of Mr. Samuel Sprint, who tried to amalgamate the two. Chauncy was not the sort of man to consider amalgamation. He opposed the idea, routed Mr. Sprint, and then tempestuously left for London where he was given charge of an Independent Meeting House in Mark Lane. This was a fashionable place of worship. The Lord Protector's grand-daughter worshipped there, so did the Lord Protector's brother-in-law, so did the employer of Isaac Watts, Sir John Hartopp, and his lady, and their friends Sir Thomas and Lady Abney of Theobalds. Dr. Johnson, who included Isaac Watts in his

Lives of the Poets, noted that 'by his natural temper he was quick of resentment; but by his established and habitual practice he was gentle, modest, and inoffensive'. It was a penetrating observation to see that Watts's sweet disposition was the result of self discipline. Thus he was no scolder, and for that alone he would have been welcomed at the Mark Lane conventicle but it also happened that the worshippers were not all that fond of their pastor. Dr. Chauncy practised on bodies as well as souls and remained a physician all through his ministry. It has seldom been a successful combination. Moreover he was also a voluminous writer and publisher of polemics and he harangued his flock until they were wearied by his tirades. As his biographer noted, he 'so tormented his hearers with incessant declamations on church government 'that they left him' '. Dr. Chauncy took the broad hint and resigned. Isaac Watts was invited to succeed him and did so on the death of King William III and the accession of Queen Anne. He was not up to the task, his health began to fail, his drive to study, not unlike that of the young John Milton, seriously weakened his natural force. Within a year he was obliged to take on an assistant.

It was at this period that he published a collection of his verses; *Horae Lyricae*. It was this that caught Dr. Johnson's attention. 'His ear,' he wrote, 'was well-tuned and his diction was elegant and copious.' A year later, in 1707, he published *Hymns and Spiritual Songs in Three Books*. The first were paraphrases of Holy Scripture; the second, poems on 'Divine Subjects'; the third poems for and about the Lord's Supper.* The whole work took the religious world of Dissent by storm. They rejoiced in his simplicity, his tender faith, and his serene piety. Virtually by himself he had begun a form of devotion, that which we know as hymn-singing. The learned Dr. Johnson, a particularly loyal member of the Church of England, which did not yet accept hymn-singing, noted that the subject matter of Watts's devotional verses was small and that he tended to be repetitive. Yet he did not deny its quality. 'It is sufficient for Watts to have done better than others what no man has done well.' He analysed Watts's great success: 'He was one of the first authors that taught the Dissenters to court attention by the graces of language. Whatever they had among them before, whether of learning or acuteness, was commonly obscured and blunted by coarseness and inelegance of style. He showed them that zeal and purity might be

---

* In his concentration on this Sacrament he was in total contrast to his predecessor, for the title of one of Dr. Chauncy's polemical blasts was 'The Unreasonableness of Compelling Men to go to the Holy Supper'.

Frail, sweet and pious little Isaac Watts, who expressed 'zeal and purity' in 'polished diction' (*National Portrait Gallery*)

THE

PSALMS

OF

DAVID,

Imitated in the Language of the

NEW TESTAMENT,

And apply'd to the

Chriſtian State and Worſhip.

By *I. WATTS.*

The FOURTH EDITION.

Luke xxiv. 44. *All things muſt be fulfilled which were written in ⸺ the* Pſalms *concerning me.*
Hebr. xi. 32. ⸺ David, Samuel, *and the Prophets.*
Ver. 40. ⸺ *That they without us ſhould not be made perfect.*

LONDON:

Printed for JOHN CLARK, *at the* Bible *and* Crown; *and* RICHARD FORD, *at the* Angel: Both *in the* Poultry.

M, DCC, XXII.

The title page to Watts's paraphrased Psalter, 'making David a Christian'

expressed and enforced by polished diction.'

It was Watts who, in a free paraphrase of Psalm 90 and always sung to the beautiful setting of Dr. Croft, gave to England and the former British Empire a second national anthem, sung on all state and solemn occasions:

> 'O God, our help in ages past,
>   Our hope for years to come,
>   Our shelter from the stormy blast,
>   And our eternal home.'

His paraphrase of Psalm 72 is almost as memorable:

> 'Jesus shall reign where'er the sun
> Does his successive journeys run;
> His kingdom stretch from shore to shore,
> Till moons shall wax and wane no more.'

In fact, his hymn-books contain a treasury of easily remembered lines:

> 'There is a land of pure delight,
>   Where Saints immortal reign;
> Infinite day excludes the night,
>   And pleasures banish pain.'

> 'Death, like a narrow sea, divides
>   that heavenly land from ours.'

> 'When I survey the wondrous Cross,
>   On which the Prince of glory died,
> My richest gain I count but loss
>   And pour contempt on all my pride.' . . .

> 'Were the whole realm of nature mine,
>   That were a present far too small;
> Love so amazing, so divine,
>   Demands my soul, my life, my all.'

This extraordinary little man – he was barely five feet tall, 'graced with no advantages of appearance', and much enfeebled physically by over-study – produced hymns which are timeless. Some, of course, were not so happy. His *Divine and Moral Songs for Children* are more of a curiosity and unacceptable today, though in their time they ran, literally, through hundreds of editions. And, like any other poet, he could fall flat on his face.

> 'Now to the earth I bend my song,
>   And cast my eyes abroad,
> Glancing the British Isles along,
>   Bless'd isles confess your God.'

The undermining of his constitution and generosity of friends combined to free him for a far longer life than ordinarily he could possibly have expected. Only nine years after he had taken on an assistant, and the conventicle had been twice moved to other sites, ending at St. Mary Axe, Watts was invited to visit two loyal members of the congregation who had become close friends. Sir Thomas Abney had been Lord Mayor in 1700, and he and Lady Abney lived at Theobalds, once the property of the Cecils but then used as a hunting-lodge by King James I, who exchanged Hatfield for it. It was a beautiful house, warm and peaceful. Watts much enjoyed and benefited from his visit, and so the kind Abneys proposed their invalid pastor return for another visit, and this time permanently. The congregation at St. Mary Axe would not hear of him leaving them, and so a compromise was reached. The assistant was made co-pastor and Watts would come into London when he had the strength and occasion to do so. It was a happy arrangement which was to last for the rest of Watts's life. Even after Sir Thomas died in 1722, and Lady Abney moved to Stoke Newington, Isaac Watts went with her. A contemporary described his enjoyment of the Abneys' hospitality: 'Here he dwelt as a family, which for piety, order, harmony, and every virtue, was a house of God. He had the privilege of a country recess, the fragrant bower, the spreading lawn, the flowery garden and other advantages to soothe his mind and aid his restoration to health.' Indeed the Abneys kept him alive until he died on the 25th November, 1748, at the age of seventy-five. By then he had published education manuals, highly popular devotional works, and philosophical books such as his *Logic* of 1725 which became famous and was used at Oxford as a textbook for years. He also published more sacred verses including a lovely paraphrased Psalter, lighting up the Psalms with what his followers called 'Gospel meaning', a process which he described as 'making David a Christian', which was quaint considering the history and character of that particular Hebrew monarch. By then his learning and piety and his self disciplined sweet nature had brought him a wide circle of admiring friends and an honorary D.D. degree from Edinburgh. The frail clothier's son has a monument in Westminster Abbey, and there is another in Southampton where he had stuffed his head with learning as a boy and often gazed over the blue Solent. At his burial in London an onlooker observed, with the superstitiousness of which Dr. Watts would have disapproved, that there was an electric storm and it seemed as if Heaven itself had received him with 'joyful clamour'. But, doubtless, Heaven had.

★

Watts quickly had successors in this new field of liturgy. One, whose *Hymns and Spiritual Songs* were published as early as 1720, was Simon Browne (1680–1732), a melancholy minister of the same connection of the Independents. He and Watts were allied by doctrine as well as by versifying, neither believing the doctrine of the Trinity was necessary to salvation, and casting their vote that way with a minority at a meeting of Dissenting ministers held in London. Each was distressed and perplexed by the majority decision. But while Watts passed quietly to the Unitarian position, his fellow minister did not. About the same time as the meeting, Browne's wife and son both died, and he himself, in fighting off a highwayman, accidentally strangled him. It was all too much for a man already disposed to severe depression. He told his friends he had no more sense than a parrot and tried to persuade them he was 'a mere bear'. They stood by him, but he could take no joy in anything. This he made all too evident when asked to say Grace at the table of a friend. Several times he begged to be excused. Thinking it better for him, the guests remained standing and prevailed upon him to say Grace. In great distress he cried: 'Most Merciful and Almighty God, let thy Spirit which moved upon the face of the waters where there was no light, descend upon me, that from this darkness there may rise up a man to praise Thee.' Convinced his soul was lost, he resigned his pastorship, retired to the place of his birth, Shepton Mallet in Somerset, and lived a dozen more years in forlorn dejection, passing his time by translating the classical authors, compiling a dictionary and writing books for children. He died in 1732, sixteen years before Dr. Watts, leaving several daughters and for Christians a much favoured hymn:

> 'Come, gracious Spirit, heavenly Dove,
> With light and comfort from above;
> Be Thou our Guardian, Thou our Guide,
> O'er every thought and step preside. . . .
>
> Lead us to Heav'n, that we may share
> Fulness of joy for ever there;
> Lead us to God, our final rest,
> To be with Him for ever blest.'

★

Another contemporary and friend and fellow divine of Watts was Dr. Philip Doddridge (1702–1751), the twentieth child of a London tradesman. He was also sickly in health and a forceful writer. His *Rise and Progress of Religion in the Soul* had great influence in the Evangelical movement. And, too, he wrote a number of popular hymns; amongst them one for Communion: 'My God, and is thy Table spread'; two for general use, 'O God of Bethel, by whose hand' and 'Ye servants of the Lord'; and the Advent hymn 'Hark the glad sound! the Saviour comes'. His hymns helped and sustained an old friend, Col. James Gardiner, who was slain in the sunrise six-minute battle of Prestonpans when Prince Charles Edward's Highlanders cleared the Hanoverian dragoons from the field. Doddridge's best-remembered Advent hymn was used on another historic occasion, though whether through ineptness or blasphemous bad taste it will never be known. In 1853, at the direct order of a President – Millard Fillmore – with no pretensions to learning or culture, Commodore Perry of the United States weighed anchor off Japan, and sought to force that sovereign state of great antiquity and civilisation to abandon her policy of isolation and enter, willy-nilly, into trade and diplomatic relations. Driven by the imperialistic dreams of young America and determined to 'improve' people whether they wanted it or not, he told the Japanese he would be back in one year to see the thing done. He was. More black frigates than before dropped anchor off Japan and Divine Service was held aboard the flag-ship. Perry's choice of hymn was extraordinary. The American band struck up the *Old Hundredth*, and to it the company sang Philip Doddridge's hymn: 'Hark the glad sound! the Saviour comes.'

★

Of all the Nonconformist hymn writers of this century the most prolific was Charles Wesley. He and his brother John revitalised the Established Church by an evangelism so forceful that some people were led away from the Church and those who were left behind reformed themselves. Their father was a Lincolnshire parson, himself a convert from Dissent to the Establishment. Though he just managed to accept William III as his sovereign, Mrs. Wesley did not. She was one of a family of twenty-five, and a firm woman. She resolutely refused to say 'Amen' when, at Family Prayers, her husband prayed for the reigning sovereign. For this he formally threatened to deny her her conjugal rights, but she remained stubborn, and so, we presume, won her point. Parson Wesley abhorred both the location and the inhabitants of his parish. The dislike was returned. To his rage, the Rector's property was damaged and his cattle maimed by invisible enemies. His Rectory was set ablaze at night. His family was saved, but he lost half the house and many of his goods. When he went to vote in the Lincoln election for the Tories against Dissent, he was mobbed by his own Whiggish parishioners who banged drums and fired guns beneath the window where he was staying. Gustily he recorded: 'They intended me mischief. If they got me in the Castle Yard they would squeeze my guts out. However, God preserved me.' God did not, however, save him from a Whig creditor who suddenly pressed for payment, and had him lodged in Lincoln Gaol, until he was rescued from that indignity by the Archbishop of York.

Against this frenetic background nineteen children were born. Those who survived infancy were first educated by Mrs. Wesley, and afterwards, in fits and starts, by their volatile sire. Of the seven girls only one made a fairly happy marriage; the rest were disastrous. Of the boys, Samuel was the oldest. He was a clergyman and master at Westminster School when little Charles arrived there as a pupil under his brother's care and at his cost. John, or Jackie as he was called in the family, was four years older and leaving Charterhouse for Oxford. It was during Charles's time at Westminster that a kinsman, Garret Wesley of Dungan, co. Meath, selected him for adoption as his heir. It was a handsome offer but Charles promptly declined, saying he preferred to stay in England. Another relative was selected for adoption, and in due course of time he inherited the rich Irish estate and became the first Lord Mornington and a grandfather of the great Duke of Wellington. Charles enjoyed school and did well, but he only paid conventional allegiance to Christian beliefs, and when he left brother Samuel to go up to Oxford to join brother John, he impatiently demanded: 'Would you have me a saint all at once?' It appears their father was not puritan. As boys they played cards and backgammon, chess, billiards and tennis, and went to race meetings, taverns and the theatre. John had left Christchurch and was already a don of Lincoln. Charles, as an undergraduate at Christchurch, wanted to spread his wings; but he knew the family circumstances. Willy-nilly, he was destined to become a parson.

John at Lincoln had founded 'The Holy Club'. This was High Church in its doctrine and adherence to Order, and, as one would expect from young men, its notions were generally contrary to those of the Establishment. The members were later called Methodists, an expression used before to describe a group of Roman Catholic apologists of the 1680s, and now used as a loose term to describe such Dissenters as the followers of Whitefield or members of the Countess of Huntingdon's Connection. Only gradually did John Wesley accept the name, for he was no Dissenter, and both he and Charles lived and died, like their father and their brother Sam, as priests of

John Wesley, the great orator of Methodism and translator of several hymns
(*National Portrait Gallery*)

(3)

PREFACE.

1. SOME years ago a Collection of Tunes was published, under the title of *Harmonia Sacra*. I believe all unprejudiced persons who understand music allow, that it exceeds beyond all degrees of comparison, any thing of the kind which has appeared in *England* before: The tunes being admirably well chosen, and accurately engraven, not only for the voice, but likewise for the organ or harpsichord.

2. But this, tho' it is excellent in its kind, is not the thing which I want. I want the people called *Methodists* to sing true, the tunes which are in *common use* among them. At the same time I want them to have in one volume, the *best Hymns* which we have printed : and that, in a *small* and *portable* volume, and one of an *easy price*.

3. I

iv   PREFACE.

3. I have been endeavouring for more than 20 years to procure such a book as this. But in vain : Masters of music were above following any direction but their own. And I was determined, whoever compiled this, should follow *my* direction : Not *mending* our tunes, but setting them down, neither better nor worse than they were. At length I have prevailed. The following collection contains all the tunes which are in *common use* among us. They are pricked *true*, exactly as I desire all our congregations may sing them : And here is prefixt to them a collection of those hymns which are (I think) some of *the best* we have published. The *volume* likewise is *small*, as well as the *price*. This therefore I recommend preferable to all others.

JOHN WESLEY.

SELECT

That this part of Divine Worship may be the more acceptable to God, as well as the more profitable to yourself and others, be careful to observe the following directions.

I. LEARN *these Tunes* before you learn any others; afterwards learn as many as you please.

II. Sing them exactly as they are printed here, without altering or mending them at all; and if you have learned to sing them otherwise, unlearn it as soon as you can.

III. Sing *All*. See that you join with the congregation as frequently as you can. Let not a slight degree of weakness or weariness hinder you. If it is a cross to you, take it up and you will find a blessing.

IV. Sing *lustily* and with a good courage. Beware of singing as if you were half dead, or half asleep; but lift up your voice with strength. Be no more afraid of your voice now, nor more ashamed of its being heard, than when you sung the songs of *Satan*.

V. Sing *modestly*. Do not baul, so as to be heard above, or distinct from the rest of the congregation, that you may not destroy the harmony; but strive to unite your voices together, so as to make one clear melodious sound.

VI. Sing *in Time*: whatever time is sung be sure to keep with it. Do not run before nor stay behind it; but attend close to the leading voices, and move therewith as exactly as you can; and take care you sing not *too slow*. This drawling way naturally steals on all who are lazy; and it is high time to drive it out from among us, and sing all our tunes just as quick as we did at first.

VII. Above all sing *spiritually*. Have an eye to God in every word you sing. Aim at pleasing *Him* more than yourself, or any other creature. In order to this attend strictly to the sense of what you sing, and see that your *Heart* is not carried away with the sound, but offered to God continually; so shall your singing be such as the *Lord* will approve of here, and reward when he cometh in the clouds of heaven.

John Wesley's Preface to *Select Hymns* followed by some good advice on hymn singing

Charles Wesley, the 'Sweet singer of Methodism', author of more than six thousand hymns, looking down from the wall of the boardroom of the Methodist Missionary Society (*Methodist Recorder* – photographer E. W. Tattersall, St. Albans)

the Church of England. John left his fellowship to become his father's curate; then, in 1735, he accepted work for the Society for the Propagation of the Gospel in Georgia. By this time Charles had proved himself an exceptional and felicitous Latinist and had paying pupils, but he could not be a college fellow without being Ordained and he approached it with the enthusiasm of a goose anticipating Michaelmas. Then John proposed he accompany him to the Colonies as Secretary to the Governor of Georgia, General Oglethorpe. America was an adventure. Charles hesitated no longer. He was made deacon and ordained priest, packed his bags, and left for Georgia. John in Georgia did not make himself very popular. Nor did his brother. Charles disliked being half-secretary, half-parson in a dirty frontier settlement of huts dignified by the name Frederica. He summoned the frontiersmen to public prayer by rolls on a drum, and was rigidly obedient to prayer-book rubrics or rules no matter how inconvenient to everyone concerned. In fact, he proved himself his father's son by provoking such hostility amongst his flock that once he was shot at. Sensibly he resigned, and the Governor in accepting his resignation, gave him the kindly advice not to drive himself and others too hard and to 'abandon celibacy'.

John, too, returned to England two years later and joined his brother in London. It was there, on Whit Sunday, 1738, that Charles was 'converted', as he described it. John experienced the same exultation in religion on the following Wednesday, and both, fired by their mystical turning to God, began a mission as preaching evangelists.

John was a brilliant orator; Charles a garrulous but not ineffective extempore preacher. He was a curate in Islington and came under censure from the Bishop of London for re-Baptising a woman who had been previously Baptised by a Dissenting Minister. The Islington Churchwardens physically prevented him from preaching there again by blocking the way to the pulpit. They had the law on their side as Charles was an unlicensed curate. He had to leave. He found work in a Kent parish and preached and preached. The Archbishop cautioned him that open-air or field-preaching was not quite the thing. Charles returned to Oxford and preached there. Then an enraged proprietor of a field through which he had walked to preach on Kennington Common brought an action for trespass. It cost Charles nearly £20 and it taught him a lesson. For years after he followed John as an itinerant missioner, but he never knowingly broke the law of Church or State. Not only did the brothers practise field-preaching, but they visited the gaols. Charles was particularly good at this, and would go to the scaffold with condemned criminals and rejoice at their repentence, though he saw no reason why they should not be hanged. For years the brothers made enormous journeys, preaching out of doors in all weathers and indoors if they were invited. Charles did it for seventeen years, going twice to Ireland. He liked the Irish, and reported in Kinsale in 1748: 'The presbyterians say I am a presbyterian, the churchgoers that I am a minister of theirs, and the catholics that I am a good catholic.'

In 1749 he at last followed the advice of General Oglethorpe and, at the age of forty-two, married the young daughter of a Breconshire squire. But matrimony made no difference to his wanderings. Mrs. Wesley rode behind him pillion, and did so for seven years until Charles's health and the approach of middle-age made him give up his journeyings. They first settled in the West Country. They had eight children but only three survived. Sarah the daughter remained unmarried and was a woman of great culture who moved in literary circles. Both her brothers became famous musicians and the family moved to London from the West Country in 1771. There was a large music room in their new house equipped with two organs. The young Charles, aged twenty-two, and his brother Samuel, aged thirteen, began to give successful subscription concerts. Each went on to notable careers as executants and composers. Charles became organist to that cultured voluptuary the Prince of Wales, and musical preceptor to his daughter, Princess Charlotte of Wales. Sam grieved his parents by becoming a Roman Catholic and composing a Mass and dedicating it to Pius VI. The eighteenth century was a no better time, however, for the Roman Church than any other. Over a period of twenty-seven years the Supreme Pontiff slowly lost control. His Church reached its lowest point since the Middle Ages, and, at the very end of the century, he died in France a prisoner of Bonaparte. Not surprisingly Sam's conversion was only temporary. He remarked that 'the crackers of the Vatican are no longer taken for the thunderbolts of heaven'. Then Sam met with an accident, tumbling into a deep hole in the road and damaging his brain. He refused surgical help yet lived to be accepted as the greatest organist of his day, unrivalled as an extempore player, and he married and begat four children, one of them out of wedlock, Samuel Sebastian Wesley, who became an eminent composer of sacred music and of many great hymn tunes.

The ageing Charles Wesley bore family reverses with fortitude. He was becoming increasingly near-sighted and, his friends admitted, amazingly absent-minded again. But he lived his regular life as before, riding out daily, clothed the same way, summer or winter, and keeping in close contact with his brother. He and John had differences. Charles was dismayed when John began to 'ordain' ministers; he even disapproved of lay-preachers, and female lay-preachers in particular; and he was positively censorious of ministers not ordained by a bishop daring to celebrate the Sacrament. But they remained on close and affectionate terms and wrote endlessly to each other. They also wrote hymns which were not only declarations of faith but teaching instruments, part of the evangelistic mission. John's original verses were unimportant, but his translations from the German hymn writers included 'Lo! God is here! let us adore!', 'Thee will I love, my Strength, my Tower', and most famous of all, 'Put thou thy trust in God, in duty's path go on'. John was the great orator of Methodism. Charles was its 'sweet Singer'. Few have written as many hymns. He wrote between six and seven thousand, besides a large quantity of secular poetry. He turned out his verses, stanza by stanza, day after day, in a mellifluous tide, all concerned with the Faith he professed and taught and tried to practise. Most are now never read, let alone sung. Some are very personal, so self-revealing that they make the reader feel an intruder into a very private piety.

> 'This is my shame, my curse, my hell;
> I do not love the Bleeding Lamb.'

But a large number of his hymns are still sung, especially in Evangelical circles, and his finest hymns, sung all over the world and by every denomination, are quite imperishable, for in them he showed an amazing depth of feeling and variety of expression. It is of interest to arrange twelve titles in the order in which he wrote them. There is but one example each for the 30s, the 50s and the 60s. All the rest are from the prolific 40s when Charles Wesley was in the prime of life physically, preaching every day on his immense journeys up and down the land from 1749, and a married man.

> 1739 'Hail the day that sees him rise, Alleluya!'
> 1740 'Jesu, Lover of my soul'
> 1740 'Come, Holy Ghost, our souls inspire'
> 1740 'Christ, whose glory fills the skies'
> 1742 'O for a heart to praise my God'
> 1742 'Come, O thou Traveller unknown'
> 1746 'Rejoice, the Lord is King'
> 1747 'Love Divine, all loves excelling'
> 1749 'Soldiers of Christ, arise'
> 1749 'Forth in thy name, O Lord, I go'
> 1759 'Let saints on earth in concert sing'
> 1762 'O thou who camest from above'

This splendid poet of feeling had a robust sense of humour; something John Wesley lacked although, quite unintentionally, he could be funny; for example, he wrote of a Methodist Conference which 'concluded in much love, to the great disappointment of many'. And he noted in his *Journal*, of the burial of a lady in Dorking: '. . . a lovely woman, snatched away in the bloom of youth. I trust it will be a blessing to many, and to her husband in particular.'

Charles also enjoyed the bliss of a happy married life with a lady who outlived him by thirty-four years, reaching the age of ninety-six. His brother was less fortunate, marrying an evil-tempered party, who interfered with her husband's work, nagged him ceaselessly, and once, 'foaming with fury', tore out locks of his hair. Mrs. John Wesley was a terror. A candid friend once described her as one of 'a brace of ferrets'. The only favour she ever did her husband was to leave him in a rage in 1776, and he never saw her more. Yet Charles lacked John's vitality and strength, and, with age, he grew gravely enfeebled. His anxious brother bade him take more fresh air and exercise. But Charles could not even use a pen to reply. His daughter wrote for him. More medical advice came from John, who appeared to be a physician manqué and gave case histories. Let his brother take ten drops of elixir of vitriol in a glass of water and ride out daily; or, if this failed, he should have a large onion slit cross-ways and bound to the pit of his stomach after eating. Should these remedies not prove satisfactory, Charles was to remember the lady of Paris who lived several weeks without swallowing a grain by applying thin slices of beef to the stomach. But fresh air, daily exercise, elixir of vitriol, split onions, and slices of beef were of no avail. Charles Wesley died on the 29th March 1788, and was buried in the churchyard of the parish where he had lived, not in a Dissenting grave. John was up in Cheshire and could not get to the funeral in time. He rather disapproved of his brother's last act of conformity. He published an obituary notice

> 'Mr. Charles Wesley, who after spending four score years with much sorrow and pain, quietly retired into Abraham's bosom. He had no disease; but after a gradual decay of some months *The weary wheels of life stood still at last.*'

But his own weary wheels continued to revolve and he greatly missed his brother, his constant companion in religion despite their differences, and strictly speaking, by a matter of four days precedence in 'conversion', the founding father of the Methodist movement. John was to work alone until he reached the great age of eighty-eight and he felt his loss keenly. Two weeks after Charles's death he was taking a service and found that the chosen hymn was one of his brother's greatest poems. With breaking voice he announced:

> 'Come, O thou Traveller unknown,
>   Whom still I hold, but cannot see,
> My company before is gone,
>   And I am left alone with thee;'

It is said that the poignancy of the moment overcame him, that he sat down and wept into his hands until he could compose himself sufficiently to continue the service.

★

John Wesley was not revered by everyone. No-one of such personality and such conviction, and of such achievements, could fail to make enemies. But the enmity of Augustus Montague Toplady, a hymn writer of some merit, and possessed of a keen intellect, was quite unreasonable. It was also ironic in that the sixteen year old Toplady, as an undergraduate of Trinity College, Dublin, was converted from the Established Church to Wesleyanism on a hot August evening by a mission sermon preached in an Irish barn, and he was so thankful for being saved that he wrote a fervid letter to John Wesley himself. It was the last letter of its kind to pass between them. Perhaps the evening had been too warm, and it was, of course, in Ireland where emotions are easily kindled, and within a few months the young man was not only back in the Established Church but in the most enthusiastic, un-eighteenth century Calvinistic part of it. He had been born in England in 1740, probably never having seen his military father, who was killed, either of tropical fever or in action, at Admiral Vernon's hopeless siege of Cartagena, the heavily fortified Caribbean seaport of Colombia in South America. His mother indulged him. Her brother, Uncle Julius, Rector of St. Paul's Deptford, was less soft and fond. He sent Augustus as a day boy to Westminster School, where he wrote pious sermons and essays, and tried his hand at hymns, and concocted farces which he actually submitted to Garrick for production at Drury Lane. Such precociousness simply offended his ill-tempered uncle. Mother and son removed themselves from the Rectory to Ireland. There Augustus continued to develop his gifts. Garrick must have disappointed him, for he appears to have given up farces, but he was undoubtedly clever, a versifier, a philosopher, a talented writer of prose. Religion bothered him at first; but, having resisted the temporary seduction of Wesleyanism, he decided to be ordained. This was arranged by a kindly Bishop of Bath and Wells who made him deacon, and he began work as an assistant curate in Blagdon in Somerset in June 1762. On being ordained priest at the canonical age of twenty-four he removed himself to an assistant curacy near Hungerford, and soon obtained the presentation to a benefice in Devonshire which he gave to himself. Whether he bought the presentation, which was simony and illegal, or had it indirectly through his mother's purse, is not known. As it troubled his conscience there must have been something shady about the affair, and he felt more at ease when, as was the common practice, he managed to exchange that living for another, the vicarage of Broadhembury in the same diocese of Exeter. He was an exaggerated believer in predestination, for when he heard that his previous parsonage house had burnt to the ground and his successor would have to pay for another, he noted: 'What a providential mercy was it that *I* resigned the living before this misfortune happened! Oh God, how wise and how gracious art Thou in all Thy ways!'

He was destined to remain parson of Broadhembury for the rest of his days. Not, of course, that he stayed much in Devon. Bath was not far distant with its many attractions, not the least of them the salon of a tall and stately widowed Amazon with raddled cheeks, author of *Mrs. Macaulay's History of England*, who had many distinguished admirers. Indeed she was peculiarly honoured by having her sculpted life-size figure in marble placed within the sanctuary of a London church, plus an empty vault ready for her remains, whilst she was still very much alive. Toplady became one of her many correspondents. There is no mention in his writings but it is unlikely that he was silent when, at the age of forty-seven, Mrs. Macaulay astonished England by marrying again, this time a twenty-one year old surgeon's mate who was the brother of a noted quack doctor, and her empty vault and full-sized marble statue were hurled from their sacred position. Through Mrs. Macaulay, Toplady would have made the acquaintance of Dr. Johnson, and he had a circle of literary as well as Calvinistic friends. Being the most militant of Calvinists, and the cause's most brilliant apologist, saucy with his pen, unmatched in his flow of logical thought, he was often in London, centre of literature and theological causes. It is said he mixed freely in society, but there is no mention of whether or not he made an agreeable companion. He was ruthless with those with whom he disagreed, and had a purblind hatred of John Wesley because Wesley rejected Calvin's doctrine of the elect. Toplady rushed into print. 'A Letter

To Mr Wesley' (1770) was his first blast of venom, accusing him of coarseness and evasiveness, and raking up gossip about his supposed misconduct. Wesley replied. A second blast of venom was issued by Toplady in 1772: 'More Work for Mr. Wesley', which accused him of lying and satanic guilt, and shamelessness. Wesley briefly replied that he would not 'fight with chimney-sweepers' and, mixing his metaphors, went on to call Toplady an 'exquisite coxcomb'. In 1774 Toplady produced a monumental 'Historic Proof of the Doctrinal Calvinism of the English Church', which was brilliantly written but far too controversial.

Simultaneously he began to show symptoms of consumption. He obtained permanent leave from his benefice and settled in London, where he looked after the French Calvinist Reformed Church in Orange Street and began to contribute to *Gospel Magazine*. In October 1775, he contributed one of his own hymns and his most immortal achievement: 'Rock of ages, cleft for me.'* Allegedly Toplady had written the hymn twelve years before publication whilst sheltering at Blagdon from a storm in a rocky gorge called Burrington Combe. A romantic accretion to the story claimed Toplady lacked a notebook or any sort of paper but that he found at his feet, quite fortuitously, a playing card, of all un-Calvinistic things, and he wrote the hymn on the back of it. It had four stanzas of four verses each in the original, so he must have been hard put to get it all in as he scribbled in the thunderstorm. However, the card is said to be still preserved, as a sort of Protestant Relic, in the United States. It was uncharacteristic of an author always eager to be in print to wait twelve years before publishing his great devotional poem; but the story lives on. At first it enjoyed little success but afterwards it spread through the Christian world. It was a favourite of the Prince Consort who quoted it in lucid moments as he lay dying from typhoid in Windsor Castle. Gladstone wrote a Latin version: 'Jesus, pro me perforatus', which was not up to the standard of the original; nor were Gladstone's other exercises in translating the hymn into Greek and Italian. Toplady wrote 133 hymns in all. He sent one to Lady Huntingdon, who had her own Dissenting sect, which was not a success. It began morbidly

> 'When languor and disease invade
> This trembling house of clay,

---

* With the hymn he attached a calculation 'introduced for the sake of spiritual improvement'; namely, that if sins multiplied with every second, at ten years old, a boy would be chargeable with '315 millions and 36 thousand sins'. It is not known how he arrived at this precise figure.

The militant and saucy Augustus Toplady, author of 'Rock of Ages' and foe of John Wesley (*National Portrait Gallery*)

'Tis sweet to look beyond the cage,
And long to fly away.'

Amongst the others was 'Deathless Principle Arise', a rhetorical address to the human soul and therefore of curiosity value. James Montgomery, of whom we hear in the next chapter, put some of Toplady's hymns on a level with Charles Wesley's, but Montgomery was wrong. Toplady's only memorial is that one hymn, his masterpiece. It atoned in some measure for his return to John Wesley-baiting when he became editor of *Gospel Magazine*, two months after he had contributed 'Rock of Ages'. Like all consumptives, Toplady burnt brightly with a brief blaze of light before he was snuffed out. In June, 1778, he rose from his deathbed, and ordered chairmen to carry him to his pulpit in the Orange Street conventicle. There he preached a vigorous sermon, and went home, and died. He was thirty-eight.

There are two versions of his death. One is that his physician spoke encouragingly of his prospects of recovery at which Toplady bade him hold his tongue, adding: 'No, no, I *shall* die, for no mortal could endure such manifestations of God's glory as I have and live on', and that he died singing his own hymn 'Deathless Principle Arise'. The other version, claimed by the Wesleyans, is that 'he died in black despair, uttering the most horrible blasphemies'. Thirteen witnesses testified that he had done no such thing. Neither deathbed scene seems very likely. His dying sermon was published the week after his death. In it he affirmed all his controversial writings, saying he would alter not a word, especially those relating to that 'old Fox tarred and feathered', John Wesley. He was buried in Tottenham Court Chapel. A marble tablet commemorated him. His only abiding achievement was inscribed on it:

'Rock of Ages, cleft for me,
Let me hide myself in thee.'

★

The remaining pair of eighteenth century English hymn writers whose works are universally known were as Evangelical as any of the others. John Newton and William Cowper were from different backgrounds and totally different in personality and character. Yet their providential meeting and subsequent friendship enabled them to produce a volume of verse entitled *Olney Hymns* which, at the end of the century, matched in importance the hymnal of Isaac Watts and the compilation of hymns and psalms made by John Wesley.

John Newton was the older. He was born in London in 1725, the son of an extrovert, Jesuit-trained sea captain and a delicate Dissenting woman. His mother taught him to read by the time he was four. At six he had begun Latin, had learned off by heart many of Dr. I. Watts's *Children's Hymns*, and was destined for the Dissenting ministry. At seven his mother disappeared, leaving him in the care of neighbours. She was consumptive and went to be nursed by a relative at Chatham named Catlett. There by the standards of the time she was correctly nursed; put in a hot, dark room with all windows and cracks and even the keyhole sealed, nourished with a broth of snails, and drastically purged. She died; coughing away her life in flecks and streams of bright arterial blood. Her only son, as one biographer put it, 'lost a valuable parent'. A year later his father returned from sea and took him to meet a prosperous grazier who had a number of young unmarried daughters. The captain came to an arrangement and married one of them. She was young and disinclined to be physically cruel to her stepson; instead, like David Copperfield, he was emotionally starved. 'In short, I was neglected.' To carry the Dickens simile further, he was packed off to a school at Stratford, and not the sort that Dr. Watts's old father had kept so successfully in Southampton, but under a master every bit as bad as the terrible Creakle. Fortunately after a year this barbarian left and was replaced by a gentler usher.

At the age of eleven John went to sea with his father and heartily disliked it. He was set apart from the crew and he dreaded his parent. At the conclusion of six voyages, when Captain Newton retired, or, in his own term, 'swallowed the anchor', John had become a seventeen year old rebel with a turbulent spirit, given to obscenity and profanity, his religion not merely gone but replaced by a vehement rationalism. He appeared to relish blaspheming the God his pious mother had taught him to love. The old captain made provision for him through a Liverpool merchant. John was to go out to the West Indies and learn how to manage a sugar plantation. There he would have slaves to do his bidding; anything he wished to eat and drink, and plenty of freedom. John lost the chance of it by paying a short visit to his mother's kinsfolk the Catletts at Chatham, for there he lost his heart to the fourteen year old daughter of the house, Mary Catlett, dallied too long, and missed the coach to Liverpool by several days. His prospects were gone and his father enraged and, to cap all, he was at that moment seized on by the press gang and thrust in the lower deck of H.M.S. *Harwich*, a Fourth Rate ship of the line with a complement of 350 men, under the command of Captain Philip Cartaret R.N. Conditions below were indescribable. War with the French was expected. The ship's log at that time recorded that she rode at anchor in the mouth of the Thames in strong gales of snow, while the seamen re-fitted her sails, and scraped and revarnished masts and spars and decks and the ship's sides. John was fortunate in one respect. Word reached his father that he had been pressed for service. But his father did no more than to write to Captain Cartaret and beg him to begin the boy in the Royal Navy. The Captain obliged. He sent for John Newton and made him a midshipman on the spot. It was an easier life than that of a common seaman but still fearful.

War was declared. H.M.S. Harwich engaged the enemy several times, losing much tackle but only one life. When she went to refit for a long cruise, Newton could only think of Mary Catlett, and, believing himself unable to endure being without her for several years, he deserted. Caught within hours, he was clapped in irons while Captain Cartaret considered his punishment. He decided it was to be in two parts. First Newton was publicly flogged in the eyes of his 349 shipmates, a solemn dramatised disgrace, then he was stripped of his rank, degraded and put at the beck and call of those who had been his messmates. He was filled with such hatred that he seriously contemplated murdering the Captain and committing suicide. Rage then gave way to despair. He was certain that he would live his whole life as a ship's slave and never marry Mary Catlett. Then fortune smiled on him. At Funchal in Madeira a most unusual event took place. The Fleet Commodore impressed two skilled seamen from merchant ships lying there in port and ordered that they be replaced by two men from H.M.S. Harwich. Newton begged to be allowed to go. Captain Cartaret consented, either out of kindness or, more likely, to rid himself of a potential nuisance. Newton took a small bundle of personal belongings, and found himself back in the merchant service. He had one book: Barrow's *Euclid*. The ship he joined was a slaver. Slaving was still a respectable trade and there was nothing about slave ships likely to shock a young man who had served on the lower deck and in the gun room of a man-of-war, and who had himself been in irons and flogged. But Newton did not care for his new captain and the mate. As they traded along the coast of Africa, he determined to take work with a well-to-do resident trader named Clow on a hilly little island off Benanoes (or Bananas), and Clow arranged for his discharge from the merchant service. It turned out to be a dreadful mistake. Clow had a black mistress who was at once jealous of Newton because he was white and a potential danger. She plotted against him, turned Clow against him and, when he fell ill with fever and within her power, she mercilessly neglected him. For two years he was treated worse than any slave, overworked, underclothed, terribly underfed. He became, he later said, like an animal. He hid in shame when slave traders came ashore from their ships. His reason hung on only two threads; his battered Euclid which somehow he kept despite everything, and his dreams of Mary Catlett. Then his circumstances altered. A new trader arrived and established himself beside Clow and, not listening to Clow's statement that Newton was idle and a thief, and declaring it was bad for the blacks to see a white man enslaved, he offered Newton work. More than this, he gave him clothes, food and self-confidence, and trusted him to look after his affairs at a station on the mainland, bartering for slaves with rice, palm oil, and iron, and looking after the bought natives in transit to the coast. Newton sufficiently recovered his health and his spirits to write to both Mary and his father. He heard nothing from her. Her parents knew of his feelings and, dismayed by his lack of prospects, had forbidden her to write. But old Captain Newton replied in the best way possible. He told his Liverpool friend, a ship-owner, that John was somewhere on the coast of Africa and must be got home. Thus it came about that a ship, *The Greyhound*, working her way down the west coast of Africa trading for gold, ivory, dyer's wood and beeswax, called at the Benanoes, and her captain asked if anyone had ever heard of a John Newton. Newton hesitated, but only fractionally. He went aboard with his Euclid destined for home and Mary. It was to be a long journey. *The Greyhound* was on her way out; trading was slow. The ship was not laden until twelve months had passed and they had voyaged over one thousand miles further south. Then, in January 1748, the last cargo was taken aboard, the hatches battened down, the ship provisioned, and she set sail for home. It involved using trade winds and a voyage of more than seven thousand miles. Thoroughly bored, young Newton put his mind to the business of becoming an expert in profanity; his blasphemy a reasoned revolt against God's existence. He was so excellent at it that he quite appalled the captain of *The Greyhound*.

Divine retribution, as Newton later considered it, was not far away. The ship met with disaster after disaster. A violent storm almost caused her to founder. Provisions and men were swept overboard. The survivors hacked away tackle and jettisoned cargo. They caulked sprung timbers with blankets and clothing. They kept at the pumps continuously. As well as they could they steered *The Greyhound* into the eye of the howling winds and met the mountainous seas. It was then that John Newton spoke 'The Lord have mercy upon us'. He was at the pumps. He suddenly realised the significance of what he had said. He considered it the moment of his conversion. Certainly it was as dramatic as that of Saint Paul on the way to Damascus. There seemed little hope. After the tempestuous winds dropped, *The Greyhound* was left a sodden, rolling hulk, at least three hundred miles from the nearest landfall by someone's estimation. It was only an estimate. They were lost; beginning to suffer hunger; dependent on sufficient wind to keep their ship under way, praying it would not be too strong and blow the remaining sails to ribbons; still pumping day after day after day; drifting, reduced to near starvation, using scraps of wind to labour along for four long weeks. Then the captain's navigation, or luck, or Almighty God brought them to a landfall, Lough Swilly in Northern Ireland; and only two hours after they had limped into the safety of the lough, a gale blew up that must have dashed them to pieces had they been off-shore at sea. John Newton, the blaspheming, free-thinking reprobate, sought evidence that he had been 'converted', and, having found it to his entire satisfaction, he ever afterwards kept the anniversary of the day he had involuntarily prayed during that sea storm.

On reaching England he was offered the command of a ship. The Catletts withdrew their opposition to his marriage to Mary. In February 1750 he married his 'dearest darling' as he called her, down in Chatham, they set up house in Liverpool, and John went to sea again, this time as a slave-trading Captain. He was perfectly able to reconcile this 'genteel employment' with his refound Evangelical faith. All he felt, as the slaves were offered to him, was the burden of responsibility to choose wisely; strong and healthy, not too old or too many children. And he endeavoured to avoid wanton thoughts by not looking at the naked female slaves as they came aboard but fixing his eyes on a point above their heads, and abstaining from meat during voyages. The Middle Passage from Africa over the Atlantic was always perilous. There was the danger of shipwreck, through freaks of weather or overloading; danger of fever that carried off the cargo, of the crew falling so weak and ill that the slaves would easily revolt, danger of mutinous seamen. Letters helped. Mary had little skill in writing and none in punctuation, but he valued those of her letters that got through. There was none now from his father. The old captain was drowned while sea-bathing in Hudson Bay in 1742. John heard the news when he reached Antigua on his first voyage to the Indies.

When not trading or taking on and loading cargoes or navigating the ship, John passed the time improving himself. He struck up an acquaintance with Latin again, re-teaching himself by reading Virgil and Horace, Terence and Livy, even Erasmus. He learnt theology of the Calvinistic variety. The crew were in awe of their energetic rumbustious Captain who would fell any man he heard swearing. Twice on Sunday it was 'hats off' and they had Divine Service read to them. He remained remarkably well, avoiding the contagions and infections which so attacked his crew and cargo until the summer of 1753, when he caught a fever. He shook it off, made port, saw his 'dearest darling' and went off directly to take command of a new vessel. It suited him well. Preparations were under way for a round trip to Africa and the Indies and back again. He had the opportunity to return home for a time before sailing and he and Mary were quietly drinking tea one evening when he crashed to the ground in a seizure. The fit lasted for an hour, then he regained consciousness. The physicians advised him not to take up his new command. Impulsively, at the age of thirty, he decided to quit the sea for ever, to swallow the anchor and live on his savings until work turned up. Was it, he asked, Divine Providence that he did not sail? The officer appointed Captain in his place was hacked to pieces on his own vessel in a slave revolt not many months afterwards.

His Mary was ill. He took her to Chatham where she could be looked after. He himself went sermon-tasting, learnt Greek, and enjoyed bear-baiting and bowling and card-playing. Later he gave up such frivolities but he was less censorious than most Evangelicals of his day. He rather disapproved of Hell Fire sermons. 'Love and fear,' he said, 'are like the sun and moon, seldom seen together.' It showed an unusual gentleness of spirit in that age. Dr. Johnson, on gloomily asserting he was very probably damned, and asked to define it, replied forcefully: 'Sent to Hell, Sir, and punished eternally.'

Newton found work, entering the Liverpool Customs Service in a well-paid post. Mary recovered and joined him in the north and John continued as one of the two Tide Scriveners for five years. He had a good deal of leisure time, added Hebrew and some Syriac to his other languages, met Whitefield and Wesley, and went to see famous Evangelical Divines of the Establishment including Grimshaw, Patrick Brontë's predecessor at Haworth. He felt called to the Ministry, but which? He was urged to propose himself for the Church of England and offered a curacy in Yorkshire. The Bishop of Chester who had been disposed to ordain him then said he could not. From the Archbishop of York he 'receiv'd the softest refusal imaginable'. The Archbishop of Canterbury likewise refused. John Wesley tugged the other way. Newton should be an itinerant preacher. Then he was urged to become a Congregational Minister and actually served as one in Warwick for three months. He was invited by a Presbyterian Church in Yorkshire to become their minister. Then, in 1762, giving up all idea of ordination, he wrote a series of eight letters about his life to the present – the first draft of a book named *An Authentic Narrative* which was to make him famous. A young clergyman from Christchurch Oxford passed it to Lord Dartmouth, a leading Evangelical, and in the course of time, Newton was offered the assistant curacy of Olney in Buckinghamshire: that is charge of the parish and the use of the vicarage, as the vicar was an ordained pen-cutter named Moses Brown who wrote poetry and held a college chaplaincy as well as his vicarage and thus was an absentee. Lord Dartmouth already had a distinguished career in the House of Lords. He was more interested in a faithful observance of his religion than in hunting and racing and balls, and he had the influence to persuade a bishop to ordain his nominee. And so the convert with a rich experience of sea life, described as 'an odd, unclerical little man with a big nose', but with immense energy and humour and strength of conviction, of so compelling a personality that Coleridge was later to use him as the prototype for 'The Ancient Mariner', was ordained at the hands of the Bishop of Lincoln, presented to gentlemen of distinction by his noble patron, arrived to take charge of Olney parish, and stunned a clerical neighbour who was neither an enthusiast nor an Evangelical by genially informing him, 'I am one of the most astonishing instances of the forbearance and mercy of God upon the face of the earth'.

Newton was a different type of Evangelical from most. He looked much more back to the hell he had lived through, than forward to the Hell he might reach. He went from cottage to cottage in Olney, where there was a thriving industry of lace-making, cheering up his parishioners rather than filling them with dread. He was liked for his sense; calculating that every village had its idiot, was it surprising that Olney, twelve times the size of many villages, should have a dozen. No more than any other clergyman was he universally loved. There were bully boys in the town who were fiercely opposed to the parson. Indeed, when he attempted to restrain the annual riotousness of the Gunpowder Treason and Plot celebrations, a crowd of defiant parishioners, inflamed by drink from The Bull and other inns, marched on the Vicarage to smash all the windows. The parson wisely sent out an appeasing message and a shilling for the ringleader, who marched his men back to The Bull. Newton was a very pastoral parson, but his most notable work at Olney was as a result of the publication of *An Authentic Narrative*, for it not only at once put him in line for preferment – and Lord Dartmouth at once offered him the Presidency of a new College or University in Georgia with the living of Savannah, and another friend offered him the living of Cottenham – but it put him in touch with dozens of enquirers of all classes. He refused both offers of preferment, but made it his business to care for his new friends, some of whom made pilgrimages to see him, and he became spiritual director to many of them. Amongst them was the distinguished London divine Martin Madan, formerly a barrister-at-law and co-author with Charles Wesley and Whitefield of 'Hark, the herald Angels sing', and re-arranger of two hymns by Charles Wesley and the Quaker, John Sennick, into 'Lo! he comes with clouds descending'* and who later was forced into retirement because he supported polygamy. Before that, however, he became a link in the chain that was to bind John Newton and William Cowper, for he was Cowper's 'Cousin Madan'.

Newton first met Cowper in 1767. He and Mary had been on holiday in Yorkshire. Their host returned the visit to Olney and proposed that Newton become acquainted with another family clergyman named Unwin who lived not far away in Huntingdon and who had staying in his house Martin Madan's cousin William Cowper. It was possibly an exaggeration to describe old Mr. Morley Unwin as Evangelical, for this inferred a degree of zeal and Unwin was very eighteenth century in his lack of zeal. Indeed he was so idle that to his parishioners' fury he never performed any clerical duties at all, and was theologically suspect for he politely doubted the divinity of Christ. John Newton dutifully rode over to meet this fireball of the Established Church, only to find he was several days too late. Mr. Unwin had tumbled from his horse and cracked his skull, muttered deliriously for four days whilst his wife, son and daughter, and William Cowper, hovered waiting unavailingly for the vital Evangelical affirmation of faith which would guarantee his salvation, and had died unsaved. The distraught family needed Newton's counsel.

Mr. Cowper had been their lodger for some time. It was convenient that he should be for, poor man, he had lived an acutely miserable existence. The Cowpers were gentlefolk. William's father

---

* *Helmsley*, the popular tune for this popular hymn, is an adaption of an eighteenth century ballad known as 'Miss Catley's Hornpipe' or 'De'il tak' the wars that hurried Billy frae me'. Sheridan used it for his plaintive song: 'When sable night each drooping plant restoring.'

was a Chaplain to George II, his grandfather a Judge of the Common Pleas, and his uncle Lord Chancellor and the first Earl Cowper. William's mother was a Donne of Norfolk and thus related to the eccentric Dean of St. Paul's who wrote such metaphysical poetry. His mother had meant all the world to William. She died, as Newton's mother had done, when he was six; and forty-seven years afterwards he was to write that not a day passed without him thinking of her. Again like Newton, he had been sent off to a school. There he did not suffer at the hands of a sadistic schoolmaster as Newton had done. His devil was a lout of fifteen who tormented him so vilely that Cowper never looked up beyond the bully's buckled shoes. At the same time he discovered, or was told, or imagined that he had some form of intimate sexual deformity; and he was at once convinced he was different from everyone else and somehow rejected. Things looked up for him when he went to Westminster School. As much as was possible he was happy there. For all his sickliness he played cricket and football and did well. He could turn out respectable Latin verses and better English ones. He was happier after he had left school and began reading law. He was happy to fall in love with his cousin Theodora, write poems to her, and think of her wistfully when they were parted. He never did well at the bar. He never married Theodora. He had lost his nerve too long before.

In 1752 he began to suffer from severe melancholia. He had no routine, no briefs, nothing to prevent the melancholia from deepening to anguish. Then he was saved by reading George Herbert's poetry and writing prayers. He grew more composed. A visit to a cousin in Southampton helped still more. He was taken bathing, wore sailor's trousers and went sailing. His spirits rose. Suddenly he felt able to take joy in life again. Here his history lacks substance. It is known he mourned his father who died in 1756, and a close friend who was accidentally drowned; that he had friends with whom he dined, and that he preferred literature to the law. But there is a lacuna because it seems that he did virtually nothing for ten years except wait for one or other of two government posts promised him by a cousin when they should fall vacant. Both fell vacant in 1763 and he was offered the more valuable, that of Reading Clerk and Clerk of the Committees in the House of Commons. It was virtually a sinecure and would keep him in comfort for life. Overscrupulousness, or feelings of inadequacy and anxiety, made him ask his cousin if he could have instead the less lucrative piece of patronage, that of Clerk of the Journals of the House of Lords. His cousin agreed. All seemed well. But then Cowper heard that he would have to face an appointing committee and he was thrown into an agitated fever. Remembering what Southampton had done for him before he went to Margate for the summer. It did no good, because on his return his nerves collapsed; he hid himself from his friends, gave up prayer, gave up food, and in despair he tried to kill himself, first by an overdose of laudanum, then by drowning, then by his penknife,* finally by hanging. But he could not take his life. Instead he grew even wilder and more incoherent, and he went mad. His brother John, a Cambridge don, was sent for. Cowper raved about his inescapability from utter damnation, and so his Evangelical cousin, Martin Madan, was sent for as well. They determined to commit Cowper to Dr. Cotton's Home for Madmen at St. Albans, a robust eighteenth century name for a private lunatic asylum, kept by a medical man who was a convinced Evangelical, and a versifier in the tradition of Isaac Watts. Dr. Cotton calmed his patient with sedatives, and, after much rest, treated him with tenderness and calmed his religious terrors with 'the things concerning salvation'. Within five months Cowper was well enough to find sufficient appetite to eat and drink with pleasure. He was given the Bible to read and what in its day was a famous book, James Hervey's *Meditations among the Tombs*. A whole year later, Dr. Cotton pronounced him well enough to leave.

Cowper left, a convinced Evangelical, and, with a modest income guaranteed by a family trust, he took lodgings in Huntingdon under the friendly eye of his brother John only fifteen miles away at Cambridge. It was his own wish not to live in London, or see the friends of his youth. Instead he chose to live in the country, and country people then lived totally different lives from the inhabitants of the metropolis. Their social life was not the same, not even the time they slept and ate and took exercise. Their speech was notably different, and their clothing generally so. Their contact with affairs was through old copies of *St. James's Gazette* or very expensive letters. Cowper felt that the differences, the remoteness, would be beneficial. But then he found himself lonely in his lodgings. The emotional demands of being an Evangelical were considerable to a man with such a frail nervous system. Always he had to be at concert pitch to maintain that state of grace which he believed he had achieved by his 'conversion'. He badly needed the company of like-minded souls to shore him up. Divine providence, as he believed

---

* This is not so ridiculous as it might at first appear. Clive of India ended his life on the 22nd November 1774 by cutting his throat with a penknife in a lavatory at 54, Berkeley Square. Samuel Whitbread did the same forty-one years later at 34, Dover Street.

it was, gave him the friendship of a young man named Unwin whose mother and sister were good Evangelicals and who lived a snug existence of order and comfort and piety. All the Unwins, even the lethargical and non-Evangelical old Mr. Unwin, took to Cowper and his quiet but sincere religion and his liking for literature and music. Within three months Cowper had entered the monastic enclosure of their lives. They prayed and read together, breakfasted and dined and took tea together, walked together for up to four miles a day at the slow pace their clothing dictated, Cowper ungainly like a harvestman insect but attentive always to the ladies, especially Mrs. Unwin. When alone he read, wrote verses and letters, or rode out for exercise. He also took a great interest in the garden. Planning and digging and sowing and planting and weeding soothed him more than anything. His quietude had deepened and lasted two years until, on the 2nd July 1767, old Mr. Unwin died.

Cowper's fright at what might happen was only appeased by Mrs. Unwin's assurance she would not desert him. He wrote to a Hertfordshire cousin, Miss Cowper, a few days after the funeral, that Mrs. Unwin's behaviour had been that 'of a mother to a son'. It was a curious situation, for Mrs. Unwin's children were grown up and, at forty-four, she was only eight years older than he. Moreover she was bereft of intellectual accomplishments, unsubtle and, by most standards, limited. Yet she shared his religious views and supplied what he most needed, support and strength, and had a common-sense way of going about things. Moreover she was a most constant and reassuring and sensible person. John Newton, when he came to visit the Unwins and was asked his advice by the bereaved family and the pale poet, at once bade them visit Olney Vicarage where they would be welcomed by his Mary. This they did, and they were so struck with Olney they decided to move there. A vacant house on the south side of the market green was taken for them, and six weeks to the day after Mr. Unwin's death they left Huntingdon for ever, living at the Vicarage while their new home Orchard Side was decorated, and establishing a new form of cloistered existence which was to last for several years. John Newton was to be Cowper's guardian in his faith. Cowper was to assist as he could in the parochial work, Mrs. Unwin was to continue as Cowper's prop and stay. The two men appeared strangely unalike; the small Newton, with his big nose and roaring and piercing eye and wild, romantic history; the taller but more timid Cowper with his gangling gait, and valetudinarianism, and his fearful experience of mental anguish. Yet they shared a conversion of striking vividness, and each was devout.

There was no one of Cowper's class in Olney. Quaintly he was known as 'Sir Cowper' or 'Squire'. But this separateness, more rigid in the eighteenth century than most, did not prevent him from carrying the Evangelical banner. He found himself drawn into the whirlpool of Newton's energetic zeal. They spent eight hours a day in each other's company. Cowper went with him to minister to the sick and the dying, taught in the Sunday School, visited the poor, accompanied him on his long walks and rides to preach in neighbouring parishes.

It was perhaps natural that both should turn their literary talent, Newton's so much less than Cowper's, but still valid, to spreading the Gospel and feeding Evangelical sheep with sacred poetry and hymns. They were in the tradition of Watts and Doddridge and the Wesleys. The cottage workers sang simple Lace Tellings as they bent over their clicking bobbins, and Newton had a habit of writing a weekly hymn to put to a Lace Telling tune and be sung at the Great House, a large hall where he held extempore prayer meetings and gave addresses and Bible classes, as distinct from the Divine Offices offered daily in the Parish Church. Busy as never before in his life, Cowper yet found time to write verses. When he could he took solitary walks in the countryside, far preferring it to Olney itself. There was one neighbouring village named Weston Underwood for which he had a special affection. Situated on an upland above the meads and crack willows beside the plenteous Ouse, it was so quiet a place that, if the rooks were silent, footfalls could be heard in the dusty village streets. Cowper would go there and think out his verses under the trees.

Within Orchard House and its little garden life was as orderly and unremarkable and placid as that of the Unwin home at Huntingdon. The young Mr. Unwin had been ordained and left the household. The three who remained were so ensconced that the need to move out, because a servant had smallpox, and live temporarily in the principal inn, The Bull, was greatly upsetting. Had they been abruptly moved to the middle of Arabia they could scarcely have felt it more. Equally vexing to Mrs. Unwin, who was determined Cowper should at least have peace in the home, was the servants' propensity to back-slide in their religion once they had become useful to her. The respectable seemed incompetent; the competent insufficiently converted. When eventually they were suited they found themselves very comfortable. The grounds of the Vicarage touched on the little garden of Orchard House, so a wicket was made to facilitate the exchange of visits. These were frequent. The sea captain Evangelical and his 'dearest dear' were in and out of Orchard

House less often than the poet Evangelical and his ladies were at the Vicarage, but they met at least once a day and generally much more often.

To the conventional ordinary man of the eighteenth century both households would have appeared quite extraordinary, for masters and servants exchanged intimate details of the present condition of their salvation and discussed with each other the nearness or distance of an acquaintance from the Mercy Seat.

Extempore prayer, even extempore preaching, could suddenly interrupt a quiet half hour's reading or sewing by the fire, or even a stroll in the countryside. There is no indication as to how ascetic they were in eating and drinking, but to the average person, accustomed to mountainous meat meals and great quantities of port or claret, they must have been lean feasts. From time to time John Cowper took the coach over from Cambridge to see his brother. Being an average sort of rationalist clergyman don, embarrassed by enthusiasm, and fond of his comforts, he must have found the visits to Olney insupportable. But he loyally did his duty to the family.

The years passed. John Newton's energy never flagged. Cowper's zeal did. He began to suffer spiritual aridity. Evidently they were symptoms of his disease, but no-one then would have diagnosed them, or, for that matter, treated him. He suffered fairly silently but occasionally he felt it keenly. He wrote to his aunt, Mrs. Madan, that he regretted he no longer felt as he had done at his conversion, 'When the name of Jesu was like honey and milk upon my tongue and the very sound of it was sufficient to sustain and comfort me'. Then his faith and his sanity were challenged by a message from Cambridge in March 1770. His brother John was dying. Would he go to him? Cowper's old faith soared up like a rocket. He took the next coach and went straight to his brother. He begged him to repent; give up his well-worn conventional religion and truly repent. For days he worked to bring his brother to the ecstasy of Final Perseverance, and either because he was convinced, or he was too weary to stand out against such zeal, his brother declared that Divine light had enfolded him, he felt saved. William was almost beside himself with relief and excitement.

After John's glorious death he suffered a relapse of faith himself. He could no longer take pleasure in religion, nor in anything else. His life continued as before but his motive for leading it had left him. Newton did what he could for him. So did Mrs. Unwin. Neither succeeded greatly. They observed his melancholy with distress and increasing anxiety. Each sensed it needed but the smallest, unlooked for, event to trigger off real madness, and kept his life on as even a keel as possible. Miss Unwin became engaged to be married, a joyous event for everyone except Cowper. He felt obliged to ask Mrs. Unwin to marry him as they could scarcely live together after her daughter's departure. Mrs. Unwin accepted his proposal. It pressed the trigger. On January the 24th, 1773, Cowper's reason fled. He could not bear the thought of marriage. Newton was woken at five in the morning by a message from Mrs. Unwin. He dressed and hurried through the garden wicket, and found Cowper raving. Doctors were sent for, Dr. Cotton was consulted by post. The Newtons spent a great part of each day at Orchard Side 'astonis'd and griev'd' at their friend's sufferings. They had their own troubles. Mary's mother died as did one of her sisters. A man greasing the church bells had his thigh broken. Bellringers were found dead drunk on duty. One of the lace makers went off her head and had to be taken to the local Bethlehem or Bedlam. But apart from Mary Newton's enforced absence they were constant in their attentions upon Cowper for a full three months. They took him out walking or for a drive in a chaise. He scarcely responded. Mostly he was indifferent, drawn within himself, sometimes showing signs of agitation and great mental stress. Yet in rare lucid moments he would accept the consolations of religion and it was then that, miraculously, he wrote some of his most memorable hymns. 'Hark, my soul! it is the Lord' and 'God moves in a mysterious way' were written by a man in anguish. So was that hymn for Holy Communion, in which we see the inspired imagery and desperateness of the madman, 'There is a fountain filled with Blood'. And so, wrung from him by the pitifulness of his condition, was the hymn that confirmed his place as the greatest hymn writer of the age.

> 'O for a closer walk with God,
>   A calm and heavenly frame;
> A light to shine upon the road
>   That leads me to the Lamb!
>
> Return, O holy Dove, return,
>   Sweet messenger of rest;
> I hate the sins that made thee mourn,
>   And drove thee from my breast.
>
> The dearest idol I have known,
>   Whate'er that idol be,
> Help me to tear it from thy throne,
>   And worship only thee.

So shall my walk be close with God,
Calm and serene my frame;
So purer light shall mark the road
That leads me to the Lamb.'

This deeply moving prayer from the heart of a man in despair was composed just before one of the two Cattle Fairs held yearly on the Market Green in Olney. It was a boisterous occasion, on Easter Monday 1733, and Cowper, holding his ears from the noise of lowing beasts and of dealing and the rowdiness of drunken stockmen, and farmers, and pedlars, shrieked that he was damned, damned irrevocably. He was hurried from Orchard Side through the little wicket to the Vicarage, and there he sank into total madness. Six months later he was still at the Vicarage; usually persuadable but always morose and fearful and never far from the edge of the abyss. The Newtons decided to take a fortnight away and went on a preaching tour in Warwickshire. But on their return they found poor 'Sir Cowper' greatly deteriorated. He was obsessed with guilt and Abraham's sacrifice of Isaac. He tried to kill himself and was prevented just in time. Mrs. Unwin was unremitting in her labours to bring back Cowper's sanity. Newton could do little save pray, though for and not with his friend, because Cowper believed himself beyond the power of prayer. Only Mrs. Unwin could help him, as his one contact with normality, and she gave herself to nursing him day and night. She had small reward because he often shrank away from her, and, besides this, she bore the burden of public calumny. The people of Olney now openly expressed their disapproval of their association. Parson Newton was told it had been bad enough at Orchard House. For such things to go on in his Vicarage was worse. Newton was firmly loyal to his friends. He outfaced his parishioners and doubtless told them about beams and motes. At any rate, the muttering died down. He was also very generous, refusing to let either pay for their keep and insisting they were Mary's guests. And he was very patient. Cowper was darkly gloomy all the time. Newton noted when one day he smiled as he was feeding the Vicarage fowl. It was his first smile for sixteen months. Having such a permanent guest must have been a severe strain. In fact, Newton and his Mary were saintly about the whole episode. She was frequently unwell herself and had to have leeches applied to her feet. Then she was obliged to go and say goodbye to a dearly loved sister who was moving to remote Scotland. Her consolations were long letters from her husband, as uxorious as ever: 'Since the Lord gave me the desire of my heart in my Dearest Mary, the rest of the sex are no more to me

'The old African blasphemer' John Newton (*Olney Museum*)

OLNEY HYMNS,

IN

THREE BOOKS.

BOOK I. On felect Texts of SCRIPTURE.

BOOK II. On occafional SUBJECTS.

BOOK III. On the Progrefs and Changes
of the SPIRITUAL LIFE.

———————————Cantabitis, Arcades, inquit,
Montibus hæc veftris : foli cantare periti
Arcades. O mihi tum quàm molliter offa quiefcant,
Veftra meos olim fi fiftula dicat amores !

VIRGIL, Ecl. x. 31.

And they fang as it were a new fong before the
throne ;—and no man could learn that fong,
but the redeemed from the earth. Rev. xiv. 3.

As forrowful—yet always rejoicing, 2 Cor. vi. 10.

L O N D O N:

Printed and Sold by W. OLIVER, Nᵒ 12, Bartholomew-Clofe ;
Sold alfo by J BUCKLAND, Nᵒ 57, Pater-nofter-Row ; and
J. JOHNSON, Nᵒ 72, St Paul's Church-yard.

M DCC LXXIX.

The title page to *Olney Hymns, 1779*

This publication, which, with my humble prayer to the LORD for his blessing upon it, I offer to the service and acceptance of all who love the LORD JESUS CHRIST in sincerity, of every name and in every place, into whose hands it may come ; I more particularly dedicate to my dear friends in the parish and neighbourhood of *Olney*, for whose use the hymns were originally composed ; as a testimony of the sincere love I bear them, and as a token of my gratitude to the LORD, and to them, for the comfort and satisfaction with which the discharge of my ministry among them has been attended.

The hour is approaching, and at my time of life cannot be very distant, when my heart, my pen, and my tongue, will no longer be able to move in their service. But I trust, while my heart continues to beat, it will feel a warm desire for the prosperity of their souls ; and while my hand can write, and my tongue speak, it will be the business and the pleasure of my life, to aim at promoting their growth and establishment in the grace of our GOD and Saviour. To this precious grace I commend them, and earnestly entreat them, and all who love his name, to strive mightily with their prayers to GOD for me, that I may be preserved faithful to the end, and enabled at last to finish my course with joy.

Olney, Bucks,
Feb. 15, 1779.

JOHN NEWTON.

2 5   CON-

Extract from John Newton's Preface to *Olney Hymns*

The tormented William Cowper, who wrote his greatest hymns in his hours of deepest despair (L. F. Abbott, 1792, *National Portrait Gallery*)

than the tulips in the garden.' He wrote this at the beginning of May, 1774, when Cowper and Mrs. Unwin were still at the Vicarage. It was not until the end of that month that Cowper grew sufficiently calm to go back to Orchard Side. It had been a long haul for them all: a winter, a spring, a summer, an autumn, another winter and spring again; more than twelve months. Cowper was given a hare by a kind neighbour and the gift delighted him. He found solace in watching and taming the hare, so much so that others were pressed upon the Squire. He gravely thanked them but took only two more, and for a very long time the three hares, named Tiny, Puss and Ben, absorbed his interests. Though he would never be the same again, Cowper's nerves were slowly soothed. He returned to his old love of gardening; adding carpentry and drawing; wrote occasional verses and fed the pigeons. The Newtons found great pleasure in adopting a niece, Betsy Catlett, and they persuaded Mary's old father to give up his house in Chatham and go to live with them.

John Newton was slowing down. He preached and wrote as before and rode round the countryside far more than the average parson; but he had begun to like to smoke a pipeful, and grew stout as the temptation to overeat met with too little resistance. For all that, he was a modest eater for the age, and, though only fifteen years ordained, he was accepted as a leader of the small and influential group of Evangelical parsons in the Established Church. Inevitably it seemed he must be offered preferment again. He was, in 1779, six years after Cowper and Mrs. Unwin had returned to Orchard Side from their year at the Vicarage. He was offered the living of St. Mary Woolnoth, in the City of London, a parish with barely one hundred parishioners, but an eclectic congregation of great influence and interest. He went with his Mary through the wicket gate to discuss the matter with his old friends at Orchard Side. They decided he must accept. But before he left the parish the patron of his new living undertook to publish the hymns both the two friends had been preparing for so long, the *Olney Hymns*. It consisted of sixty-eight by Cowper and two hundred and eighty by Newton. The latter, though he did most of the work, wrote far less poetry, yet of his contributions one has achieved a peculiar eminence in the modern world. 'Amazing grace! How sweet the sound That saved a wretch like me' is only found in four of the thirty-eight principal hymnals used by English speaking Christians today; but in the early 1970's, set to an early American melody, it was recorded as played by the band of the Royal Scots Dragoon Guards with the melody underlined by a single pipe of the regimental pipe major, and sold millions and millions of copies. The old and middle-aged as well as the young kept it at first position in the ten best-selling records for a record time of nine weeks. Doubtless it would have amazed the author, but also, probably, pleased him. He always liked to impart the intense gratitude he felt for his own conversion to as many people as possible. And his best hymns are chiefly remembered because they contain abounding joyousness: 'How sweet the name of Jesus sounds', a litany of praise much valued by many Christian denominations, and 'Glorious things of thee are spoken', a thunderous affirmation of faith emphasised by the last two lines, from which the title of this volume is taken:

> 'Solid joys and lasting treasure
> None but Sion's children know.'*

The parting was sorrow for all four. There were promises of visits and letters. Newton had an idea Cowper might not love his replacement at the Vicarage and commended the friendship of his pipe-smoking crony, the Independent Minister of Newport Pagnell. Then as he settled in London he watched the great progress of Cowper which secured his position as 'the first poet of the day', publications of *Poems by William Cowper of the Inner Temple, Esq.* in 1782, *The Task* in 1785, the immortal *John Gilpin* in 1786, and his translation of Homer in 1791. All of this would have given the older man great pleasure, as would the knowledge that Cowper had been made more secure financially in 1785 by the gift of an anonymous donor who settled on him an annuity of £50. Cowper never knew it, but the donor was his first and only love Theodora, still unmarried after all these years. Newton also watched with anxiety when Cowper and Mrs. Unwin moved to his favourite village of Weston Underwood where he had Roman Catholic friends, the Throckmortons. He need not have been alarmed. No-one who had gone through so fierce an Evangelical fire as William Cowper was likely to embrace popery. Then Newton would have felt the pain of the news of Cowper's third and worst collapse into madness, triggered off this time by the death of Mrs. Unwin's son. In his dementia he hanged himself but Mrs. Unwin again saved him. She arrived in the room in time and cut him down. His recovery was rapid but never complete and he was always subject thereafter to strange delusions. Then Mrs. Unwin had a series of paralytic

---

* This hymn is generally set to the tune *Austria* which is the tune of the Austrian National Anthem *Deutschland! Deutschland! uber alles.* . This greatly startled the German Emperor, Kaiser Bill, when, visiting his godmother at Windsor and attending Divine Service, he found himself singing Newton's hymn.

seizures, each worse than the last. She became exacting. Friends and relations considered it would do both of them good if they went to live down in Norfolk under the guardianship of Cowper's cousin Johnson. When Mrs. Unwin at last died, Cowper received the news with little emotion. He scarcely had sufficient strength. He grew weaker, and died peacefully on the 25th April, 1800.

Of all who mourned Cowper no-one was more sincere than his old friend John Newton, who though on an eminence as counsellor to such people as William Wilberforce, Charles Simeon of Cambridge, and Hannah More of Cowslip Green, was himself a sorrowing widower. In 1788 Mary Newton had discovered she was suffering from cancer. No surgeon dared operate. She lived quietly, taking a little laudanum, and comforted by Newton. She developed a disgust for butcher's meat, then even for poultry and fish. All she could manage was small birds, but they were out of season in the markets and Newton appealed to country friends to do what they could. By the time the markets were full of small birds again Mary's appetite had gone altogether. She lay almost twelve months, reading the Bible and the hymns of Isaac Watts, Charles Wesley, her good friend William Cowper, and her John. Then, quite abruptly, she rejected her faith entirely for a fortnight. Newton could do nothing for her, but to his immense relief it was only a phase through which she passed. He was more than simply distressed when she died. He was troubled because he feared his great love for her had been slightly idolatrous. Friends tried to help. More successful was the suggestion of his adopted daughter Betsy that they spend a time in travelling. In the summer of 1791, when Cowper's *Homer* was published, they travelled by stage and by chaise more than seven hundred and fifty miles. This enabled him to bear his loss, and he returned to a full and busy life, always slightly astonished that he seemed destined for an old age. Cowper's death was another sunderment, but he could not grieve for his old friend who had known such distress. He confided in Hannah More of Cowslip Green that the poet 'for twenty-seven years knew not one peaceful day'.

His Betsy became engaged to an optician. It was as well, quipped Newton, for his eyesight was going and such a son-in-law would be useful. But the prospect of matrimony had a serious effect upon Betsy, as it had, once, upon poor William Cowper. Her nerves fell to pieces. All sorts of remedies were tried. But in the end she had to be sent to Bedlam. Newton, virtually blind, was desperately sad and anxious. One of his servants took him daily to Bedlam, and there, outside the ward of Betsy's confinement, he waved a handkerchief and bade his servant look for an answering signal. No matter how cold or wet the weather he would wait and wait until Betsy made her signal. She was fortunate. Within a year she had recovered her senses sufficiently to be discharged. Within two years of that she married her optician and they both moved in to live with the ageing Newton. Though blind he still preached. Tactful friends suggested it was too much for him. He was indignant. 'What! Shall the old African blasphemer stop while he can speak?' He became absent-minded and his senses increasingly failed him. He awaited death with some impatience, declaring it was like waiting for a stage-coach which, for some reason or other, failed to arrive. But it did come at last on St. Thomas's Day 1807.

Cowper had been buried in Norfolk with this couplet carved on his tomb:

> 'His Highest honours to the heart belong,
> His virtues formed the magic of his song.'

Newton wrote his own epitaph

> JOHN NEWTON, Clerk
> Once an infidel and libertine,
> A servant of slaves in Africa:
> Won by the rich mercy of our Lord and Saviour
> Jesus Christ,
> Persevered, restored, pardoned,
> And appointed to preach the Faith
> He had long laboured to destroy.

He lay with Mary Newton in his London church until 1863 when their remains were transferred to Olney, where he and Cowper had written their marvellous hymns.

They were remembered seventy-five years afterwards by another poet who also loved hymns and had a deep personal piety. Not yet Poet Laureate nor knighted; in fact a bare thirty years of age, John Betjeman stood beside the spired church where the old sea captain and the nervous poet had worshipped for so long together, and he wrote

> 'Oh God the Olney Hymns abound
>   With words of Grace which Thou didst choose,
> And wet the elm above the hedge
>   Reflecting in the winding Ouse.
>
> Pour in my soul unemptied floods
>   That stand between the slopes of clay,
> Till deep beyond a deeper depth
>   This Olney day is any day.'*

---

* From *Collected Poems* of John Betjeman by kind permission of John Murray (Publishers) Ltd.

CHAPTER THREE

AUTHORISATION

THE great success of *Olney Hymns* ensured that it would have imitators. The Wesleyans had the *Wesleyan Hymn Book*; the usual hymn book of the Independent and Congregational Churches was Isaac Watts's *Psalms and Hymns*; the Unitarians, hard thinkers and deep prayers, were to publish a hymn book in 1819 which excluded the word 'soul', "because the doctrine of the soul had no rational foundation"; yet no hymn book in the modern sense was authorised for use in the Established Church.* Evangelical parsons like Toplady and Newton did not trouble themselves unduly about such formality but other clergymen did. Most of them were old-fashioned High Churchmen, known in their day as 'High and Dry' because of their sober dread of emotionalism in religion, which might lead to an enthusiasm they found ill-bred and disgusting. Worse it might take people off into Dissent. Anything but metrical psalms and the hymns included as canticles in the Book of Common Prayer were anathema to them, and in 1817 one Yorkshire clergyman was summoned to appear before the York Consistory Court for using a hymn book which he and his organist had concocted between them and had printed. The plea that this was illegal was allowed by the Archbishop who, Solomon-like, politely requested that the book be withdrawn and, at the same time, offered to sanction a revised edition which he said he would print at his own expense.

This prelate, Edward Vernon, afterwards took the name of Harcourt when he inherited the vast estates of his kinsman, the third Earl of Harcourt, and he represented something of a break with his

---

* John Wesley had produced the first Church of England hymn book, a third of the contents by Isaac Watts, at Charlestown in 1738, but it was in no sense authorised.

eighteenth century predecessors, particularly the rollicking devil-may-care Archbishop Lancelot Blackburn who, so it was alleged, numbered among his numerous illegitimate progeny a Bishop of Norwich. Harcourt had of course the right connections; being the youngest son of the first Lord Vernon and married to a daughter of the first Marquis of Stafford; besides which he was rich and had many important political friends. Otherwise, in such an age of patronage, he would not have been a bishop for fifty-six years living under five successive sovereigns, and being Lord High Almoner to George III and Queen Victoria. Nor would he have been able to do so well for four of his eight surviving sons; one being a Prebendary of Carlisle; another, a Canon of York; another Chancellor of York Minster; and, the fourth, a barrister, Chancellor of the Diocese of York.* Nevertheless he much disapproved of ostentation and of contentious prelates, modestly refusing the offer of a renewal of the Harcourt peerage when he took his inheritance, and was respected for his caution and love of compromises. He voted against Catholic Emancipation with a majority of his fellow prelates in the House of Lords, not because he was against Emancipation, but because he disliked the wording of the bill; and he avoided being caught up in the conservative vote against the Reform Bill by prudently remaining north in his diocese. There was no-one better to be a member of the Commission set up by Lord Grey, a Whig of conservative mind, for the necessary reforms of the Established Church now that the Wesleyan connection had taken from its congregations almost all shop-keepers and artisans and large sections of the poor. Harcourt lived an amiable and useful life for forty years as Archbishop, showing great generosity when, twice during his primacy, York Minster suffered severe fire damage. He preached his valedictory sermon in the Minister in November 1838, but lived on at Bishopsthorpe until 1847 when, in his ninety-first year while he was walking with his chaplain on a wooden bridge over an ornamental pool, the wood shattered and both found themselves up to their chins in icy water. 'Well,' he said cheerfully as they were hauled out, 'I believe we frightened the frogs!' but the drenching proved too much for his aged constitution, and, within a month, on the evening of Gunpowder Treason and Plot, the good old man died. The hymn book which he sanctioned, and for which he paid the expense of publication, was Harcourt's important contribution to English

---

* The remaining four boys were a Member of Parliament, a Lieutenant-Colonel, a Vice-Admiral and an Admiral.

Hymnody; the first officially recognised hymn book of the Church of England. It was named *Cotterill's Hymns* after the clergyman who had been cited in the York Consistory Court and was a carefully revised edition of his previous work. To aid him in his revision, and to add to its contents, Cotterill invited the assistance of a versatile poet, James Montgomery, whose contributions were so important and who led such an unusual life that both invite attention.

Montgomery was born in Ayrshire in the Lowlands of Scotland in 1771. It was an important year. Walter Scott was also born then, so was Robert Owen the social reformer, and so was Sydney Smith, an eccentric parson, gifted contributor to the *Edinburgh Review*, unexcelled for his drollery, once urging a colleague appointed as first Bishop of New Zealand to be sure to have cold clergyman on the sideboard to meet the taste of his native guests, and, to his friends 'a spirit as joyous as Nature on a sunny day'. Possibly the most significant event for mankind in 1771 was Richard Arkwright's production of the first spinning wheel. Montgomery's parents were Scots but his father's family had long been living in the Ulster plantation. There is one of those customary allusions, found in many families, to having belonged once to the great and powerful; and the young James heard his great grandfather had inherited an estate and dissipated his fortune with vice. James's father was a common labourer of co. Antrim, but then he became a Moravian and married a Moravian and in some way managed to get himself made a Moravian Minister. This was the reason for James being born in Ayrshire. At the time the only Moravian settlement in Scotland was there. Nevertheless the family returned to Ulster when James was four, and he had only reached six, when his parents deposited him in a totally strange Moravian boarding-school at Fulneck in Yorkshire, and, like a pair of depraved Mrs. Jellabys, they took themselves off to do good works to the natives of the Barbados.

The deserted boy made the best of a bad job, though he did not care for the schoolwork and preferred writing verses. This became a passion. He composed epics; one on King Alfred; yet another on the world, in which the fallen archangel Satan had his wings clipped by the Archangel Michael. He went through childhood and the beginnings of adolescence with no holidays from school and little if any contact with his undutiful parents. The Moravians saw no merit in his verses nor evidently did they consider him fit for the ministry, and, as a lad of fourteen or fifteen, they apprenticed him to a baker. Being left alone to fend for himself gave him a tough independent spirit which made him find the life of a baker's boy intolerable. He still scribbled verses, and his pockets were full of them when he decided to bolt and seek his fortune elsewhere. Besides the bundle of poems his total capital was three shillings and six pence. He met with some luck, but not much. A poem carefully written out and presented to Earl Fitzwilliam brought him his first literary earnings, a guinea. He found he could not manage. Homeless, virtually an orphan, quite alone in the world, and with no character testimonials, he was fortunate to be taken on as a shopboy in a chandler's at Mirfield.* Once more he felt entirely out of his element. Neither baker's nor chandler's suited his temperament. Again he bolted with his poetry and, after a few days of liberty and increasing hunger, he found work in the general store in the little village of Wath-upon-Dearn. This was close to Rotherham, an ancient town which had begun to change its character by the introduction of an iron industry. Montgomery was treated well by the village store-keeper but now he was eighteen and he longed for the literary life. There was only one place for him – London. His master let him go. A year later he was back in Wath. No publisher had given him any encouragement whatsoever. His old job was still open to him and gratefully he took it. It must have been about this period that any contact that existed between James Montgomery and his parents came to an end. When he discovered the facts is not known, but his mother died of yellow fever in 1790 and his father met with the same fate one year later.†

In April 1792 Montgomery saw an advertisement in *The Sheffield Register* for a clerk and book-keeper in the office of the newspaper. It was not much of an opening, but he took it; and from the moment of his introduction to Joseph Gales, described variously as the newspaper's proprietor and printer, a bookseller and auctioneer, the boy's luck changed. He was twenty-two and living in exciting if dangerous times for a journalist. The American colonies had revolted in a seven year war and declared their independence. The beginning of the French Revolution had seriously upset the United Kingdom, which was already suffering from the birth pangs of the First Industrial Revolution. The use of pit coal instead of wood in smelting iron ore was making England an industrial nation. The invention of the puddling-furnace greatly improved the manufacture of brass in

---

* Later the site of the Community of the Resurrection, which was founded in the diocese of the hymn writer Bishop Walsham How of Wakefield (*q.v.*) and the home of a number of hymn-writing Church of England monks.

---

† Doubtless Mr. and Mrs. Montgomery had the best intentions, but their unfeeling abandonment of their only son at such a tender age moves one to wish, uncharitably, that they had ended up on the Bishop of New Zealand's side-board – as 'cold clergyman'.

Birmingham and cutlery in Sheffield, where Montgomery now lived, and in the very year he moved there coal gas was first used for lighting. The foundation for the cotton industry had been laid. The wool mills, traditionally worked by water, could now be powered by steam. New inventions were threatening cottage industries. Agriculture was altering, too. The flight from the land had begun. The 'dark Satanic mills' were going up. War with France seemed likely. In fact it broke out in 1793, raged for twenty-two years, and tripled the national debt. Warren Hastings was being impeached for maladministration in India in a trial that had begun in 1788 and showed no signs of ending. The authorities were watchful for signs of unrest. Jacobins and liberals threatened the old stability.

Joseph Gales was a liberal. His opinions as expressed in *The Sheffield Register* were unacceptable. Two years after Montgomery arrived as general factotum in the office he found himself alone. His master and friend had been forced to leave the country, just ahead of the Sheffield police. In those two years Montgomery himself had often contributed pieces, commentaries, descriptions of town functions, and, most important to him, verses. Now he rallied his co-workers, successfully found a backer, and, as working editor, promptly issued the paper under a new, unproscribed name, *The Sheffield Iris*. His politics were less liberal and the *Iris* became profitable. A year later he borrowed money to buy out his backer, and he also became a general printer. He was to be proprietor and editor for thirty-one years. Bad luck dogged him in that he was wrongfully prosecuted and imprisoned for printing a ballad about the Fall of the Bastille which had, in fact, been printed by Joseph Gales. He was prosecuted a second time for the way in which his paper described a local magistrate reading the riot act, and again he served time in York prison. He whiled away his time in gaol by writing subversive poems under a pseudonym, and a long four-volume novel; but he was prudent enough to destroy them all when he was released. The political feeling of the time was so high that the prosecution of newspaper proprietors and editors became commonplace. At one time *The Sheffield Iris* was the only newspaper being printed in the town, but Montgomery was more poet and idealist than a realistic journalist. He could not take and keep the advantage, and in 1825 he sold the paper and concentrated on writing poetry and criticism. Like his contemporary the aged Archbishop Harcourt of York, he was too kindly and too impatient to make a good reviewer; and his poetry was given more praise than perhaps it deserved. Yet his contribution to hymnody was considerable. It has

James Montgomery, the Scot deserted by his parents and adopted by Sheffield, where this statue of him stands (*Sheffield Newspapers Limited*)

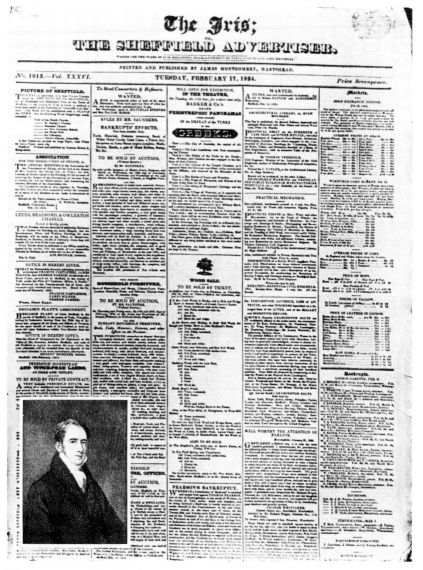

The newspaper, *The Iris*, for editing which Montgomery (inset, painted by John Jackson, R.A.) served two prison terms (*Sheffield Newspapers Limited*)

been claimed that more than one hundred Montgomery hymns are still being sung. Those with undisputable popularity suggest he was in the second, not the first or the third, rank of poets, but that his understanding of praise and worship was keen and full of feeling. 'Hail to the Lord's Anointed!', 'Lord, teach us how to pray aright', 'Go to dark Gethsemane', 'Palms of glory, raiment bright', 'For ever with the Lord!', 'Prayer is the soul's sincere desire', 'Songs of praise the Angels sang', 'Lift up your heads, ye gates of brass' are well-written thoughtful hymns. His very best, perhaps, were the Christmas hymn: 'Angels, from the realms of glory', the Communion hymn: 'According to thy gracious word' and the prayer for the priesthood: 'Pour out thy Spirit from on high'. Montgomery achieved a recognition in his own day. In 1835 Sir Robert Peel offered him a pension of £150 a year.* The citizens of Sheffield honoured and respected him and when, still unmarried, he died quite unexpectedly at the age of eighty-three, the corporation gave him a public funeral and had a monument, designed by John Bell, put over his grave.

★

An even more prodigal hymn writer of the first half of the nineteenth century was James Edmeston, a fairly drab character who seemed untouched by the excitements of the times in which he lived. He was a Londoner and the grandson of an Independent Divine from Stepney, but in adolescence he gave up both Dissent and Stepney for a more fashionable address and regular work in the Established Church. He was assiduous in his religious observance and eventually became a churchwarden. He was also assiduous in work, becoming a respected if not aspiring architect and surveyor in Surrey, and having the Victorian 'reformer' Gilbert Scott amongst his articled clerks. And Edmeston was an assiduous visitor to the London Orphan Asylum, enjoying the company of the inmates and doing a great deal for their welfare. It was for the orphans that he wrote no fewer than two thousand hymns, publishing selected collections from his work under such titles as *Sacred Lyrics*, and *Infant Breathings*. Yet, for all his drabness, and singularity, and assiduity, he was inspired to write one estimable hymn which is still included in every major hymn book in English:

---

* Montgomery was fortunate. The recommendation and offer came towards the very end of Peel's first Administration which only lasted 140 days. The following Whig Administration lasted six years and 138 days.

> 'Lead us, heavenly Father, lead us
>   O'er the world's tempestuous sea;
> Guard us, guide us, keep us, feed us,
>   For we have no help but thee;
> Yet possessing every blessing
>   If our God our Father be.'

This, with its subsequent two stanzas, has a guaranteed immortality denied his remaining one thousand, nine hundred and ninety-nine hymns.

★

A contemporary, Richard Whately, who also wrote long-forgotten hymns, had an infinitely more interesting and colourful life and personality than jejune James Edmeston. The Whately's of Nonsuch Park, Surrey were not undistinguished. Richard's uncle Thomas was a Member of Parliament and he held the singular office of Keeper of His Majesty's Private Roads, and Guide to the Royal Person in all Progresses. Richard's father was ordained, held pluralities and bought himself a Doctorate in Civil Law. Richard's mother was a Miss Jane Plumer of Blakesware Park in Hertfordshire, her widowed mother's dower house, where the housekeeper was grandmother of the unhappy Charles and Mary Lamb. Richard himself was the youngest of nine children: five daughters and four sons, all of whom lived to maturity and most of them to a great age. He appeared long after his parents supposed their family was complete, and he was so puny at birth they gave him up for lost. He survived. He grew a little stronger. His nurse considered each day of extra life an unexpected gift. The boy clung on to it tenaciously. His earliest memory was of being weighed against a turkey – 'to the advantage of the bird'; and never once as a child did he have an appetite, only learning the sensation of hunger at the age of twelve. Slight, ailing, timid, retiring, and left very much to himself, he had but two passions, mental arithmetic and natural history, and he showed exceptional promise in both. At six years of age he quickly and correctly calculated how many minutes old he was. By that age, too, he knew his father's garden intimately, and would spend hours observing insects and birds, and training domestic ducklings to perform tricks. At nine he was sent off to a school in Bristol, where the majority of the boys had parents connected in some way with the West Indies. He was out of place, and felt it. Then his father died and his mother moved with her five daughters to reside permanently in Bath. All these changes, with the onset of puberty, combined to increase his loneliness and, simultaneously, as sometimes happens, he lost his astonishing powers of calculation, though he was still an acute observer and, as the years passed, his ability to concentrate grew formidable. He liked to be out in the fresh air and was fond of walking, though he seldom kept to a path but went in a direct line over the countryside, caring neither for hedges, ditches, streams nor bogs. He also enjoyed angling and later took to game fishing and shooting. As a result, his thin, delicate frame fleshed out and he became a clumsy, common, ungainly, bear-like young man. Most of his pleasures being solitary, his natural shyness increased. By the time he left school he was happy enough with two or three companions, but could not tolerate ordinary society. This gave him an abruptness in conversation which many found disconcerting. The apparently gauche barker of a boy went up to Oxford in 1805.

So fierce was Whately's concentration and single mindedness that he failed to jump nimbly from subject to subject in conversation, and thus he became absent-minded. Moreover he could not be bothered to absorb the day to day facts which make human intercourse more interesting and comfortable. He never knew who had died nor who was married to whom, nor if they had children. He even failed to know the departure time of coaches or their destination or even where they came from. He confided to his Journal: 'If I had had no uncle or aunt, I should probably have been ignorant of my mother's maiden name.' In the same Journal he confessed how much he had suffered from shyness – 'If there was no life but the present, the kindest thing that one could do for an intensely shy youth would be to shoot him through the head!' This strange and gifted undergraduate believed, perhaps rightly, that his natural disposition was to be idle. In order to conquer it he rose early to light his own fire and read before Chapel and breakfast. In 1808 Whately took a double first class.

Fastidious Oxonians agreed that he was a good scholar, but would not say he was 'accomplished'. He began to take pupils and read for a fellowship. Method passed surely into eccentricity when he doubled his work for the fellowship by devising a means of making one day into two; rising at three and concluding his 'first day' at noon; undressing and sleeping in a darkened room for two to three hours, when he rose for the 'second day'.

He achieved a Fellowship of Oriel in 1811 and was ordained priest in the year of Waterloo, though he made no sign of possessing more than a usual piety, indeed, rather the opposite, for he shocked a congregation one Sunday by hanging one leg out of the pulpit as he preached because he found it more comfortable. He had few friends;

among them, until they disagreed about Catholic Emancipation, were Keble and John Henry Newman. He was a friend of Dr. Arnold of Rugby for life; Arnold being described in *John Bull* as 'Whately's bottle holder'. In fact he was not popular with his peers, who did not care for his inability to see another viewpoint nor for his asperities. However, his pupils liked him. Young men usually find eccentrics engaging, and Whately with his gruff manner, unconventional behaviour, his enormous appetite for food which he consumed by the plateful, and for going at a subject and worrying it as a terrier shook a rat, was no ordinary clergyman-don. He did not even dress like one. He was called the White Bear, because on his long excursions across the country he wore a white hat and shaggy white coat, and was always accompanied by his white dog named Bishop. Whately's tutorials were famous. The big man lay on a sofa, smoking his pipe, and booming at his pupils on the most abstruse subjects. In the vacations he took them on reading parties, where he insisted on talking Latin, and kept them to a strict regimen which always brought good results. He took them fishing, too, and developed the habit of taking a gun on his walks with which he blazed away at passing birds. Europe was a battle-field until after 1815, so these reading parties generally took place in the Lake District or the Isle of Wight. Whately himself, however, occasionally went abroad, once to Oporto to chaperon an ailing sister. He enjoyed scenic grandeur but would not step a yard out of his way to see anything of artistic or antiquarian merit.

In 1820 the young Fellow of Oriel was bilious and advised to try the waters at Cheltenham. There he met an Oxford acquaintance with his sister. In his abrupt way he decided to marry the lady if she would have him. Bravely she did. His academic career flourished and he began a literary career by publishing: 'Historic Doubts respecting Napoleon Buonaparte.' In 1822 an uncle presented him with a good living in Suffolk. He accepted, but, as the air did not suit Mrs. Whately, he put in a curate, and visited the parish only two or three times a year. In the long vacations he and his wife would go to the seaside or to relations at Tunbridge Wells or to see Dr. Arnold at Rugby. In 1825 he was made a Doctor of Divinity and Principal of Alban Hall. In 1829 he was elected Professor of Political Economy. Then in 1831, when on a visit to Rugby, he received a letter at the breakfast table from Earl Grey, a man not among his correspondents nor even an acquaintance. Indeed they had never spoken to each other nor even met. Yet here was the Whig Prime Minister proposing that the White Bear of Oxford, a notoriously ungainly clerical scholar who had once shocked the Bishop of Norwich by receiving him with his feet on the table while he puffed a tobacco pipe, be offered illustrious preferment, the Archbishopric of Dublin.

Clerical gossip had already suggested that the eighty-seven year old Bishop of Norwich would be translated across the Irish Sea. It had indeed been proposed by Earl Grey, but the old bishop declined, asking that his son, an archdeacon, be given the preferment instead. This was to no avail. The archdeacon never did reach the episcopal bench, though he hounded the Whig ministers with 'piteous, menacing and at last unbalanced letters'. Another rumour, and this was ironic under the circumstances, was that Lord Chancellor Brougham had proposed Dr. Arnold to the Prime Minister. So he had. But he had also suggested, as an alternative, the eccentric Dr. Whately, and Earl Grey had preferred the second before the first, and the guest at the Rugby breakfast table before his host.

Whately said nothing at first. He went a walk with his white hound, Bishop. He really did not want Dublin. The swift move from priest to archbishop and to responsibilities in the House of Lords was not for the likes of him. He liked his work at Oxford where people tolerated his absent-mindedness. He had quite sufficient money. He lacked any desire for distinction. It would give him no pleasure to be addressed as His Grace, the Most Reverend the Lord Archbishop of Dublin. Then his dog Bishop climbed a tree as was his habit, and a stranger walking nearby remarked on it. Was it allegorical? Diamond-hard heads like Whately's scarcely admitted such fancies. Yet he went back to Dr. Arnold's house and said he was going to Ireland.

In October 1831 he sailed over to be consecrated bishop and enthroned as Archbishop. An hour before the service it was discovered he had not formally resigned his living in Suffolk, and he had to do so if the law was not to be violated. This was seen to by ecclesiastical lawyers and the postponed service eventually took place. The Archbishop sailed back to England to collect Mrs. Whately and the family. It was a bad time for bishops. Because so many had voted against the Reform Bill they were held in contempt. The Archbishop of Canterbury asked the Home Secretary for an armed guard to protect Lambeth Palace. Bishop Philpotts of Exeter had his palace filled with men of the 7th Yeomanry and he, like the Bishop of Carlisle who was threatened by a mob of eight thousand demonstrators, was burnt in effigy. The Bishop of Lichfield and Coventry had to alter a route to avoid being thrown in a horse pond. The Bishop of Durham was reviled in his see-city; the Bishop of Bath

Richard Whately, the White Bear of Oxford turned Archbishop of Dublin

and Wells stoned. Bishop Copleston of Llandaff, Whately's old tutor and friendly correspondent, was warned to avoid big towns and kept a brown billycock and greatcoat handy so that, if necessary, he could escape in disguise. The new Archbishop of Dublin on his way south to Oxford met an ugly crowd at Birmingham, and only escaped through the cleverness of his coachman. Then, on his return to Holyhead three days later, whilst they waited for the packet to Dublin, he escaped another kind of peril. Walking with a friend in a badly lighted street he saw his friend who was leading disappear into a deep pit in the road. He wrote indignantly to Bishop Copleston about the iniquity of not fencing off dangerous holes: 'I saw him suddenly vanish, and heard a heavy fall, followed by a plop which I thought was probably his hat. When drawn out, his first word, on recovering his senses, was to explain his joy that it had not happened to me!'

Bishops at that time were not subject to great pressure of work. They had chaplains to assist them with essentials. Sacrament of Confirmation was irregularly celebrated, and generally *en masse* rather than to each candidate in turn. There had to be time for attendance at the House of Lords, holding receptions, ordinations, and dinners. And Whately had every intention of continuing to visit Tunbridge Wells whenever he could. Yet he realised that as Archbishop of Dublin he had special responsibilities, and would have far less time to himself than he had had at Oxford, and he made adjustments accordingly. He took a country house, Redesdale, about four miles from the city, where he supped, slept and breakfasted, and used his palace in Dublin only for the lesser part of the day where he had to be on ceremony. His new regimen involved rising between seven and eight and thinking of sermons* or letters to be written or literary undertakings as he dressed. He then gardened for an hour, a relaxation he added to the pleasures of walking and fishing and shooting and observing natural objects. After that came a late breakfast with his family and friends and clerical household with whom he liked to discuss or to pontificate upon subjects as diverse as the habits of snakes, logic, mathematics, and Thucydides' account of the Plague at Athens. At Dublin Palace he worked on the affairs of his diocese, the Irish Church, and the Irish nation. After dinner he returned to Redesdale to hear music, play chess or backgammon, above all to read. It was his chief recreation and he read with avidity

---

* Evidently he did little actual preaching for he confessed to a fellow Bishop: 'You may guess how pressed I have been with business when I tell you I have had a sermon in hand six weeks, and have but just finished it.'

and great rapidity, engorging even those books he seemed to skip through so that he squeezed out all the meat and taste they had. At an early hour he returned to his study and there would write until very late at night. Whately remained as eccentric as ever. He still charged in a direct line over the countryside overcoming any obstacles that lay in his straight path. He was still followed by a favourite dog or two. He ate hugely, if anything more than before.

In dress he was less particular than his fellow bishops and, though Prelate of the Order of St. Patrick, he managed to arrive at his first royal levée without the Order, to the considerable annoyance of King William IV. Yet his absent-mindedness was chiefly in these lesser matters. His massive concentration was on more important enterprises. Anyone who wished to see him attended his weekly receptions. Formal dinner parties permitted him to exercise his patronage of such causes as The Dublin Association for Discountenancing Vice. He never hesitated to put pressure upon the Lord Lieutenant and through him upon the Prime Minister in England to moderate the 'turbulent' attitude of the English towards Ireland and not to take political refuge behind an outbreak of Asiatic cholera by declaring it a national judgment. He frequently wrote letters. To Pusey he said his heterodoxy consisted chiefly in waiving a good many subtle questions agitated by various 'ans' and 'ites' and 'ists'. To Bishop Copleston he confessed his distaste for Orange flags and decorating Dutch William's statues, comparing it to 'keeping a trophy in repair' and lacking in the good taste or feeling which should prevent Englishmen meeting in Paris to celebrate Waterloo. 'Take care,' he finished, 'that this letter does not set your house on fire, as it would mine, if found in it.'

In administering his own diocese he was far more orthodox. Discovering that no Confirmation had been administered in the Dublin diocese for years, he arranged for regular personal Confirmations. He instructed his clergy to celebrate the Lord's Supper. He personally examined some of the candidates presented for Ordination once they had been screened by his chaplains. He travelled when time spared about the diocese. He made triennial visitations; and, on one, he urged incumbents to learn to speak Irish more, employ Irish-speaking curates, so that the Church could minister to everyone, not simply the English-speaking, Protestant minority. Neither the content of these sort of charges, nor his abrupt way of making them, made him very popular with the clergy. He cared not a jot, and, as some of them found, beneath the gruffness could lie great consideration and kindness. One of his chaplains went through a long spiritual crisis, gave up his Orders, and became a Unitarian, but Whately never scolded him, and pensioned him privately for the rest of his life. In contrast to such gentleness he showed a savage sense of justice, proposing that 'any female receiving relief should have her hair cut off'. In the abstract it seemed logical. A head of hair was worth from five to ten shillings which was at least two weeks' relief, and women would be discouraged from claiming.

The same cold hard logic told him that the stipends of the Roman Catholic clergy who cared for the vast majority of the Irish should be matched by the State, and, if necessary, from the revenues of the Established Church. It was he as much as anyone who pushed through the Irish Church Temporalities Act in July 1834. Amongst other measures it abolished two of the four Irish Archbishoprics and eight of the Dioceses were to be amalgamated with neighbours at the next vacancy. The Act did not do as Whately and other serious reformers wished and earmark the money saved for the payment of Roman Catholic priests, but it was some measure of reform. The Tory clergymen were furious. Newman called it sacrilegious. When, four months afterwards, the Houses of Parliament were destroyed by fire, they considered it the judgment of Heaven. When the Whig ministry fell only one month after that, they were sure that it was. The new Tory ministry brought in a Tithe Bill for Ireland during which the surplus revenues of the Irish Church were endlessly discussed. Archbishop Whately was a realist. He wrote to Lord Wellesley, the new Tory Lord Lieutenant: 'If you could collect all the Protestants of Ireland into one district, one bishop and a proportional number of clergy and a proportionate endowment would suffice.' As it happened Lord Wellesley's tenure of office was short. Divine providence also seemed to frown on the Tory ministry. The bill was defeated in the Commons and the Tory ministry was out. When the Whigs returned to office they just squeezed an Irish Church bill through the Commons but it was thrown out by the Lords. No Irish reform has ever been an easy matter.

The Archiepiscopal round of Ireland, London, Tunbridge Wells was broken in 1839 by a visit to the Continent. He took his whole family and then visited the field of Waterloo, dined with Queen Victoria's uncle, the King of the Belgiums, and travelled to the Rhine, thence to Switzerland, Northern Italy and back through France. In 1841 they were in the tiny German pumpernickel Duchy of Nassau where Whately wrote to his domestic chaplain: 'There are multitudes here of small orange-coloured slugs: shall I bring some over to fill sinecure places in Ireland?' A year later his old friend Dr. Arnold died. Whately sent Mrs. Arnold his commiserations and a warning that the Doctor's sermons be carefully preserved before publication; 'lest some readers should be scared away . . . by too violent a shock to their prejudices.'

In 1846 the Whately family took one of Dr. Arnold's sons on their annual peregrination, this time as far as Austria where the Archbishop fished with great success and enjoyed throwing a boomerang, 'at the same time holding forth on the mathematical principles which its flight illustrated'. Their approach was in some way signalled ahead and as the Archiepiscopal equipage lurched past, people looked out for the bewigged figure topped by a tricorn hat and knelt to receive his blessing. What precisely Whately did is not recorded.

They returned to find Ireland facing famine, a disaster which lasted three years and more. By March 1848 a million people were on relief. By the end of it over half a million had died, and another half had fled to England, and upwards of two million had gone to foreign countries. The Archbishop gave his entire stipend to the general relief and made other large contributions. He also worked ceaselessly to alleviate the sufferings of the people in his diocese. In 1850, when the famine was well past its peak, the Archbishop accompanied a sick son to Paris and sent him on to Nice for recruitment. Then he spent much of his summer at Cromer and was not in the least perturbed when the Pope issued a Bull appointing a Roman Catholic Hierarchy in England.

More and more he took pleasure in the company of his children and grandchildren. His daughter and son-in-law, with the family, were often at Redesdale and were a considerable help to him as he approached the sear and yellow of his life.

The first indication of Whately's weakening strength was a severe inflammation of the tongue, particularly nasty to such a perpetual talker. Then a form of creeping paralysis manifested itself and his left hand began to shake with palsy. He was an adherent of homoeopathy for other people. For himself he had little faith in any sort of medicine. He managed as well as he could, the paralysing disease continued its slow and relentless progress, and he had accidents. One in 1858, when he was receiving an eminent American missionary at the Palace, was both painful and embarrassing. Intending to present his guest with one of his own works translated into Armenian, he tripped over the carpet and crashed to the floor. Being large and heavy, the shock was considerable. He noted in his Journal: 'At first it was apprehended that all the front teeth would be lost; but by great care the evil was averted.' That same year he showed he still had his sense of humour. He wrote to a friend, 'I have just lost a sister at the age of eighty. It seems strange to me to outlive so many of my own family. For though in years I am much the younger, in point of wear and tear I may be reckoned the oldest. Hot water is not my proper element; and I have long been in it'. In 1860 afflictions increased. His youngest daughter, a bride of scarcely four months, died in March. The bereaved family moved from Dublin to Hastings. There, in April, Mrs. Whately was carried off by a pulmonary infection. The Archbishop went to his relatives in Tunbridge Wells. Troubles amassed. His son-in-law and family moved to the Continent because of ill health. Another daughter was advised to do the same. Only one daughter was left to the grief-stricken and trembling old man who now began to develop ulcerous legs. In 1863 he gave his last charge in Dublin Cathedral. He was very feeble, and the ulcers gave him great pain: in his words 'It was as if red hot gimlets were being bored through the legs'. In that state he gave his ordinands their final divinity exam, and it was beyond him to ordain them. His strength ebbed away. Even the excursions in his garden-chair at Redesdale exhausted him. Chess and backgammon were no longer diverting. He could not hold a book nor hear one word read.

The family gathered as families dutifully did in the nineteenth century. Whately, who had hated to be fussed and had always looked after himself, was now helpless and utterly dependent for everything on his servants and chaplains. On Sunday September the thirteenth he lay asleep. Gradually it occurred to those who were sitting with him that he had died. A tearful daughter kissed his cheek. Whately at once opened his eyes and, in great irritation, stated that sleep was sovereign and an invalid should never be woken up. After some reflection he apologised to his tearful and alarmed daughter. On September the fourteenth he received Holy Communion for the last time. The disease made slow progress. He could no longer bear a wheelchair or even his usual bed. For sixteen more fearful days he lay on a waterbed covered by a fur cloak. Then on October the eighth, an artery burst in one of his ulcerated legs, and he quietly bled to death in the middle of the morning. The sickly and puny child not expected to outlast infancy had lived into his seventy-seventh year.

He was an Englishman who accomplished much for the Irish Church and for Ireland. As a scholar he contributed much to logic. His published sermons would scarcely find a reader today. Yet he wrote a number of hymns, some in Latin, most in English; and one of them, only one, inspired surely by the old Compline antiphon 'Salva nos Domine, vigilantes; custodi nos dormientes; ut vigilemus in Christo, et requiescamus in pace', keeps his memory green throughout Christendom. To the present writer's knowledge, Richard Whately is the only author of hymns who was widely admired for only *half* a hymn; generally sung to the Welsh traditional melody 'Ar hyd y nos' or 'All through the night'. His half runs:

> 'Guard us waking, guard us sleeping;
>   And, when we die,
> May we in thy mighty keeping
>   All peaceful lie:
> When the last dread call shall wake us,
> Do not thou our God forsake us,
> But to reign in glory take us
>   With thee on high.'

It is a seemly memorial: the confident hope of an imperfect man, an old-fashioned, rugged, weak Archbishop in turbulent Ireland, that, as at the very last, all will be well.

★

The writer of the first half of the hymn, Reginald Heber, shared with Whately a number of things in common, but not many. They lived at the same time, that is in the same period of transient history, though Heber was four years older, and died much younger. Each tended to sickliness in youth, though Heber was 'as fat as a little mole' at birth, and Whately so skinny and feeble that he was given up for lost, and both grew through their invalidism to strength. Both became clergymen, which the Oxford fellowship of one one and the offer of the family living to the other made a necessity. Both were consecrated bishops rather against their wish, but their cathedral cities were approximately five thousand miles apart. Both were men of common-sense and character, but while Whately was brusque, Heber seldom showed anything but exquisite politeness. They fused in their memorable hymn, 'God, that madest earth and heaven'; half, Whately's only real contribution to hymnody; half a minute part of Heber's large contribution.

The family of Heber was an ancient one. Reginald's father, another Reginald, succeeded his brother as Lord of the Manor and patron of the Rectory of Morton in Yorkshire, and from their mother inherited the Lordship and Rectory of Hodnet in Shropshire. Reginald senior was himself ordained and, from being Rector of Chelsea, he moved in 1770 to a Peculiar, the moiety Rectory of Malpas just on the Cheshire-Shropshire border, within close waiting distance of the family living in Hodnet, in an exceedingly pretty part of England, surrounded by a clutch of friendly squires and parsons, and excellent for sport, it being hedge and ditch hunting country, superb for short-legged, robust gallopers, and there being ample meres and rivers and streams for angling and fishing. The little market town had two Rectors because seven hundred years before the Norman Lord of Malpas died without a male heir, and both his daughters seized on and persisted in their right to present a priest to the parish church. So Malpas had two priests for the one church; one, Rector of the Higher Mediety; the other, Rector of the Lower; and conceivably as much accord arose as discord did from such a complicated arrangement.

Young Reginald the hymn writer was born in Malpas Higher Rectory* on the twenty-first of April 1783, subsequently being Christened in the Malpas font which, for some unknown reason, was later transferred to St. Chad's Church in Shrewsbury.

It was an amazing world in which to be born, undulating with change in society, politics, agriculture and manufactures, philosophy and theology. Reginald was the eldest of three children of his father's second marriage. He had a half brother, Richard, with whom, despite the difference in age, he was always on the most affectionate terms. After two years he had a full blood brother Thomas, and two years after that a sister, May. This completed the family at the Higher Rectory. When Reginald was born, Richard, or Dick as he was always called, went away to school in Middlesex, but simply because he was of the age to go and not because, like the wretched little John Newton, he had an indifferent or cruel stepmother at home. Whether or not it was wise to entrust him to the care of such a divine as George Henry Glasse is not for a non-contemporary to judge. Glasse certainly had accomplishments which might have recommended him for the moiety Rectory, being chaplain to the Earl of Radnor, the Duke of Cambridge, and the Earl of Sefton successively, as well as Rector of Hanwell and an elegant casuist; publishing translations from Greek into Latin, *Samson Agonistes* into Greek, and *Miss Bayley's Ghost* into a Latin version, which was sung by the irrepressible Irish poet Tom Moore as a

---

* This building, at the time of writing, is now the only parsonage in Malpas and the fine Rectory, with the brass plaque marking the door of the room where the plump Heber baby was born. But, like so many excellent parsonages throughout the length and breadth of England, it will, before the time of publication, fall into the maw of the modern Church of England which, by forcibly rehousing its clergymen in snug though characterless parsonages, stands a chance, in the end, of producing a fresh brand of parson.

masquerade. Catholic in his works, Glasse also contributed to the *Gentleman's Magazine* and *Archaeologia* pieces of antiquarian and archaeological interest, an impressive medley of sermons, and a popular work *Louisa; a narrative of fact supposed to throw light on the mysterious Lady of the Haystack.* He also contrived to run through an inherited fortune so successfully that, unable to face his creditors, he ended all by hanging himself at the Bull and Mouth Inn in St. Martin's-le-Grand in London. This anticipates. To Dick Heber in the 1780's Glasse gave the advantage of a firm foundation in Greek and Latin and confirmed his liking for books which turned out to be less advantageous. Dick had begun collecting as a little boy. Dr. Glasse influenced him to amass a classical library. At Oxford he added drama and poetry, then belles-lettres. He became an MP, helped to found the Athenaeum Club, and in literary circles was known as 'Magnificent' Heber; but none of this, not even the affectionate dedication to him of the sixth canto of Scott's *Marmion,* ever mattered so much to him as books, for he was a book magpie, travelling widely to collect books, and, when he died unmarried, he left eight large houses in England and on the Continent all overflowing with books, as well as other bibliographical deposits here and there over Europe. It took three years to dispose of them all.

This rich generous elder half-brother was Reginald's companion in the holidays and looked after him. Despite his fitness at birth, Reginald was not strong as a child and had a tendency to catch any ailment that was in the area. He even managed to contract gaol fever in sleepy Malpas from which he almost died. But he grew stronger with the years, and, though bookish, he enjoyed the usual pleasures of boyhood; skating and sliding in the frosts, shooting, riding and occasionally hunting for fox and hare. In the spring and summer there were birds' eggs to take, and birds to trap, and collections to make of plants and butterflies and other insects; there were always angling and eeling, otter hunting when the water was warm, and September brought steeplechasing. In 1787 the family living of Hodnet became vacant. Rector Heber of the Higher Mediety decided to hold the two in plurality, and remain at Malpas, which he did in fact until his death. The French Revolution led to widespread demonstrations against the Jacobins in England. They even reached such cut-off country areas as Cheshire and Shropshire. In 1793 when Reginald was ten Tom Paine was burned in effigy as a revolutionary at Malpas Cross; bands played 'God save the King' – who fortunately was enjoying a lucid interval between crises of lunacy; the guzzle-guts of the parish had the time of their lives; and the High Rectory children amused themselves making mop-guys of Tom Paine and a French General on the top of their otter-hunting poles.

Children were then self-contained as family units, but Malpas happened to be a centre from which they could visit other children from time to time and most of their parents' friends in the area had children of their own. The Earl of Cholmondeley who had the Castle was a bachelor until 1791, and so his daughter, loyally named Charlotte Georgiana for the Queen and the King, and her two brothers, were a mite young at first for the Heber children. But there were plenty of others who grew up as they did until it became time for them to leave home to marry or settle elsewhere. There were their kinsmen the Vernons at Hodnet and the Leycesters at Stoke-upon-Terne Rectory. There were the Hills of Hawkestone Park, a huge and handsome Queen Anne house, possessing its own chapel with an intriguing allegorical ceiling showing the Flight of Error before Truth, set in parkland of fine trees, and coverts, and causeways and tunnels, and ruins, a grotto containing a wax figure, a Druid's Cavern, Hermitage complete with seated hermit reflecting upon mortality, and banks of rugged, rich-red sandstone.* There lived Sir Richard Hill who was unmarried, together with his married brother and heir, John, with his wife and family. They had a quiverful of children, no fewer than sixteen, of which seven were boys,† and the four youngest were reasonably close to Reginald and his friends. The Hebers' closest companions were the Williams-Wynns at Wynnstay not far into Denbighshire, a family descended on the Wynn side from Rhodri Mawr, King of Wales and, on the Williams side, from Cadroc the Handsome, a tenth century chieftain of Anglesey. Sir Watkin and Lady Williams-Wynn had two girls and three sons; the eldest another Watkin, the same age as Dick; the youngest, Henry Watkin, a month older than Reginald. Henry and Reginald were only six years old when Watkin in his seventeenth year succeeded his father as fifth baronet. Old Sir Watkin's death caused consternation in the area, not least amongst the sportsmen because his recently collected pack of hounds for hunting hare and fox had to be broken up and the kennels were not re-established until the new Sir Watkin reached his majority in 1793. Besides the shared friendships of their youth – there were amateur theatricals and balls at Wynnstay, expeditions all over the place, and plenty of out-door sport – the

---

* The house itself was dismantled and its pictures and library dispersed in 1895.

---

† Five of these brothers fought at Waterloo and all survived it. One even brought back his charger unharmed from the wars, and would ride it about Shropshire for years after the battle.

Williams-Wynn and Heber families were later to be connected by marriage, and in other important matters.

But life was not by any means all play. At ten Reginald began to attend the Grammar School at Whitchurch, a busy market town only six miles from Malpas, and less by the fields and tracks over which the boy rode his pony. The headmaster there gave him the inestimable gift of caring for poetry. He read it, learnt it, and began to write it. At thirteen he was sent off to a boarding-school. Perhaps by 1796, the Reverend George Henry Glasse had reached a less reputable stage in his spendthrift career; or maybe Dick gave a discreet warning from Oxford which otherwise might not have reached Cheshire; or possibly the Rector of the Higher Mediety of Malpas and of Hodnet believed in change and had had another tutor recommended to him. Whatever the reason, young Reginald was packed off to a school in Neasden near Willesden in North London, in the care of a Dr. Bristowe, about whom nothing deleterious has ever yet been alleged. By then the boy had become so prodigal with his pocket money to anyone in need, that it was considered necessary to sew his bank notes for the half year's allowance into the linings of his pocket before he was sent off by coach to London. It showed a part of the sweetness of his disposition which, increasingly, drew remark. At Dr. Bristowe's he was known to wander off and read Spencer's *Faerie Queene* rather than join in the games of the other boys, a provocative act which, in many small schools, would have made him very unpopular. And though he was not good at dates in history and less good at syntax than might have been expected, he had an excellent sense of history and of cause and effect of events, and such a gift for expressing himself in, and understanding, the classical tongue that again he was set apart from his schoolfellows. Yet none of them disliked him for being different; and they loved to hear him recite the old ballads, and tell them adventure stories as they sat by the fire on winter evenings. One of them, John Thornton, the son of an MP, became his friend for life, though they separated in 1800, Thornton going up to Cambridge, and Reginald Heber, after a hectic holiday in Malpas, going racing at Shrewsbury and Threapwood and attending a Masked Ball at Wynnstay, going up to Oxford.

He entered Brasenose, the college where his father had been undergraduate, then fellow and tutor, and where Dick had been, too. There he began what everyone expected of him, a brilliant career at the university. In his first year he won a prize for Latin verse, an exercise on the new century entitled *Carmen Seculare,* in which he cleverly made mention of lightning conductors, electricity, the steam engine, ballooning, and even the Japanese name for the Bering Straits, but which, despite the promise it showed, is now totally forgotten. Two years later he submitted *Palestine* for the university prize in English verse. By then he had a wide circle of acquaintance; amongst them Dick's friend and advocate Walter Scott, himself an established translator and ballad collector, and poet, with the first volume of *The Border Minstrelsy* behind him and *The Lay of the Last Minstrel* just begun. He breakfasted with Reginald in college on the day the poem had to be recited and asked to see it. He had but one critical comment; Heber had failed to mention the extraordinary fact that no tools were used in the building of the Temple. Heber put it right at once, adding two and a half verses:

> 'No hammer fell, no ponderous axes rung;
> Like some tall palm the mystic fabric sprung.
> Majestic silence.'

That, said Scott, would do. It did. The prize poem was highly applauded. It won an unusual distinction for university prize poems in attracting a public for a considerable time, and, twelve years after its first recitation in 1803, 'Palestine' was made into an oratorio by the musician Professor Crotch.

In 1803 the short-lived peace between Great Britain and Bonaparte broke down. Volunteers were raised all over England. Dick, who was looking after the family estate in Yorkshire, was commissioned colonel of the volunteers at Craven. There was a Corps at Hodnet, another at Malpas. Reginald Heber was asked to write a special march for the latter. He complied with a martial quatrain:

> 'Swell, swell the shrill trumpet clear-sounding afar,
> Our sabres flash splendour around,
> For freedom hath summon'd her sons to the war,
> Nor Britain has shrunk from the sound.'

The following year was of great importance to Heber. His father died at Malpas and the rich rectory of the Higher Mediety passed to the Reverend Sir Philip Grey-Egerton, ninth baronet of Egerton and Oulton, who, putting a curate into his living of Tarporley, moved into his new rectory, and celebrated the birth of his son and heir there that same year, calling him De Malpas, a name which has continued to be used in the family from time to time ever since. Dick Heber, as his father's heir, decided the Hodnet living should be kept warm by curates until Reginald reached the canonical age of twenty-four to be ordained. Their mother and sister Mary moved to Hodnet Hall, a long two-storeyed thatched house of great antiquity with a dovecot in the park.★ Reginald finished at Oxford, being elected a Fellow of All Souls, and went down to Shropshire at Dick's bidding to take temporary command of the Hodnet section of the Shropshire Volunteers. He drilled the men and marched them once to Shrewsbury, but they were a boozy lot who soldiered for the pay and parading was no more in their line than it was in their commander's. They were at their best when they had a military band to help keep time, but the bandsmen proved volatile and quarrelsome and refused to agree about which march should be played. The resulting cacophany which Reginald called 'detestable' might have been amusing if Bonaparte had not been massing an invasion force at Boulogne. Mercifully for Reginald his commission was a short one and someone else took command of his Falstaff's company. However one particular advantage of his brief military career was Reginald's introduction at a dinner party to the daughters of Jean Shipley of St. Asaph† with one of whom, the younger, Amelia, or Emily as she was usually named, he struck up a warm friendship and whom he later married. Amelia's elder brother also made a happy marriage to a sister of Reginald's friend Henry Watkin Williams-Wynn. But the other Shipley sister was less fortunate. Her life reads like the plot of a Gothic novel. She was married thrice: first, 'at her father's desire but against her wish, to a savage paralytic'; then, after long period as a widow, to a neighbour who died within a year; last, to a clergyman, to whom she left a fortune after a married life of only several months.

Released from the volunteers, Reginald undertook with his school friend John Thornton that which was still required by custom from young gentlemen to round-off and polish them: a Grand Tour. It might seem foolhardy to go abroad at the height of the war with France, but total war had not been thought of, a certain degree of civilisation obtained; for example, the French Empress continued to order plants from her London nurseryman and they were conveyed to her safely by courtesy of the Royal and the French navies. Even so, with the French Emperor rampaging over Europe it was not possible to follow the route of the peacetime Grand Tour. Instead the two young men were adventurous. They went to Scandinavia and Russia,

---

★ The present Hodnet Hall is Victorian, built by Reginald Heber's eldest daughter and her husband Algernon Percy when Dick 'Magnificent' Heber died unmarried.

---

† William Davies Shipley was appointed to the Deanery of St. Asaph of which his father was Bishop. His work there permitted the Bishop to be an absentee for most of the year, and he himself was described by a relative as living a life 'full of enjoyment in hunting and shooting, – rollicking, popular, and good natured, – though not really ecclesiastical.'

down to the Crimea and back through Hungary, Austria and Prussia. In Russia, which they both admired, they heard of the victory at Trafalgar which finally obliged Bonaparte to give up his plans for invading England. Instead the Grand Army assembled in the East. A brief six weeks after Trafalgar the French Emperor defeated the Emperors of Austria and Russia at Austerlitz, a brilliant victory which marked the apogee of his power, and, it was said, killed off the morose William Pitt. George III was blind and going off his head again. The Prince Regent was about to put his hand on the helm. Napoleon's triumph was the breaking straw for the British First Minister. 'Roll up the map of Europe,' he exclaimed dramatically, 'we shan't need it again'; and he went into a rapid decline, at the early age of forty-five. Though the area in which they took their Grand Tour was quickly the scene of campaigning, Heber and Thornton thoroughly enjoyed themselves.

They finally reached England again on October the fourteeenth 1806, landing at Great Yarmouth on the day Napoleon won the field of Jena against the Prussian armies. The war seemed very distant from little Hodnet. The tenantry and villagers fêted '*Master Reginald's Coming Back Safe*'. The triumphal arches of greenery and the address of welcome brought home to Reginald the potential difficulties of being a Heber Rector of Hodnet. Technically his brother was squire, but he was so seldom at Hodnet that Reginald would be virtually squarson, and far more would be expected of him than of most country parsons. He confided his doubts to John Thornton, who urged him to go ahead with his former plans and be ordained. Reginald did so, was presented by Dick to the rectory of Hodnet, married Emily Shipley, and settled first with his mother and sister at Hodnet Hall, then at the parsonage house at Moreton Say, a tiny hamlet close to Hodnet, while he had a Rectory built on the high ground above the church and close to the Hall. He still had qualms about reconciling his work as a parish priest and his work as an author and as Dick's deputy. It would seem he was being over-scrupulous. He built schools, held regular and well attended services and was a good well liked squarson; even managing to remain on amicable terms with the Hills of Hawkestone although they were now his parishioners with a vault beneath his church* and one vexing member of the family was the eccentric itinerant preacher Rowland

---

* One monument commemorates Richard Hill, an ambassador and statesman in the reign of Queen Anne and so skilful at negotiating between conflicting prejudices, loyalties, and interests, that he is described as 'a gentleman of very clear parts and a favourite with both parties'.

Hill,* who, quite understandably, went home from time to time.

There the family received and comforted him but he was a running sore to Rector Heber. This independent preacher was an intellectual of sorts, but also a fanatic who preached with great passion his individualistic and unacceptable Gospel message to which he occasionally added a curious postscriptum on the value of inoculation against cow-pock. Moreover he stolidly refused to be contained by the accepted parochial system, and he wandered about England and Wales preaching eloquently, emotionally, and persuasively to large congregations in other parsons' parishes. Because of this irregularity he had been refused ordination by six bishops in succession until a seventh inadvisedly made him deacon. But that was the end of it. The Archbishop of York sent out a fiat that on no account was Rowland Hill to be ordained priest. Disciples gave him centres in Gloucester and in London and to his 'chapel' in London he had thirteen Sunday schools with more than three thousand children on their registers; but still he wandered abroad, and Heber disliked his out of doors preaching at Hodnet, where, because it was his home place, his harangues met with ridicule and heckling and even caused violence. Dealing with this particular problem demanded much patience from Heber but he gave it unstintingly.

He was also afflicted by zealous Nonconformists. Later in life he showed greater tolerance to Dissent, but, as a young incumbent, he noted: 'The Methodists in Hodnet are thank God, not very numerous, and I hope to diminish them still more.' His younger brother, Tom, was ordained, and he arrived to help with parish work and the diminishing of Methodists, until he was appointed Perpetual Curate 'with the style and dignity of Vicar' of the hamlet of Moreton Say where Reginald and Emily had lived before moving into the rebuilt Rectory at Hodnet. There, soon after his licensing, Tom died suddenly of a haemorrhagic disorder of the brain, and his family was cast into the deepest mourning. This was in 1815, Waterloo year, but not even the great victory could make up for their loss at Hodnet Hall and Rectory. Then, quite unexpectedly, came a financial crisis. It

---

* Not to be confused with his nephew Rowland Hill, who distinguished himself in the Peninsular Campaign and was ennobled as Baron Hill of Almarey and of Hawkestone, Salop, fought at Waterloo, was Commander-in-Chief from 1828 to 1842 when he was raised to a Vicountcy and was adored by the county who toasted 'our hero Hill, may the Hills of Hawkestone be as everlasting as the Shropshire hills!' He was a particular friend of the Parson of Hodnet who addressed to him a poem beginning:
'Hill! whose high daring with renewed success
Hath cheered our tardy war –.'

was not too severe. The abundance of local banks in Britain at the time lacked the stability which was to come later. Reginald partially banked with the Old Bank in Nantwich, a market town in Cheshire, which failed in 1816. It took quite a time to recoup his losses. The year after, 1817, he was bidden to Wynnstay by his old friends to meet the hero of the nations, the Duke of Wellington. Reginald missed him, recording somewhat peevishly that the Duke 'had left the house before I got there, having paid a visit of about ten hours instead of three days as had been expected'.

Heber's work as a parish priest was rewarded by preferment. Doubtless owing to the influence of his father-in-law, Dean Shipley, he was made a prebendary of St. Asaph as early as 1812, but it was a personal tribute when his university invited him to be the Bampton lecturer in 1815, and when he was appointed Preacher at Lincoln's Inn in 1822.

In letters and memoranda a charming sketch of life at Hodnet Rectory was drawn by young Miss Maria Leycester a daughter of Oswald Leycester, Rector of Stoke-upon-Terne,* only one and a half miles from Hodnet. The Leycesters and Hebers became friends and Maria was frequently at Hodnet, walking over the heath or riding there on her pony, named for the immortal nymph with butterfly wings, Psyche. Maria Leycester was a pretty, intelligent, affectionate girl, full of enthusiasm for subjects as diverse as Roman antiquity, which she determined one day to see in situ, and black bantams of which she preserved several, naming two of the cocks Bonaparte and the King of Rome. The Hebers' were very fond of her and she became deeply attached to them, writing to a friend of the great contentment she found at Hodnet; 'To be sure splendour and luxury sink into the ground before such *real* happiness. . . .' When time allowed, and it often did, they rode out together, walked together, took tea on the lawns on summer evenings, dressed up and acted *Bluebeard*, a play of the Rector's, or mimed French proverbs with the curate, Mr. Stow. They all listened to the Rector telling stories and reciting verses, or reading aloud *Waverley* and *Guy Mannering* and *Ivanhoe*, which he and they knew were written by his old acquaintance Walter Scott, although, at first, they were published anonymously, and their authorship generally attributed to his own brother, 'Magnificent' Heber. Miss Leycester at the age of

---

* Parson Leycester belonged to an old Cheshire family. One of his direct ancestors as Squire of Toft was a close friend of John Byrom (1692–1763), a giant of a man who seldom found a horse of convenient size, spent his life teaching a type of shorthand he had invented, and wrote as a Christmas gift for his daughter, the carol 'Christians, awake, salute the happy morn'.

(top left) Reginald Heber, Shropshire Rector, instant hymn-writer and Bishop of Calcutta; (top right) Maria Leycester, later Maria Hare; (bottom) Hodnet Rectory

nineteen took tuition in German from the Rector, and quite evidently adored him. She confided to one young lady: 'How happy I am to be able to say I *love* him! I may thank *Mrs. R. H.* for that.' It was a safe enough passion because her really deep affections were for his curate. At length Mr. Stow declared himself, and asked if he might speak to her father. She consented. Parson Leycester did not. On no account would he hear of such a marriage for his daughter and he forbade the idea. So Mr. Stow went into temporary exile, taking the Chaplaincy of Genoa and he and Maria pined.

Besides his parochial duties and social pleasures, Reginald Heber continued to write, always in the best tradition of the country clergyman of the Church of England. He worked, in a desultory fashion, on a Dictionary of the Bible, and he edited the works of Bishop Jeremy Taylor and wrote his Life. He also contributed to literary journals. But it was as a poet that he justified the promise first shown as an Oxford undergraduate. He wrote a good deal of secular poetry, three extensive 'fragments': *Morte d'Arthur*, *The World Beyond the Flood*, and *The Masquerade of Gwendolen*[*a], and forty-six shorter poems on a miscellany of subjects. He also wrote tolerable translations of Pindar but, without doubt, he is best remembered for his hymns which he appeared to spin off with remarkable ease. In 1819 a Royal Letter was issued by the Prince Regent[†b], presumably at the suggestion of advisers, for he was not of a godly disposition, that alms be collected in all churches on Whitsun day for the Mission Field. Dean Shipley of St. Asaph was to preach that day at Wrexham and, on the day preceding Whitsun day, he asked his son-in-law to favour him with an appropriate hymn to marry with the subject of his sermon. Heber at once agreed, moved to another table in the same room and wrote the grand mission hymn 'From Greenland's icy mountains'. At least, he wrote three stanzas with eight verses in each, and presented the hymn to his father-in-law. Dr. Shipley was amazed, as well he might have been, and his amazement increased when, looking over his shoulder, Heber declared himself dissatisfied. The hymn seemed to him to be unfinished. Despite Dr.

---

[*] An uninspiring piece with such stage directions as '*Enter two* Goblins *bearing a casket*', '*Enter two* Genii of Fire *with a vase*', and plenty of thunder and flower-strewing.

[†] George III was in his last year and still unfit to govern. His bouts of silence alternated with excited chattering. Sometimes he preached to his servants and went through a performance of celebrating Holy Communion. On the whole he was not too unhappy. He played Handel on the harpsichord and flute, and sang a good deal, and, though increasingly deaf and old (he was eighty-one) he managed 'to find amusement in the inexhaustible resources of his distempered imagination', under the care of his Queen, and when she died, of his son, the grand old Duke of York.

Shipley's insistence that it was perfectly adequate, he returned to the other table and wrote straight out the last stanza 'Waft, waft, ye winds, his story', then declared himself satisfied. The whole exercise, including the interruption about whether or not there should be a fourth stanza, took twenty minutes. The manuscript was immediately printed and sung the following day in Wrexham Church to the tune of a popular ballad ' 'Twas when the Sea Were Roaring'. It was a great success. An adroit local printer, procuring Parson Heber's manuscript by unknown means, sold thousands of facsimile copies.

Though Heber had the distaste of the great majority of his class for Evangelical emotionalism, and, considering himself a High Church Tory, admitted to having scruples against hymns in the public liturgy, he found himself enchanted by a copy of the *Olney Hymns* which fell into his possession less than a fortnight after the Wrexham Mission service. He was also impressed by its usefulness. He realised that the Established Church could not afford to do without so powerful a teaching engine as hymn-singing, and he conceived the entirely original idea, using a few hymns he had already written and writing others, of producing a hymn for each Sunday and Feast and Solemn Day in the English Prayer Book Calendar from Advent Sunday onwards, to which he added a miscellany of evening hymns, hymns for funerals, an introit before the Eucharist, a hymn before the Sacrament, and a thanksgiving for recovering from sickness. He was encouraged by his friends and correspondents, particularly by the Poet Laureate Southey, and by Canon Milman of Westminster,★ and, over a period of time, he completed the work. The hymns were mostly written in a child's school-book opposite sums done by his daughters. No poet can set out on such a methodical course and expect uniformity of success; but in his total collection of fifty-seven hymns, all written and used at Hodnet, some published in the *Christian Observer*†, the remainder, not until after his death, he wrote some very special poems. One, 'Brightest and best of the suns of the morning' was originally sung to the tune of a Scottish ballad

---

★ Milman was himself encouraged by Heber to write hymns for St. Margaret's, Westminster. Amongst them was his Palm Sunday hymn 'Ride on! Ride on in majesty'.

---

† As this was a decidedly Evangelical organ it is surprising that the High Church poet should contribute to it. Suffice it to say Heber had the wisdom to realise the value of a wide circulation and he would produce hymns for the Church of England Calendar if they were acceptable. He also made a point of publishing most of them anonymously or under unidentifiable pseudonyms.

'Wandering Willie', and was intended for the Feast of the Epiphany.
Another, written for the Feast of St. Stephen, 'The Son of God goes
forth to war', became an instant success.* 'Virgin-born, we bow
before Thee', for the twenty-third Sunday after Trinity, and 'Bread
of the world in mercy broken', for Before the Sacrament, though still
deeply loved and much used, had a flavour of the High Established
Church which made them a trifle exclusive; but three of his hymns in
particular have been used by virtually every sect which calls itself
Christian and holds to the Creed and Sacraments; his half of the
hymn shared with Archbishop Whately, but an evening hymn in
itself although only one stanza, 'God, that madest earth and heaven';
and another one-stanza hymn, 'O, most merciful! O, most
bountiful', intended by Heber to be used as a motet to be sung as an
Introit before the Holy Communion; and, finally, his triumph, his
perfect paraphrase of Revelation 4, 8–11, for Trinity Sunday:

> 'Holy, Holy, Holy! Lord God Almighty!
> Early in the morning our song shall rise to thee;
> Holy, Holy, Holy! Merciful and mighty!
> God in three Persons, blessèd Trinity!'

For this majestic anthem which, through its four stanzas, followed
precisely the lines laid down by St. Ambrose so long before for a good
hymn of praising and attempting to explain the inexplicable, Heber
would always be remembered.

Thackeray in his *George the Fourth*, called Heber one of the good
knights of the time and one of the best of English gentlemen; a poet,
the happy possessor of all sorts of gifts and accomplishments, birth,
wit, fame, high character, and competence; a beloved parish priest.
But it distorts the true portrait to see Heber as a mere child of
fortune. Like the careful scrutiny of a written testimonial to see what
is in but more, what is left out, we can achieve a balanced picture by
recalling Heber's difficulties; those things which do not spring from
fortune. Chief amongst them was the death of their first child and
daughter, Barbara. It seems from the fact that Heber took his wife to
Chester for her confinement that trouble was expected. At all events,
the baby was not strong and in less than a year she succumbed to a
very hot summer which wasted her away. There were to be other

---

* In a Victorian children's story of spectacular sentimentality it is named 'The Tug-of-War
Hymn' because the common soldiers liked it and named it thus. Briefly; an officer's only son
met with an accident. He was hideously crippled. Death came slowly. The barracks were
hushed. Towards the end the little sufferer begged that the men might sing the hymn beneath
the sick-room window. They complied, and, when they reached the seventh stanza – 'A noble
army, men and boys', a hand slowly drew down the window blind. This is a précis of a long
'Story of a Short Life' by Mrs. Ewing.

children, but all daughters, no son. Heber's own health was not as good as it had been. There was mention of erysipelas perhaps contracted on his Grand Tour. Probably this was a wrong diagnosis, for erysipelas, being contagious, would have spread to others, and there is no evidence of this happening; moreover it was a dangerous disease before the discovery of sulphonamides, causing fevers, even pneumonia and nephritis. More probably Heber suffered from psoriasis about which little is known save that it is not contagious and is thus a 'clean' skin disease. Heber could not have known this, and psoriasis is as unpleasant as any other dermatosis; causing itching, inflammation, scaling, nervous irritability, and a sense of being different from other healthy people. Moreover, though it gives the appearance of being susceptible to treatment, it is virtually incurable. Considering that Heber lived at a time when these facts were unknown, and the stench and dirt of the eighteenth century were no longer the fashion, and rather to the contrary, people were becoming fastidious, he must have suffered considerable mental stress about his skin trouble, even if most of it was imagined. He certainly tried cures, taking the waters at Harrogate, sea-bathing, and using mercury and a number of other internal and external medicines.

And in the end, his cosy, country life, made the more interesting by occasional visits to local friends, and when he had the time to make the long journeys in those days before railways, trips to Chester and London and Oxford, an existence for which he was so eminently suited despite his first fears to the contrary, was suddenly threatened.

Charles Watkin Williams-Wynn, the middle brother of the three who had grown up at Wynnstay when the Heber children grew up at Malpas Rectory, had been M.P. for Montgomery for some time and, in 1822, he was made a member of Lord Liverpool's Tory Cabinet as President of the Board of Control, an office which later became Secretary of State for India. Charles Williams-Wynn knew Reginald Heber well and his sister was married to Emily Heber's brother. Therefore, it was natural that, when that summer of 1822 the Bishop of Calcutta died, he asked Heber if he might put forward his name to the East India Company and then to the King. It was a proposal to which Heber reacted less with false modesty than with sincere shock. The Bishop of Calcutta did not merely look after the Christians in and around that city. His responsibilities included the vast Indian territories ruled by John Company's Governor-General, which stretched from Ceylon to the Himalayan foothills, it also covered

Burma, and because there was no other Bishop of the English Church in the Eastern Hemisphere even Australasia was reckoned to be under his jurisdiction. It was a vast diocese which would require endurance more than mere stamina, excellent health, and great vigour. It would mean either separation from his family or risking their health in the Indian climate notoriously unfavourable to Europeans. There were other risks besides heat and disease. The natives were by no means always friendly. There were dangerous animals, insects and reptiles to face. He himself would have to cover immense distances in his work and live more in temporary and primitive bungalows and tents than in civilised houses. His second daughter was only one year old. The physicians he consulted could give him no satisfactory answer when he asked if so frail a baby could withstand the long voyage out and the new climate. His friends were gratified by the honour done to him but none wished him to accept and leave them. Maria Leycester was appalled, and the more so when Heber said if he went he would chivy Martin Stow from Genoa and take him as chaplain to India. Old Mrs. Heber at Hodnet Hall was in her seventy-second year and greatly distressed. Should he accept there was little chance of her ever seeing him again. He was persuaded to refuse the suggestion, but Williams-Wynn was persuasive. He refused to accept the refusal. He pressed his old friend to reconsider. Eventually, though with declared reluctance, he allowed his name to be put forward. A month later he panicked. He begged Williams-Wynn to cancel the whole idea. Once again he was pressed. Once again he gave way. Early in 1823 the Directors of John Company submitted Heber's name to the King who was in bed in the Brighton Marine Pavilion screaming, according to the wife of the Russian Ambassador, from the pains of rheumatic gout, and being bled copiously in his Moorish, Tartar, Gothic, Chinese and Indian surroundings, and totally incapable, one must suppose, of engendering much interest in the transfer of the Rector of Hodnet to an episcopal throne on the Ganges. Nevertheless he agreed, and Reginald Heber was committed.

He faced the melancholy prospect of leaving everything and almost everyone he loved. He was to take his wife Emily, their baby daughter, their monthly nurse and one Hindu servant. Their luggage was crated up into twenty-six baggage cases, and conveyed to the warehouses by the Thames. He arranged with Richard for his place to be taken at Hodnet by their old friend Oswald Leycester of Stoke-upon-Terne. The Leycesters were to continue to reside in the former picturesque Stoke Rectory,* which suggests there might have been an understanding he would hand Hodnet back to Reginald should he wish to retire from India to Shropshire. As neither Reginald nor Richard had sons, the family manors and presentation to Rectories passed eventually to Reginald's daughter who married a Percy, son of the then Bishop of Carlisle, and the family of Heber-Percy lives to the time of writing in a rebuilt Victorian Hodnet Hall. It was necessary for the Heber family to go visiting, saying good-bye to all their friends in Shropshire and Wales and Cheshire; preaching farewell sermons, which wore on his nerves. There were compensations, of course, to offset the upset of leaving. Oxford made him a D.D. All Souls' had his portrait painted so that it could be hung in their hall. Friends and relatives went with the travellers up to London to see the small party off. Heber was consecrated a bishop by the Archbishop of Canterbury at Lambeth Palace on the 1st June and on the 16th June they went aboard the *Thomas Greville* with all their cabin furniture and travelling trunks to a seventeen gun salute due to a bishop, and the yards of the ship manned in his honour. There were the last good-byes and the ship weighed anchor to begin the long voyage round the Cape which took four months, and in which they met fearful weather. At last, on the 6th October the yards were manned again and the guns fired a salute as the Bishop left the ship to make the last part of the journey by road and by river to the See City and Governor-General's Headquarters of Calcutta.

The rest shall be short; as Heber had no more time to write hymns. His new life was as different from the former one in Hodnet as could possibly be imagined, but he did, however, have the congenial company in his labours of his old curate. Martin Stow was invited to give up his post at Genoa and go out to India as the Bishop's chaplain. Sadly, the consolations he brought were brief, for he lasted only a few months, dying of an undignifying indigenous disease, after a distressing, spun-out illness. He spoke of Maria Leycester in his last hours, and she, when she heard of his death, declared she was utterly bereft. She had no Hebers at Hodnet Rectory and Martin Stow was in a tropical grave. Time, of course brought solace. She married

---

* Later demolished, like the pretty Tudor church of St. Peter which he served, with the subsequent Victorian Rectory got rid of in the mass iconoclasm of the late twentieth century Church of England.

Stow's greatest friend, Augustus Hare* who, as it happened, was also Mrs. Heber's best-loved cousin.

The Bishop sadly missed his friend and chaplain in the enormously difficult task he had undertaken. What instructions he received from Lord Amherst in the imposing Government House built by a previous Governor-General are not known. It was the Company's policy not to convert those who subscribed to the greater religions of the subcontinent, and allegedly it was a feeling that they were all to be forcibly 'Christianised' which contributed in some measure to the Indian Mutiny which took place thirty-four years after Heber's arrival. But Christians of his character convert by the sincerity of the faith they hold and it appears that many Indians were convinced quite simply by the Bishop's own faith. It was he who first ordained an Indian as a priest, and he founded institutions and organisations that were to long outlive him. He was obliged to instruct pugnacious and impudent missionaries sent out by the Church Missionary Society in England that he and not the Society office in London had spiritual oversight of India and that they were responsible to him. He also kept under his protective wing several foreign missionaries from Europe. He learnt several native languages so that he could communicate with his people, and made prodigious Episcopal progresses. Chiefly he travelled by water on the great rivers of India or coast-hugging in native powered canoes or in sailing dhows or ketches right down the littoral of the Cuttack, the Northern Circars and Carnatic to Ceylon, thence to Bombay and Travancore, Cochin, Malabar and Western Ghats; and travelled overland in a multiplicity of ways – by foot, horse, pony, camel and elephant, by carriage, bullock cart, waggons, and *jampan* or sedan chair, crossing river gorges in frail baskets on an aerial ropeway, or by shaking and swaying rope and stick bridges, and down the boiling rivers

---

* Augustus Hare was one of the four sons born to a well-connected couple with handsome expectations who had eloped with the assistance of the great Georgiana, Duchess of Devonshire, to live in Carlsruhe and Italy on £200 a year. Augustus took Holy Orders, was an Oxford don, and, on marrying Maria Leycester in 1829, was presented to the college living of a tiny Wiltshire village. There he remained, apart from many excursions at home and abroad, until he caught a chill at Stoke-upon-Terne and died a few months later in Rome at the early age of forty-one. His widow never remarried, but found sufficient courage to enquire of the wife of her brother-in-law, Francis Hare, if she could possibly bring herself to spare her youngest baby and her own godchild who had recently been Christened in Rome and named Augustus. She vowed to bring him up as her very own son and was gratified but a little startled to receive a brief reply – 'My dear Maria, how very kind of you! Yes, certainly, the baby shall be sent to you as soon as it is weaned; and if any one else would like to have one, would you kindly recollect that we have others.' This boy, sent over to England 'with a little green carpet-bag containing two little white night-shirts and a red coral necklace – my whole trousseau and patrimony', grew to be the widely read traveller and stimulating literary gossip, *the* Augustus Hare.

themselves in special buffalo skin rafts. There were wars as well as other dangers for a travelling bishop with a single chaplain and their servants to contend with. Only a year after Heber's arrival John Company went to war with the King of Burma, and there was a serious mutiny of sepoys in the military cantonment fifteen miles up the river Hooghly from Calcutta.

Heber's useful life in the subcontinent was not to last long. In April 1826 he arrived on a second visit to Ceylon. He confirmed eleven Tamil converts in their own language at Trinchinopoly, and he went hot and tired to cool himself in a bathhouse. Very soon afterwards he was found there by his chaplain, drowned in the bath. He was in his forty-third year.

*

In the year George IV goutily made Heber Bishop of Calcutta, another poet, Henry Francis Lyte, became Perpetual Curate of Lower Brixham in Devon; a fishing place with bland air which, it was hoped, might benefit the parson's health. He was then thirty years old and considered delicate. He had not always been so. In fact the first memory of a schoolfellow at the Portora Royal at Enniskillen, where Henry and his elder brother Thomas arrived in 1804, was of a pair of tough lads, dropped at the school by post-chaise each dressed in tattered tartan. They looked Scots, and Henry had, in fact, been born in 1793 in or near Kelso on the north side of the Border, but they were lineally descended from a long line of Somerset squires, the Lytes of Lytescary. The eleventh squire, Henry Lyte, was a distinguished sixteenth century botanist and antiquary, and his surviving sons (again Thomas and Henry) both flourished under royal patronage; one as a genealogist and historian; the other, as one of the earliest users of decimal fractions. Presumably then the tough, ragged-looking lads were entitled to bear the Lytes' coat of arms with its exotic crest, 'the swan volant silver upon a trumpet gold'. Their father, Captain Thomas Lyte, appears to have been something of an enigma; a wandering army officer who left few trails. Nothing is reported of Mrs. Lyte; but the Captain, then quartered in Sligo, having come to an arrangement with Dr. Burrowes, headmaster of Portora School, sent his sons off to Enniskillen, and disappeared abroad for a foreign tour of duty of between three and four years. Evidently he made some provision for his sons, but it was fairly meagre. Thomas, the elder, was something of a dunce, but Henry pugnaciously protected him and made up for any slur on the Lyte name by proving himself the most able boy in the school. Indeed he showed such promise that when, after a period of three years, Dr. Burrowes somehow managed to hand Thomas Lyte back to his military father, he kept Henry on at Portora at no fee.

It was a good place in which to grow up with its shops and cattle markets and the castle. There were fish to catch in the river Erne and the two loughs, and lough islands to explore such as Devenish and White Island and Innismacsaints, each with its ruins; and plenty of birds and animals to catch, trap and snare; and, the soil being chalky, a variety of wild and handsome butterflies and flowers. The same schoolfellow who noted the arrival of the Lytes in ragged tartan commented on Henry's 'singular habits'. This is intriguing. So is the comment: 'he was popular with his schoolfellows, and left behind him a reputation of a boy of extraordinary talent, desultory and flighty; eccentric, but very amiable.' Evidently Lyte was already something of a character! He left school with a sizarship to Trinity College Dublin, which meant that, in return for serving at table and giving other help, he was given free board and tuition; but, in no time at all, he proved himself so able and brilliant that the University granted him an additional scholarship which made him quite independent. Of his father and simpleton of a brother little is now known and no more need be said. Young Henry at first read medicine, but abandoned it to read for holy orders. In three successive years he won university prizes for his English poems and he continued writing them after his ordination to a curacy down in co. Wexford in 1815. He also began to collect books, thus laying the foundation of a large library. But it seems he already showed signs of the debilitating weakness which was to dog him for the remainder of his life. Presumably he became consumptive and he soon left Ireland for the warm air of the Continent, filling his time with gentle exercise and much study of literature and theology and ecclesiastical history. His health improved sufficiently for him to return to Britain in 1817 where he chose to live in the bland south-west whence the Lyte family had originated.

At Mazarion in Cornwall he renewed his health and found an heiress who became his bride, Anne Maxwell, the daughter of a rich and scholarly clergyman of the Church of Ireland. It is alleged he also found a revitalised faith through the example and death of a fellow clergyman. Be that as it may, he took a curacy and he and Anne set up their first home in Lymington, Hampshire, where he was inspired to write a great deal of poetry and publish his first work, *Tales in Verse on the Lord's Prayer*, which ran to a second edition. From Hampshire they moved back to the West Country, first to Charleton, then

Henry Francis Lyte, a tough Scots lad who became a delicate Parson of Brixham, tutor, bibliophile and hymn-writer (*Hymns Ancient and Modern*)

Dittisham on the River Dart in Devonshire, and finally he was offered and accepted in 1823 an incumbency as Perpetual Curate of the newly created parish of Lower Brixham, the first place in England William III had stepped ashore when invited to take the throne at the Glorious Revolution. The Lytes' parsonage was called Burton House and there they settled with their three sons. He took some benefit from being beside the sea and from the soft climate. Yet he was increasingly dogged with illness. He and Mrs. Lyte were obliged to take foreign holidays to recruit his health; from one, on St. Helena, he took back two cuttings of trees which grew beside the grave of the exiled Bonaparte. They took and they grew in the parsonage garden, but they never thrived. Nor did the parson. He worked hard in his parish, helped by Mrs. Lyte and a succession of curates. He also continued book collecting, and was what might be called a Sunday poet. Yet his energy grew less and his anxiety grew more.

They were troublesome times in which to live. Lyte read his newspaper and was much concerned with the troubles which began to erupt all over Europe a bare seven years after he had settled in Brixham. In 1830 the Poles, whose country had been absorbed for centuries by Russia, Prussia and Austria, attempted to re-establish their nation and there was a military insurrection in Warsaw. There was civil war in the Low Countries, and revolution in Paris. The Bourbons were driven out to spend a dreary exile in Holyrood House, Edinburgh, and 'citizen' Louis-Philippe became king of the French; sending Tallyrand of all people, as his Ambassador to London. At home, in England, King George IV, grossly swollen 'like a feather bed' from dropsy, and suffering at the hands of physicians who purged him and tapped pints of water from punctures in his skin, and, too, from the amount of beef and fowl and chocolate he gorged and the copious draughts of laudanum in cherry brandy followed by morphia, ether, brandy and salvolatile he swallowed to subdue his discomforts, at length died, exclaiming; 'My dear boy! This is death!' His odd sailor brother, now William IV, became restless during his brother's funeral and left before the interment. For years he had gargled daily to prepare himself for making regal speeches, and had worn galoshes to prevent himself being carried off by a chance chill. He enjoyed being king, but he did not enjoy the rioting and rick burning in the countryside and the destruction of the Luddites in the industrial areas. Nor did he care for the widespread agitation for parliamentary reform. His Tory ministry was threatened by the Whigs. He had been an active sailor for many years, so he escaped the botheration of Court and Parliament by taking a cruise in the royal yacht. He sailed west along the Channel and when the yacht made Tor Bay, and the King had a mind to step ashore at Brixham, he took it as a kindly thought that the local people arranged for his foot to step on the very stone that had received William the Third's shoe when he came to claim his throne. In view of the unsettled state of things at home and abroad, and being a superstitious seaman, he probably also took it as a propitious sign. At all events, he thanked the local clergyman and his High Church surpliced choir for their kind welcome, enquired from his retinue what was available to offer in return, and promptly presented Henry Lyte with Berry House, formerly a convalescent home for garrison troops which lay half way up the hill in a far more salubrious spot than Burton House. It was a handsome royal gift and Lyte soon took possession of the property; a commodious, creeper-covered house with large gardens which were terraced right down to the sea. It was here that Lyte continued his studies and writing, especially poetry, assembling material for a second volume of sacred verse.

In 1831 all hymnographers were inspired by an article on Luther's Psalm 46, *'Ein' feste Burg ist unser Gott'*, which appeared in *Frazer's Magazine*. The writer of the article and translator of the hymn was the thirty-six year old lowland Scot Thomas Carlyle. The son of humble parents, Carlyle's talents had emerged early and been nourished, but his personality and character barred him from the profession so revered by the Scots. Foul-tempered and solitary, he was unsuited to be a school master; the sudden loss of his faith kept him from the Kirk's ministry; and he was disinclined to be an advocate. He had tried private tutoring in London, but found his real vocation as a man of letters writing a life of Schiller and an English translation of Goethe's *Wilhelm Meister*. Then he married the heiress of a tiny fortune and, after a spell in Edinburgh, they settled for six years not far from his original home in his wife's small farm or croft at Craigenputtock. It was a wretched life for her. They were quite alone save for a servant girl and a boy who went in occasionally to help; their food was infinitely monotonous and poor; and her husband either irritable with dyspepsia, or depressed, or silently absorbed in writing. He was working on a *History of German Literature*, and contributing long articles to magazines on Burns, Johnson, Goethe, Voltaire, Diderot, Schiller, and many others. His translation of Luther's Psalm as the hymn 'A safe stronghold our God is still, A trusty shield and weapon' added to his already considerable reputation. It had a rugged quality which not only exactly suited his own character and his silent, bleak environment, but also matched Luther's paraphase and Luther's solemn melody. In the Thirty Years' War the hymn had been used by the Protestants as a march, and was sung by Gustavus Adolphus at the head of his troops, to the accompaniment of trumpets, as they charged the Imperial army at Lützen where Gustavus met a glorious death in victory. For this reason Frederick the Great called the hymn 'God Almighty's Grenadier March', and it was also named 'The Marseillaise Hymn of the Reformation'. It is good to visualise Henry Lyte reading this thrilling hymn, which had been written in such a raw, unsheltered farmhouse, in the comfort of his new parsonage overlooking the waters of Tor Bay.

It was at Berry House that Lyte at last established his library, sending for his scores of books, buying many more, and always wantful. It was not, of course, as extensive a collection as that of 'Magnificent' Heber, though it was sufficiently large to require an eighteen day sale in London after his death, and was evidence of his scholarship, and his continued interest in English poetry and divinity. He specialised in early patristic writings, to which, over the years, he added an extensive and rare collection of the works of Bishop Ken and his fellow Non-jurors. He even considered preparing a new addition of their writings with a memoir on each; but the plan never matured. His chief assistant in collecting was his son, surnamed Maxwell Lyte after Mrs. Lyte had come into her inheritance.

In 1833 Lyte had sufficient verses to publish *Poems chiefly Religious*. It was fairly well received. That scourge of authors, the *Edinburgh Review*, gave it a lengthy but disparaging critical notice half a year afterwards. The anonymous reviewer first expressed unease: 'It was not without some apprehension, as well as curiosity, that we approached (this book) . . . Sounds, in which the chant of Watts's hymns was mingled with the shriller notes of the drum ecclesiastical, appeared to be floating towards us.' He continued to remark that no other body of men were so free as the beneficed clergymen of the Established Church to write good verses, and at once questioned Mr. Lyte's 'irregular dirge "On a Naval Officer buried in the Atlantic" ' in the spirit of disapprobation. Oddly, though it could never be considered to have the same quality as his sacred poems, the poem enjoyed for a time a great vogue, and Sir Arthur Sullivan composed a setting for it. But the *Edinburgh Review* writer was not yet done with Lyte. Sarcastically he remarked, 'Few

persons are more likely, and certainly none are more entitled, to
welcome the approach of evening, than an active parish priest. It
must be doubly welcome when it comes ushered in with a chain of
pleasing fancies, to sweeten and sanctify its repose:

> 'Sweet evening hour! sweet evening hour!
> That calms the air and shuts the flower;
> That brings the wild bee to its nest,
> The infant to its mother's breast.'

and quoted five other equally uninspiring stanzas. In his final salvo
he noted 'the carelessness and the inequality which are to be found in
this agreeable little volume'. A month later, on Saturday 10th May,
1834, the *Athenaeum* came to Lyte's rescue, recommending 'an
excellent unpretending little volume, with much music and
versification, much purity and freshness of thought, and none of the
blemishes which make sacred poetry so often painful and
objectionable'.

Neither of these critics noticed another publication of Lyte's in
that year 1834; *The Spirit of the Psalms*, in which he tried to give
metrical versions of the Psalter to fit the calendar and services of the
Church. It was not unlike Bishop Heber's scheme to provide hymns
for each Sunday and feast day. It was exactly like the scheme and
method of Miss Harriet Auber*, who had published her metrical
version with a few hymns added under exactly the same title in 1829.
One of her hymns, often heard at Whitsuntide, has survived: 'Our
Blest Redeemer, ere he breathed' has a strange tale attached to it;
that Miss Auber first wrote the poem, all seven stanzas as there were
in the original, on a pane of glass at her home, which was stolen at her
death, and has never been seen since. Lyte's book contained a
number of good hymns, for he was adept at seizing the central point
of a psalm and rendering it in a different way. 'Far from my heavenly
home' is based on Psalm 137; 'God of mercy, God of Grace' on Psalm
67; 'Pleasant are thy courts above' on Psalm 84; and, the most
renowned, 'Praise my soul the King of Heaven', on Psalm 113.
These were all hymns written for his people in Lower Brixham. He
worked very hard there considering his increasing feebleness. He
made a point of emphasising the parish's royal associations by
keeping Accession Day as an annual church feast. And besides his
hymns he wrote sea shanties for the fishing fleet. Mrs. Lyte's fortune
was not inexhaustible. Her husband's thirst for books was hard to

---

* The Reverend Henry Housman, in his sketch of the life and work of John Ellerton, succinctly
summarised Miss Auber's life; 'She was the daughter of the rector of Tring, and died
unmarried, advanced in years, but "full of good works" '.

slake. Money had to be found for the collection as it cumulated. And so, in the 1830's, Lyte decided to take in pupils at Berry Head. His first was James, Viscount Cranborne, the eldest son and heir of the second Marquis of Salisbury. The boy was virtually incapable of being educated. We know, from research conducted in the Second World War, that his mother probably had German measles when she was carrying him, and he suffered congenital rubella. But at that time no-one would have known the reason for his condition, which probably made it harder to bear. The poor child grew up, partly misshapen, half blind, half deaf, and so limited he could scarcely write his name. He lived to be forty-four, and later pictures are the portraits of a haunted man, locked in himself, incapable of measuring up to other men. Only those people who struggled with a devoted insistence to reach his understanding were able to help him in his solitude. Henry Lyte was chief of them; acting as his tutor in Lower Brixham until the boy grew to be nineteen years old. The demands made on the parson seemed to bring out the best in him. Nothing was too much trouble. For the young Cranborne's sake he was perfectly able to tolerate the largely illegible letters, or, rather, rough drafts on scraps of paper, which he received from the dictatorial and hectoring Marquis who believed only he knew best. Lyte was patience itself with his difficult pupil, and put himself out for him. He selected fine passages of prose and verse and from holy scripture, and engrossed them carefully in a neat, large hand, at which the boy would squinny and take in some, but not much, information. In November 1835 when James Cranborne was fourteen and the autumn gales ripped along the Channel, Lyte went by packet all the way from Falmouth to London to buy special equipment in the capital. He had heard of a French invention, a machine which embossed letters to assist the blind 'see' their letters by feel. He found one, tried it, and bought it. He also bought a special bound-up book of pages with raised letters. Teaching, thereafter, was a little easier, but most instruction was given by word of mouth. Considering the difficulty of communication it is remarkable that Lyte taught him so much. Mathematics, beyond the simplest, was not possible; nor was Greek because of its different alphabet; but Lyte tried to teach him Latin and English literature and Italian and history and geography. He brought in outside teachers for German and French. And the last teacher disgraced himself by accompanying Cranborne home for one of his rare vacations and borrowing money from the Hatfield servants which he could not repay. Lord Salisbury sent a scribble that the man should be discharged, and he was.

The Lytes all took tea at seven. There is rather a pathetic picture of the family taking it in turn to read the life of Peter the Great into Cranborne's ear-trumpet. This instrument was not very efficient and it regularly required attention. Another pathetic picture is of Parson Lyte removing the boy's orthopaedic supporting strap so that he could attempt gymnastics. It was a failure and the effort and the frustrations easily made the young man ill-tempered. In 1836 Lyte wrote to Lord Salisbury asking him to recommend people to keep his own sons company. Lyte's eldest was seventeen and already at Oxford. The next in age was thirteen, and able enough, construing Horace and working at Euclid to his father's satisfaction. The youngest Lyte was then eight. If Lord Salisbury replied, none of his scribbled drafts has survived, but it is known that, three years later, in 1839, when the Marquis took his ailing wife for a cruise in a desperate but futile search for health, he sent his third son Robert, who was in fact to succeed him as third Marquis, down to Berry Head.* Lord Robert, at nine, was half the age of his unfortunate elder brother, and himself was nervously disposed. From the age of six he had been miserable at a school close to Hatfield, referring to it in later life as having been 'an existence among devils'. Then nerves had been shattered by the death of his Irish grandmother, who was burnt alive in a fire which destroyed a wing of Hatfield in 1835, and by the foreboding that his delicate mother had not long to live. Parson Lyte looked after him while the Salisburys went abroad, and evidently liked him, though the boy had such a habit of lounging about that he had to trick him into taking exercise by interesting him in botany and geology. Which worked, and the normally torpid Robert Cecil was seen scampering over the rocks and getting 'quite rosy'. In his written report Lyte showed shrewd judgment, for no-one had ever suggested that the boy might have great promise; 'I have no doubt of him distinguishing himself hereafter in life,' he wrote to Lord Salisbury, who was astonished.† After their mother's

---

* Lord Arthur, the second son, had only lived two years; and Lord Eustace was still in the schoolroom.

---

† Lyte was perfectly right. As third Marquis of Salisbury his pupil became a brilliant Foreign Secretary of State and was thrice Prime Minister under Queen Victoria, but he never lost his indolence, not bothering to change his clothes so that his shabbiness became proverbial – when Prime Minister of Great Britain and owner of property near Monte Carlo he was refused admittance to the Casino there because he looked so disreputable – nor ever quelling his tendency to doze off, even at important meetings, so that when Ambassadors called on him he kept sleep at bay by constantly prodding himself in the leg with a paper-knife.

death it was arranged that both boys should leave Berry Head in the winter; Lord Cranborne to tour abroad with a fit and responsible tutor; his young brother to go to Eton where, apparently, he showed an extraordinary aptitude for absorbing divinity, but continued idling, perpetually 'losing' his hat so that he would not have to go out of doors. Lord Salisbury's sons had been taxing pupils, but doubtless the Lytes were sorry to see them go.

A vivid picture of Henry Lyte as Parson of Brixham in the 1840s was given by Reynolds Hole, a friend of Lyte's oldest son at Oxford, who went down to Lower Brixham in a vacation. Hole was still an undergraduate, but already showed signs of being an exceptionally rigorous all-rounder. He hunted foxes with great passion for fifty years, and was equally passionate about gardening, especially the rose, on which he became an authority and earned from Tennyson the title 'Rose King'. Besides this he had a wide circle of literary friends, from Maxwell Lyte to Leech and Thackeray, published books on roses and travel and his memoirs, contributed to *Punch* and *Cornhill*, wrote verses – amongst them some fearful and forgotten hymns*; and was a squarson for thirty-seven years and Dean of Rochester for seventeen. The young Reynolds Hole evidently had a high opinion of his host Mr. Lyte, for he wrote about him in his *Memories* fifty years later, so long after the visit that it invited candour. He called Lyte 'a true gentleman, scholar, poet and saint, who was revered by all who knew him'. The poor adored him. So did his friends the fishermen who came up sometimes to serenade their parson:

> 'We'll stay and have our breakfast here,
> We'll stay and have a 'levener here,
> We'll stay and have our dinner here,
> We'll stay and have our supper here,'

singing each verse thrice with increasing vigour, capping the lot with a ringing cry: 'And we won't go home.' This would bring a beaming Mr. Lyte from his library to shake hands with them all and ask how they did and how were their families and would they step round to the kitchen for ale. . . . Which left everyone feeling very comfortable. The parson's only bugbear, besides his feebleness, was the presence of some Plymouth Brethren in the parish. Several of his regular church attenders, even members of his choir, were seduced

---

* One of Hole's hymns, however, 'Father forgive', set to music by his friend Stainer, had a sale of more than twenty-eight thousand broadsheet copies and earned him almost £100. Unlike most Church dignitaries of the present day, Hole had no qualms at all in contributing this sum to the Transvaal War Fund.

away. Neither he nor his curate, at this time a High Church clergyman named Edmund Field★, could do anything to shatter the dour certainty of the Brethren that they were loved by the Lord Jesus and He didn't love anyone else. The curate adventurously suggested preaching on the foreshore to catch those who didn't attend church before the Brethren terrified them into a Meeting of the Elect, but, while Lyte was considering and trying to decide whether or not this would be proper, they found they had been forestalled. Some sort of Dissenting Minister seized the initiative and preached the Gospel on the sands, standing on a small turned up fish-gutting tub. The curious listeners who came along to hear him for a few Sundays were called 'Basket Christians', but when, without notice, he disappeared, so did his congregation. When we read that there were eight hundred children in the Sunday School, we must suppose that both young Maxwell Lyte and his friend Hole were drawn in to give temporary help. It was certainly too much for the parson, who stayed for the minimum time and then took refuge at Berry House.

The most regular work in the library was now on a long-neglected seventeenth-century Welsh poet Henry Vaughan, whom he was determined to reinstate in his proper place among the poets. His editing of Vaughan's *Silex Scintillans* and the Memorial he wrote of him were evidence of his own intellectual stature and his capacity to see what so many were blind to. He worked in bursts when free from parish or family duties and when he had the strength; but he was quickly deteriorating. He tried a winter in Rome and south Italy. It was supposedly the right thing to do if one had phthisis. Keats had tried it. But, as in the case of Keats, it made small difference. Lyte returned to the red cliffs of Lower Brixham. There his portrait was done by a member of the 'Bristol School', John King; a painter who was almost exactly his own age and who succumbed to apoplexy four months after Lyte died. The picture was a fair likeness, one of King's best; good enough certainly to merit engraving. In 1847 Lyte's edition of Henry Vaughan's *Silex Scintillans* with a memoir was published. It was his last secular work; and it became evident that he was close to the end of his spiritual work as well. He decided to leave his parish to the care of a curate and again the trunks were packed for Italy. On the day before they sailed he preached his last sermon and assisted at the administration of the Sacrament. Then he went home for a last quiet time in his study. An hour later he left it, having

---

★ Afterwards Chaplain of Lancing College, where he was held in great affection by generations of boys and masters.

written what is surely the most popular hymn in the English language; 'Abide with me; fast falls the eventide'. He gave the manuscript to a relative* and the next morning he left Brixham and his people and his home for the last time. His last, most powerful hymn, is frequently sung as an evening hymn, but this is really a mistake. Lyte was writing about the evening of life, as the last stanzas emphasise:

> 'I fear no foe with thee at hand to bless;
> Ills have no weight, and tears no bitterness.
> Where is death's sting? where, grave, thy victory?
> I triumph still, if thou abide with me.
>
> Hold thou thy Cross before my closing eyes;
> Shine through the gloom, and point me to the skies;
> Heaven's morning breaks, and earth's vain shadows flee;
> In life, in death, O Lord, abide with me!'

No foreign climate could help the author of these lines. Barely two months after his leaving home, when he was staying at an hotel in Nice, Heaven's morning broke for him. He summoned a servant and asked for a priest of the Church of England. Fortunately there was one in the hotel and Henry Lyte was given the Consolations of his Church. The clergyman was Henry Edward Manning, then Archdeacon of Chichester, and afterwards Cardinal Archbishop of Westminster.

★

The portrait of a lady concludes these notes on some of the writers who contributed to the abundance of hymnals which followed *Olney Hymns*. Charlotte Elliott tends to elude description, for she had the oriental disposition to *be* rather than the occidental disposition to *do*.

Writing at a time when the concept of women's liberation occasionally takes an aggressive turn, it is difficult to imagine that the ladies of a century ago wielded any power at all. There were obvious exceptions who were ladies of great consequence. Their outspoken champion, Lady Amberley, had a cemented position in Society as the daughter of a peer and the wife, no less, of the heir to 'Radical Jack', the first Earl Russell, one of the fiercest British Prime Ministers of the century. She roused the wrath of the Fount of

---

* Lyte also left a tune for his words, but the familiar tune sung on innumerable Sunday evenings, at countless funerals, and by thousands at War Memorial services, and even at football matches, was written by W. H. Monk, a musical director of the first important Church of England hymnal, *Hymns Ancient and Modern*. Monk one day read through Lyte's hymn, and though at the time he was simultaneously giving a music lesson, he composed his tune in less than ten minutes.

Honour and her Sovereign by declaring feminist views in a public lecture delivered in 1870. Queen Victoria, female ruler of the greatest Empire the world has ever seen, wrote a memorandum on the 'mad, wicked folly of "Women's Rights" with all its attendant horrors' and added with unusual venom: 'Lady Amberley ought to get a *good whipping*.' It appears from the facts that very few women really were the chattels, the downtrodden beasts of burden, and the victims of brute lust that their great-granddaughters imagine them to have been. Much in the same way as Italy is now chiefly governed by the strong mother figure in the background, so Victorian Society was largely controlled, and much of Victorian history made, by the ladies in the shade behind the men. Some ruled despotically from sick-beds. Few ladies were more demanding and domineering than the stricken Elizabeth Barrett Browning who received on a chaise-longue with her dog Flush at her feet, and whose slightest wish was granted. Few have wielded such background political power over so great a range of subjects as Florence Nightingale, and she took to her sofa in August 1857 and did not die until August 1910. And amongst these sick-bed wielders of influence, we may include Charlotte Elliott, because although her sphere of control was different and much smaller than those of Miss Browning or Miss Nightingale, it was none the less powerful. She became a force in the Evangelical Revival, that Counter Reformation of the Established Church against the Reformation of Wesley and the welling-up of Dissent.

Born into very comfortable circumstances in 1789 in Clapham, which was then fashionable and at the centre of much Low Church fervour, she quickly showed literary talent and amused herself writing light and humorous verses. At that time she was well and young and not overtly religious; but at the early age of thirty-two she began to suffer one of those unidentified but not uncommon and incapacitating life-long Victorian illnesses which laid her up for ever. After a year in the sick-room she was introduced to the Swiss Evangelist, Cesar Malan, who vexed her by enquiring if she was indeed Christian. She dismissed him as an impertinent zealot; but he had, as it were, touched a responding nerve which made her both introspective and able to concentrate her powers on sacred poetry. The household moved from Clapham to Brighton, a growing centre of religious enthusiasm, where there eventually arose a clash of such proportions between the High and Low Church elements of the Established Church that proprietary churches were built and endowed by the rich and the eccentric of both sides, and the B.&S.C.R. was an abbreviation commonly used by the ritualists and

Anglo-Catholics not to describe a railway line but for Brighton &
South Coast Religion.

The Low Church was the first on the ground and Charlotte
Elliott's father was one of the first to build a proprietary church. She
herself wielded great power from her sick-room, writing hymns
characterised by an intellectual approach to realities together with a
tenderness of feeling, deep piety, and an almost unerring use of
rhyme. These were printed as broadsheets and were read and
admired by thousands who, like her, were in some way incapacitated
and unable to lead a normal life. In this way she had great influence in
her generation, although her hymns, of which there were one
hundred and fifty, inevitably varied in quality and usefulness. Then
collections were brought out; one edited by her brother Harry, with
the plain title *Psalms and Hymns*; others under less attractive titles
such as *The Invalids' Hymn-Book*, and *Hours of Sorrow cheered and
comforted*. Charlotte was a pivot in the family, a great favourite of her
two brothers, both of whom followed their father in using the large
family fortune and their abilities to forward the Evangelical cause
and snap at anything that smacked of Popery.

The elder brother, Harry, was at first a Fellow of Trinity, but he
suffered a breakdown from overwork and was ordered abroad as a
cure. He took an adventurous route through Italy, Greece, and
Constantinople to Jerusalem, and, on his return, was ordained, and
held a curacy, then the charge of a proprietary Chapel of St. Mary in
Brighton, built by his father. There he also began tutoring in his own
establishment. His pupils included the sons of Sir Thomas Fowell
Buxton, a pious Norfolk landowner with a first-class mind, a seat in
the House of Commons, and a fortune in brewing, who was a great
cleanser of Augean Stables and an investigator without parallel into
such matters as the slave trade, savings banks, famine, hospitals, and
penal reforms.

Besides the Buxton boys Henry Elliott also tutored the sons of the
fourth Earl of Aberdeen, an accomplished nobleman of much charm
and talent who rose as a statesman to be Foreign Secretary twice, and
Prime Minister once, and, as an equally distinguished fellow of
learned societies, earned a sobriquet of 'Athenian' Aberdeen. The
eldest of his boys was conventional enough, though he produced a
son and heir, the sixth Earl, about whom *Burke's Peerage* makes the
laconic and thus tantalising report: 'after a career of romantic
adventures, (he) was accidentally drowned', at the age of twenty-
nine. The remaining three sons were a lively, promising lot. There
was Alexander, destined to be a general in the army and an equerry to

two sovereigns. There was Douglas, bookish and in Holy Orders, who became a Canon of Salisbury Cathedral. The youngest was to pass a brilliant career in the Consular Service in Trinidad, Mauritius, Fiji, New Zealand, the Western Pacific, and Ceylon, and be raised to the Peerage. How much the success of these scions of Lord Aberdeen was due to their time with the Reverend Mr. Elliot can only be conjectured.

However, we do know that, inspired by his success as a tutor, Elliott proceeded, in 1832, to found a school for the daughters of poor clergymen, in imitation of the school founded by his friend Carus Wilson at Cowan's Bridge in Yorkshire nineteen years before. Wilson's was the school held up to public ridicule by Charlotte Brontë in *Jane Eyre* and Mrs. Gaskell's subsequent *Life*, the first edition of which had to be withdrawn at the threat of libel action from that furious clergyman Carus Wilson, and it is to be hoped Elliott's proved to be more successful and less harmful to the daughters of poor clergymen. He left the running to others. His marriage, in 1833, to 'a lady of poetical talent from the Lake District', proved of absorbing interest to Charlotte, especially after the death of her sister-in-law of scarlet-fever, when she immediately concerned herself with the welfare of her nephews and nieces. Much of Charlotte's concern was wasted because two were destined for an early grave, one as a result of a fall whilst climbing a modest mountain in 1846, the other from a more dramatic accident on the Shreckhorn.

Charlotte's younger brother, Edward, followed the pattern set by his brother and was incumbent of yet another proprietary church in Brighton built and endowed by the family. He also followed Harry in providing Charlotte with constant interest in a bevy of nephews and nieces. Twice married, on both occasions to ladies of fortune, and never, in any case, obliged to depend on a clerical stipend, he still led a busy life, writing polemical sermons such as *What is the Beast?* and *The Delusion of the Tractarian Clergy*, and a rather bad memoir of 'Athenian' Aberdeen, his brother's patron.

Many of the family wrote and published hymns. Harry wrote a number himself; none was extensively used. His wife and his other sister did the same. Edward's third daughter, Emily Elliott, was more successful and published a collection in large print for use in infirmaries with the risqué but then presumably quite innocent title of *Under the Pillow*. None matched the invalid Charlotte in quantity or quality. She was queen of the Elliotts in hymn-writing. Possibly her best known in England, for in different recast versions it was familiar to hundreds and thousands of her contemporaries, was 'My God and Father, while I stray Far from my home in life's rough way'. She also wrote 'Christian, seek not yet repose', and one which brought her instant fame, and was written under rather curious circumstances. During the bustle of the Brighton household getting ready for a great church bazaar to raise money for Harry's academy for the daughters of poor clergymen, the invalid Charlotte was chagrined to be left out of things. And so, unable to do anything else, she simply wrote, and in the pre-bazaar domestic cyclone penned her famous hymn of pious resignation to the divine will:

'Just as I am, without one plea
But that thy Blood was shed for me,
And that thou bidd'st me come to thee,
    O Lamb of God, I come.'

Charlotte Elliott was to live another thirty-seven years and write many more hymns, but she never surpassed that. It enjoyed huge success, particularly on the Continent, and allegedly, 'was translated into almost every living language'. There might be something in this claim. Amongst the more uncommon languages it was first put into Samoan, and apparently rendered in Raratongen by a missionary named Buzacoth. It is almost certainly the only hymn to inspire what might be called a reply; not, of course, from the Almighty, but from America.

From over the Atlantic in 1850, sixteen years after Charlotte Elliott wrote 'Just as I am', came the rejoinder:

'Just as thou art, without one trace
Of love or joy, or inward grace,
Or meetness for the heavenly place,
    O wretched sinner, come.'

Lacking the distinction of the hymn which evoked it, it nevertheless found a place in *American Hymns Old & New*★. It was written by Mr. Russell Sturgis Cook, a Congregational Minister, barred from functioning as such by the reduction, by bronchitis, of a fine speaking voice to the barest whisper, and forced to write tracts instead. He did this with great force and energy; put into circulation more than one million publications for the American Tract Society, travelled in a frenzy all over the States and Europe, and married four wives. His hymn 'Just as thou art' might have vanished with all his tracts but for the fact that its tune took hold. This was composed by

---

★ This extensive collection with notes, in two volumes, was edited in 1980 for Columbia University Press by Albert Christ-Janer, Charles W. Hughes and Charleton Sprague Smith.

William Batchelder Bradbury, organist of the New York Baptist Tabernacle, a musician deeply interested in Sunday School hymns and skilled in writing emotional music. It was he who composed the simply, sugary tune for

> 'Jesus loves me! this I know
> For the Bible tells me so'

a mawkish infinitely popular hymn of the era composed by one of two sisters, both religiously inclined, who claimed that their rich father had lost *all* in a financial crisis, and left them only a mansion on Constitution Island on the Hudson River, where they devoted their Sundays to catechising selected West Point cadets rowed over by a servant for a lesson in divinity followed by tea and gingerbread.

It is from Charlotte Elliott on her couch in Brighton that we move to reflect on the writers of some notable American hymns. One of that country's greatest authoresses, Harriet Beecher Stowe, daughter and sister of eccentrics and an eccentric herself; tiny wife of a stocky, fat and bald hypochondriac haunted by devils and visions 'of a black colour, spotted with brown, in the shape of a flaring funnel with a nozzle'; mother of seven and tied by poverty for years to domestic toils; friend of George Eliot and Lady Byron; authoress of the amazingly influential *Uncle Tom's Cabin*, wrote in a preface to one of her books of 'the fathers and mothers of America (who) went out to give English ideas and institutions a new growth in a new world'.

It is of moment to see what some of them did with the institution of writing sacred poetry.

CHAPTER FOUR

PILGRIM CHILDREN

IT always requires a certain degree of courage for an Englishman to write about the United States and her people. There is an immensity about so much in that nation which defies any sort of compression. It is no less difficult with the subject of hymns and their writers. In that huge land-mass there are many religions; and, of the Christian and quasi-Christian sects, there are more than anywhere else in the world. Their praise of God inevitably differs and what might be a favourite spiritual to the large number of negro churches or a favourite song of all Holy Rollers and Shakers is unlikely to be a favourite in Europe. The limitation imposed in this chapter, therefore, is confined to hymns still sung in Europe originating from American writers. The six selected were all born before 1820 and all participated to a greater or lesser extent in the lengthy agonisings which both preceded and followed the Civil War of 1861–1865. This fierce conflict between the North and the South, the Union and the Confederacy, caused the bloodiest slaughter of any civil war in history. It also enabled the American Bismarck, Abraham Lincoln, to forge the United States into a nation. Scarcely anyone, and certainly no one of sensitivity and sensibility in the North or South, could fail to be touched by the events which led to the outbreak of war. They were at the forefront of most people's minds for years, and the causes of the war are still heatedly discussed today. It is sufficient here to state that there were more complex reasons than the obvious one of trafficking in slaves.

George Duffield is a good representative of a well-established old colonial family, his great-great-grandfather, originally of French Huguenot stock, having emigrated from the north of Ireland in about 1725 to Pennsylvania where he acquired extensive property.

The Huguenot-Presbyterian piety of the family produced a line of Presbyterian ministers, none without distinction. George's great-grandfather made missionary journeys through the frontier towns of Pennysylvania, Virginia and Maryland, and when an acrimonious schism came between 'Old Side' and 'New Side', he was a pugnacious supporter of the latter, and the cause of a riot when refused admission to his own church. Moreover, as he saw the Revolution approaching he declared himself an uncompromising Whig, and when it did come, he served in the Revolutionary Army as a chaplain and with such zeal that the British put a price on his head. The son of this fiery minister was a quiet and highly successful merchant who prudently married an heiress with the unusual name of Faithful Slaymaker, and for many years was Comptroller of Pennsylvania. His son, the third George, was another Presbyterian minister who, besides being a theologian, was also an author and scholar of science and languages, and very active in the Civil War on behalf of the North. Apparently he was 'conspicuous' in attempting to provide for the immense number of wounded soldiers.

The sons of the third George and the rich Miss Slaymaker were all men of mark. The youngest, Henry, rose from the ranks to be an adjutant of the 9th Michigan Infantry, and was wounded, for the Northern side, in the battle of Chickamanga. The second youngest read chemistry and medicine both in Pennsylvania and, abroad, in Berlin and Hesse where he became an accomplished expert in poisons and forensic medicine, and, on returning to the States, was frequently called upon to testify in criminal cases and wrote pamphlets on a myriad of subjects varying from *The Religion of Christ versus the Religion of the Scientist* to *Aconite Poisoning* and *The Ventilation of Sewers*. The next up in the line of sons served and was wounded in the Mexican War and survived to become civil engineer of important railway lines. Called up again to serve in the Civil War under Sherman, he led a foray against the Confederate soldiers, and, in a sharp battle, defeated them at Lebanon in Kentucky, rose to be Brigadier General in command of all forces in Kentucky, was severely wounded in two places and imprisoned, but survived the war to become, once more, a railway engineer. Less belligerent was the life of the second oldest son, a scholarly lawyer who quietly practised at the bar throughout the Civil War while accumulating an immense library and writing rather jejune works in both prose and verse.

The eldest, George Duffield IV, although considered 'wayward' by strict Presbyterians and, like his great-great-grandfather, at the centre of schism in his church, was a divine who gathered a reputation for the fervour of his preaching and the quality of the hymns he wrote. One has survived and is sung all over the world. It was inspired by an unusual occurrence, in the course of an ubiquitous affair in American life: an evangelistic Mission. Europe has produced silver-tongued persuaders, but very few in comparison to the United States. Moody and Sankey were household words not long ago – and not very healthy either, to the mind of Queen Victoria. Few in this century have not heard of the infamous Evangelist lady Aimée Semple McPherson, who ended her amazing career by leaving her clothes on a beach either for death by drowning or by disappearance into a new life; no-one knows. Dr. Billy Graham still compels with a wholesome if emotionally charged form of Christianity. Less wholesome are others with unsavoury reputations for making Bible-punching an industry through radio and television and founding their own universities, for the fee-paying 'born again' faithful.

The name Tyng is now forgotten. It meant a great deal in the slavery debates in America. Dudley Atkins Tyng was the son of a domineering and evil-tempered Episcopalian Rector, who himself was ordained but then was forced to resign his Rectory by a disgruntled congregation on account of his firm belief in abolition. The abolitionists realised his value for he was a gifted orator. They built him his own church and endowed it, and the Epiphany Church, Philadelphia was soon famous. He had a large following, and was much in demand as a leader of missions. In the emotional and physical heat of a summer mission in Philadelphia in 1858 – when Mrs. Stowe's *Uncle Tom's Cabin* and *Dred: A Tale of the Great Dismal Swamp* had inflamed the slavery issue even more than the 'auctioning' of slaves by her brother Henry Ward Beecher, from his own pulpit, so that they could achieve freedom – Dudley Atkins Tyng conducted a mission to young men with several helpers, the Reverend Mr. Duffield amongst them. Measured in conversion terms, the success was notable. It is recorded that at one point Tyng spoke in a great hall to more than five thousand men, and of this, to quote in a quaint fashion of the day, 'at least one thousand were slain of the Lord'. Resting, at home for a moment, from the chief business of organising the mission, Tyng walked in his garden to ponder. He was distracted by the sound of a cob-shelling machine worked by a mule; the beast circling endlessly attached to a capstan-like bar which separated corn from the cob. Tyng gave it an affectionate pat. This was disastrous. The sleeve of his preaching gown was caught in the boxwood cogs and he was drawn into the mill and one arm torn, with a wrench, from its socket. He was found there by family servants terribly wounded, bleeding his life away. The bleeding was almost, though not quite, stanched by a competent physician, but nothing could save him. Friends gathered by his bed as he screamed in the extremity of his pain. Duffield was there. Towards the end, in a lucid moment before he died of shock, Tyng took Duffield's hand with the one he had left and gave his last instruction for the continuing of the mission. 'Tell them', he said, 'to stand up for Jesus'. Duffield witnessed his friend and master's death and went immediately to write a panegyric for delivery at the mission. Words fell into place. At the end of his address he composed a poem which, by the custom at the time, was printed on a single sheet for the benefit of Sunday School children when it was first read out. A copy was pirated in a Baptist newspaper with a large circulation. It may aptly be described as one of the most famous of hymns, entering a large number of hymnals, and being sung in German and in Latin translations as well as in the original English. Soldiers from both North and South sang it as a march in the Civil War. And it is more widely used in mission work today than either its inspirer Tyng or its writer Duffield could ever have dreamed possible.

> 'Stand up! stand up for Jesus!
> Ye soldiers of the Cross;
> Lift high his royal banner,
> It must not suffer loss.
> From victory unto victory
> His army he shall lead,
> Till every foe is vanquished,
> And Christ is Lord indeed.'

The hymn's stirring verses, the call to conflict, the assurance of help, and the promise of a crown of life, have a solemn grandeur. The tune most usually sung to it is named *Morning Light* and is equally grand, though originally it was intended for profane not sacred purposes. It was composed almost thirty years before the poem by a young English musician, George Webb, while sailing from England to America as an emigrant. It was the setting for a drawing-room song, 'Tis dawn, the Lark is singing', and soon pirated by the Wesleyans as a fine setting for hymns, and by one particular Baptist pastor who spoke fifteen languages, but whose theology and learning still failed to make him a poet. He wrote a hymn of his own to fit the melody which had the lugubrious beginning:

> 'The morning light is breaking
> The darkness disappears

The sons of earth are waking
To penitential tears.'

Not until 1861 and the outbreak of Civil War was George Webb's *Morning Light* officially wedded in print to George Duffield's 'Stand up! – stand up for Jesus', and save for occasional separations when other composers have attempted to gild the lily it has been a very lasting marriage.

★

Probably the best poet among American hymn-writers, and next to Longfellow the most read of poets in his day, was the Quaker, John Greenleaf Whittier. Like Duffield he came from a long-established colonial family, being the descendant of a Pilgrim Father who arrived in Massachusetts from England in 1638, the year New Haven was founded in Connecticut and the first Swedes settled on the Delaware in a place they called New Sweden. His father, John, farmed land near Haverhill, then a farming village at the head of navigation on the Merrimack River, and was a gruff, unsmiling man, given to unexpected fits of generosity. His mother Abigail was devout and loving, and more easily understood that he preferred versifying to the farm work expected of him by his father. He had deep feelings for the New England countryside, and its natural beauty then quite unspoilt. He had equally deep feelings for poetry, and for a tomboyish playmate Mary Smith. Never formally educated, save for a short time as pupil of an itinerant tutor called Coffin, and an even shorter time at a village school, he virtually educated himself by absorbing any book which came his way. A local doctor earned his affection and gratitude by giving him the freedom of his library; but it was quite by chance, at the age of fourteen, that he traded something with a passing pedlar for a volume of poetry by Burns who had died only twenty-four years before. For a New England farmboy to read and understand Burns's Scots is surprising enough; more surprising is that he was enchanted by all he read and determined to write verses himself. He even managed some in Scots. The more he read, the more he wrote, ingesting and digesting travel books, history, and especially local history, even some theology, and the works of any poet he could find, particularly admiring Milton and Coleridge and Byron and the tragic Chatterton; and turning out streams of verse, some of it considered good by his sister May and his friend Mary Smith, and even praised by his mother. Doubtless some time passed before his taciturn father knew that he was writing a classic about farm life entitled *Barefoot Boy*, in addition to his

(top left) J. G. Whittier, the New England farmhand turned poet and hymn-writer; (top right) Whittier's home at Amesbury; (bottom) the Whittier homestead at Haverhill

work on the farm. John was no shirker, but not as tough as most farm lads, and, at seventeen, he severely strained himself and never wholly recovered. The one benefit he gained was his father's acceptance that he should work more with pen than with spade, though John Whittier senior never did quite understand his son's taste for poetry. The Society of Friends made no use of sacred poetry in its liturgy or even thought, and, while John always remained a Quaker, if not in deep piety, at least in their hatred of violence and slavery and the use of their distinctive clothing and mode of speech, he realised that he was a most unusual exception, lamenting that two hundred years of silence had taken 'all the song' out of the Friends. There was plenty of song in him.

He was a great admirer of William Lloyd Garrison, the reforming printer and editor of a Massachusetts local paper, *Free Press*. Garrison scourged any sort of intemperance, and with some reason for his father had been a drunken, whoring sea-captain who abandoned wife and children when William was only three; but young Whittier was really more interested in the journalist's methods as a philosophical non-resistant who relied on the power of moral principles for the conversion of opponents. Most of all he liked Garrison's sharp style and clarity of expression. He was, however, far too shy ever to approach the object of his admiration. Fortunately his sister May was not. Without her brother's permission, or even knowledge, she sent some of his verses, entitled *The Exile's Departure*, to the editor. Garrison recognised the author's lyrical powers and was sufficiently impressed to travel down to the farm at Haverhill. There he found a shy but pleasant young farmer of nineteen with no fixed future in mind save the need to write poetry. Garrison was practical. He agreed to publish the poem in his paper for a fee, which, according to the curious view of one of Whittier's biographers, permitted him 'the furtive bliss of print', but poetry then as ever, though the Queen of Arts, begrudged her votaries a living. Whittier would have to write prose as well, articles on literary and social topics, and earn a living as a journalist. To achieve this he would need a solid foundation of formal study. Garrison begged John's father to place him at a school or academy; but the old man would not countenance the idea. John could stay at home and write his verses when not required to do small jobs of which he was capable. But there was to be no investment in education. Garrison left it at that. He published many of Whittier's poems, became his personal friend, and influenced him greatly in his views on the liberal crusade in general, and on the evils of slavery in particular. He also introduced him into local literary circles which, though less sophisticated than those of the great cities, were more substantial than those caricatured by Dickens in his riotous burlesque of Mrs. Leo Hunter and her literary lions.

A member of this circle was another editor, Abijah Thayer. Garrison loyally published Whittier's lyric, but it was Thayer who commissioned a weekly poem for his *Essex Gazette*, and thus made his name better known, and it was Thayer who at last succeeded in persuading Farmer Whittier to send his son to Haverhill Academy, which had recently been founded. To help pay for this Whittier learnt to make slippers and cobble shoes, and tutored young children during the vacation; but he was only at the academy a year. By then his trickle of poems had become a rivulet. He was also writing pieces of literary criticism, short stories, and sketches. He virtually made himself into a journalist, and so acceptable was his work that, through Garrison's influence, he was appointed editor of a small magazine in Boston in 1829. Then his father fell ill. He was needed at home and resigned his work at Boston. But this was only the first of many editorships, many more honorary than practical, which he was to hold for a large part of his life. He was already well launched on that literary voyage which earned him international fame.

The death of his father had a double effect. At twenty-three he was effectively freed from parental restraint, but, because of his strong emotional ties with New England farm life, the thought of losing it made him feel more insecure and frightened than free. At about the same time, his childhood sweetheart Mary Smith married another man, and he abandoned himself to self-pity. Again Garrison rescued him by giving him something else to think about. Whittier was already against slavery as a matter of principle. Garrison, at that time corresponding secretary and salaried agent of the recently founded New England Anti-Slavery Society, and a fund-raiser in England to forward the cause, urged his younger friend to become an active abolitionist. And so Whittier spoke at meetings; he lobbied; he went as a delegate to an Anti-Slavery Convention at Philadelphia, and was one of the fifty signatories of its declaration, which was almost entirely phrased by Garrison. It was a brave thing to do. Abolitionism was not yet in the least popular. Its adherents were tarred and feathered. Garrison was once plucked by a mob from a Boston Female Anti-Slavery meeting and led round the streets with a noose round his neck, and was lucky not to be hanged. Whittier found himself cut by most of his former associates at Haverhill. But he did have supporters there who declared themselves by electing him to the Massachusetts legislature for the year 1835. That same year he and a fellow worker were mobbed. He deemed it best to sell the home farm, and in 1836 he settled near Amesbury, a few miles downstream from the Merrimack River and not far from the sea, but still in the country he loved and to which his muse responded. Burning Tyrtaen poems on any and every subject concerning slavery poured from his pen. For years he was an active abolitionist, but increasingly delicate health took him from the platforms and offices of the Anti-Slavery Society and fieldwork for the cause back to his quiet library at Amesbury. The publication of a book of his poems in 1843 put him immediately in the front rank of American poets; a place he was to hold until some time after his death. His fame grew with the years. So did his influence. Though not a politician his views were so well known and respected that the Republican Party claims him as one of its spiritual founders. When the threat of Civil War hung over the country his religious background moved him to try and evade it by any possible concession short of surrender. When it came, he wrote little. After it, he urged a humane settlement. His mood was reflected in the still countryside he described in his winter idyll *Snow-bound*, considered by the majority to be his finest achievement at that time.

Whittier never married. In middle-age he had attachments for two poetesses, one of whom died of consumption. The other led him on, married another, was widowed, returned into Whittier's life to take him to the Altar, and then angered him by her irreligious views. He lived quietly in hectic times which was probably why, despite his delicate health, he reached the great age, for that century, of eighty-five. A genial man, with a good sense of humour, he could flash with irritation like any other, and whilst he did not mind being regarded as a 'grand old man' of poetry, he did resent being thought some sort of saint, which he considered most inappropriate. His religious views were serious but not over solemn; his personal piety moving him to write a cento from his poems, more than fifty hymns, still to be found in modern hymnals. Two of them are frequently used by all Christian denominations. One is 'Immortal love forever full', with its steady affirmation ending:

> 'Alone, O love ineffable,
>   Thy saving name is given;
> To turn aside from thee is hell,
>   To walk with thee is heaven.'

Four years later he wrote a poem 'The Brewing of Soma', the sacred intoxicant of Vedic religion and ritual in India:

> 'From tent to tent
> The Soma's sacred madness went,
> A storm of drunken joy.'

Everyone is imprisoned by the knowledge of his own day. It was then believed that soma was made from the fermented juice of a tropical member of the milkwood family, *Sarcostemma viminale*, a leafless creeper with somewhat fleshy stems found in arid places. Recent research has revealed a more likely source as the beautiful but deadly crimson and white fungus *Amanita muscaria*, the Fly Agaric, praised in the *Rg-veda*, at some time between 1500 and 1200 B.C., as God of Thunder and the Divine Mushroom of Immortality, an anodyne for man, a stimulator of natural forces, and an hallucinogen. Misused, it kills. The Vedic priestly ritual was to soak a few scraps of the fungus in milk, drink it, and afterwards pass it through the bladder to make soma. Rather unusually in hallucinogenic compounds, the main active principles remain unchanged, and the stored soma is a far more powerful intoxicant than any fermented juice or distilled spirit. The same practices were followed by the people of Siberia, who knew nothing of alcohol until the late seventeenth century A.D. and yet could make themselves amazingly drunk on scraps of Fly Agaric passed through the bladder and then drunk. It seems unlikely that, had the mild-mannered, black-hatted old Quaker poet, clothed in sober subfusc, been aware of the real nature of soma, we should have ever seen the last six stanzas of his poem, which we know as the hymn which begins:

> 'Dear Lord and Father of mankind,
>   Forgive our foolish ways!
> Re-clothe us in our rightful mind,
> In purer lives thy service find,
>   In deeper reverence praise! . . .

Although Whittier was a Quaker, and 'Immortal love for ever full' was reprinted for the second time in the Boston *Congregationalist*, it is alleged his hymns had a particular appeal to Unitarians. Indeed the third stanza of 'Dear Lord and Father of mankind' has been used to emphasise the separateness of Christ, the great humane teacher, and the Divinity.

> 'O Sabbath rest by Galilee!
>   O calm of hills above,
> Where Jesus knelt to share with thee
> The silence of eternity,
>   Interpreted by love!' . . .

It has, however, been sung by, and popular with, a galaxy of

Trinitarians*.

★

In the nineteenth century, and perhaps even today, easy movement from class to class in American society has accounted for the fluid movement of certain people from one Christian denomination to another. With a few exceptions it has never been quite the thing in society to be a Baptist or a Roman Catholic. Presbyterianism, and even more so, Episcopalianism, has had a certain cachet. The Episcopalians provided two internationally known carol-writers. The first, the Reverend John Henry Hopkins Jnr., was the son of an iron-master turned lawyer, turned parson, who was elected first Bishop of Vermont, and was himself in Holy Orders, but his gifts were chiefly artistic, being a composer and poet, stained-glass designer, and editor of the *Church Journal*. He is worthy of note in this work as the author of a seemingly ancient carol of European origin. It is rather a surprise to discover that the lovely Epiphany carol 'We three kings of Orient are' was written by a New York Episcopalian priest and published as late as 1863.

The second Episcopalian carol writer was a Bostonian, Dr. Phillips Brooks; a massive man, six and a half feet high; a linguist, though not a teacher; indeed an attempt to teach Latin as a profession failed and he took to the Cloth instead; a direct and compelling preacher despite the fact that he spoke with great rapidity, an expert stenographer reckoning he uttered two hundred and thirteen words a minute. He was a reformer and humanitarian who warmed towards Lincoln and the North and, on the former's assassination, he preached a memorable panegyric on the 'Character, Life, and Death of Mr. Lincoln'. In the summer of 1865 Brooks began a year's holiday abroad. He travelled to the Holy Land and was in the old church at Bethlehem on Christmas Eve, an event which so deeply impressed itself upon his memory that two years afterwards he wrote, primarily for his Sunday School, but, in the event, for posterity, a carol addressed to Bethlehem and the Incarnation:

> 'O little town of Bethlehem,
>   How still we see thee lie!
> Above thy deep and dreamless sleep
>   The silent stars go by.

---

* The tune to which it is commonly set in America is Nathaniel Gould's *Woodland*, not to be confused with William Greatorex's *Woodlands* which is a melody used in Europe for hymns of different metre such as ' "Lift up your hearts!" We lift them, Lord, to thee'. The most familiar setting to Europeans is *Repton*, named simply because it was first used in Repton School chapel. In fact it is the tune of the ditty of Meshollemeth, 'Long since in Egypt's pleasant land', in the oratorio *Judith* by Sir Hubert Parry.

> Yet in thy dark streets shineth
>   The everlasting light;
> The hopes and fears of all the years
>   Are met in thee to-night.
>
> O morning stars, together
>   Proclaim the holy birth,
> And praises sing to God the King,
>   And peace to men on earth;
> For Christ is born of Mary;
>   And, gathered all above,
> While mortals sleep, the angels keep
>   Their watch of wondering love.' . . .

As he was a Bostonian the city took Brooks to its heart. It was the old capital of puritanism, where the intellectual rather than the aesthetic and emotional aspects of Christianity were emphasised. Unitarianism had thrived there, but Episcopalian teaching became more and more acceptable to the growing city. Phillips Brooks, described as a 'radiant Spiritual Athlete', had profound convictions combined with intellectual freedom and breadth of tolerance, and his lack of dogmatism had huge appeal. Again and again he refused preferment, but eventually, in 1891, he accepted a Bishopric at the age of fifty-seven. But he had been consecrated and held office for less than eighteen months, when a short and apparently insignificant illness carried him off. The city was stunned. Memorials were put up in statuary, educational foundations, and stained-glass. His most lasting must be 'O little town of Bethlehem'.

It is not without significance that Bishop Brooks's election as Bishop had not been entirely unopposed. He was Low Church in his views and preached in the churches of other denominations. Nor is it without significance that his father was a merchant, and his great uncle had been the richest man in Boston and the most prominent layman in the Unitarian Church. Unitarianism has always suited the American mercantile classes and the intelligentsia; with its optimism and emphasis on social progress it permits people to do good works, be rational, and prosper with a good conscience. At its worst it has an unphilosophical rigidity and aridity which caused the compilers of an English Unitarian hymnal in Warrington in 1819 to eliminate all hymns which referred to the soul because they considered any notion of a soul irrational. At its best it has always been marked by a seriousness and integrity, with what T. S. Eliot was to call a kind of 'emotional reserve' about the claims of heaven as well as the claims of earth. An apocryphal allegation states that the favourite prayer of a Unitarian begins, 'Paradoxical as it may seem, O Lord. . . .'

*

All three of the remaining selected hymn-writers were Unitarian, though one, Edmund Hamilton Sears, was a Unitarian minister who somehow contrived to have the totally contradictory and heterodox belief that Christ was, in fact, Divine. Like Presbyterian Duffield, and the Quaker Whittier, Sears claimed descent from a Pilgrim Father who reached the American colonies in the 1620's. He also resembled Whittier in that he was passionately fond of poetry from his earliest days, had a father who farmed his own property, and had the minimum of schooling because of his work as a farm lad. He began writing verses at ten years old, and although he was shy, at twelve he developed a liking for chanting poetry, his own or preferably somebody else's. He was particularly fond of declaiming Pope's *Iliad*. This gave him a taste for oratory. He practised his rhetoric in the form of sermons and lectures to imaginary congregations and audiences. He called it his 'assembly of elder bushes'. Though he lacked Whittier's lyrical genius he was more fortunate as a farm boy. Luck found him a place for a time at an academy and from there he proceeded to Union College Schenectady in New York State. He was poor and barely able to afford his fees and lodging, but by a rigid economy with the latter he stayed the course and graduated in 1834. His literary ability was very early recognised. He won a prize for poetry at Schenectady. Still abstemious and very frugal, he began to read law, then abandoned it to give outside tuition while learning theology himself at the Harvard Divinity School. When he graduated, the Unitarian Church sent him first as a missionary to the Indian frontier, then as a minister to congregations in New England. He married and he and his wife had two sons and a daughter; but the privations of his life as a student began to pray upon his frail constitution, and his reserve and natural nervousness made communication with his people difficult. In 1847 his health failed and he resigned. He succeeded best with his pen, reaching a large circle as one of the editors of the *Monthly Religious Magazine*, and with books of verse.* His sacred poetry was well known in his day, and one, the carol 'It came upon the midnight clear', has lived on. He wrote it soon after his resignation in 1849 at a time of global upheaval. In America the end of the Mexican-United States War had been considered a victory by the Imperialists and a disgrace by the Liberals, and the spread of abolitionism was already

---

* One of these volumes, *Athanasia; or Foregleams of Immortality*, was greatly admired by Elizabeth Barrett Browning.

bringing divisiveness and hatreds into many communities and homes. In far away India there were Sikh wars. There was war between Sardinia and Austria in Europe. There were revolutions in Naples, the Papal States, Venice, Milan, Prague, and Vienna, where the Emperor finally abdicated in favour of his nephew, and revolutions in many a pumpernickel independent sovereign state in Germany. Even in Prussia, the Kingdom of Iron, the barricades were up, bullets and grapeshot whistled through the capital, and the next in line in succession to the throne deemed it wise to seek temporary refuge in England. So did the King of the French, who was driven permanently from his throne and arrived at Folkestone heavily disguised in cap and goggles calling himself 'Mr. Smith'. And England herself was threatened with disorders until the Duke of Wellington took charge. And a mammoth meeting of Chartists in London turned into something of a farce. These calamities were reflected in Sears's carol, 'It came upon the midnight clear' which was universally admired and used. His third stanza ran:

> 'Yet with the woes of sin a strife
>   The world has suffered long;
> Beneath the Angel-strain have rolled
>   Two thousand years of wrong;
> And man, at war with man, hears not
>   The love-song which they bring:
> O hush the noise, ye men of strife,
>   And hear the Angels sing!'

Unexpectedly Sears lived through the troubles and worst of them all through the Civil War. Despite his delicate state of health he actually returned to take charge of a parish, but, in 1874, he was climbing a tree – on consideration, an odd thing to do for a sickly Unitarian minister of sixty-six – when a branch broke, and he tumbled to the ground. Quite unable to withstand the shock to his nervous and physical system, he took to his bed and was dead within two years.

★

A Unitarian who sat closer to the tenets of his church was James Lowell, not himself a minister but the son of one and descendant of a Bristol man who emigrated from England to the Massachusetts colony in 1639. James's mother was Episcopalian with forebears on both sides from the Orkney Islands. She had some poetic skill, and like many a transplanted Gael in New England, she believed she had second sight. She also had the conviction she was related to the brave Patrick Spens of the ballad-fame. Her eccentricities eventually grew less mild and her last days were spent in a private lunatic asylum, but she had much to do with Lowell's upbringing and was a powerful influence on his literary development.

The young James attended first a dame school and then a private school in a house not far from his home in Elmwood, Cambridge. At the age of fifteen he went on to Harvard where he spent so much of his time browsing in the library that he failed to keep up with his class, and, not caring for his independence of mind, the authorities rusticated or temporarily sent him down for the technical offence of failing to turn up at morning prayers, and committed him to the tutorship of a local clergyman. It was no setback. In 1838 the talented young man both graduated and also published his first verses in pamphlet form, *Class Poems*.

He went out into the world with no clear idea of what he should do. He was temperamental all his life, suffering the depths of depression which appear to be asked of those who favour bliss. He was a romantic and very ardent in his affections; serious though occasionally a trifle whimsical, a good critic of poetry as well as a very competent poet though of uneven quality. He made a desultory attempt to read law, but gave it up. There was a period when he worked as a clerk in a counting-house. Then he began his literary career, contributing to several short-lived magazines, and, when he had collected sufficient, publishing his poems entitled *A year's life*. A blighted romance tempted him to suicide; but he failed to pull the trigger. Then, with the resilience of youth, he found another most beautiful object of admiration, Maria Smith, a poetess and the sister of one of his Harvard friends. His admiration was returned and so encouraged Lowell that he determined to make himself independent with his pen. He achieved it in four years and the couple married on St. John's Day, the second day after Christmas, in 1844, though it is doubtful if, as a convinced Unitarian, Lowell recognised either of these Christian events. His wife was not only a poetess but a reformer and humanitarian with strong feelings about slavery. He went along with her, which either showed his earlier conservative sentiments were not strong or that he deemed it better to fall in with her wishes. At any rate he had a period when he identified himself with the radical campaigns of the time. The noble causes and effects of the American-Mexican War moved him to write in December 1844 a poem entitled *The Present Crisis*. From its eighteen lengthy stanzas, four have been plucked, and at random, to make the well known hymn sung on national occasions:

> 'Once to every man and nation
> Comes the moment to decide,

James Lowell, poet and 'best dialect verse writer in the United States', author, professor and diplomat

> In the strife of truth with falsehood,
>> For the good or evil side;
> Some great cause, God's new Messiah,
>> Offering each the bloom or blight –
> And the choice goes by for ever
>> 'Twixt that darkness and that light.' . . .

Lowell actually arranged his stanzas in five hefty verses, but they are reduced in number and length and appear with eight verses in the hymn. In the third stanza of the hymn we see an image of the disciples following Christ to new Calvaries, their way lighted by the fire of burning martyrs. It rather reduces the force of the original image of burning heretics:

> 'By the light of burning heretics Christ's bleeding feet I track,
>> Toiling up new Calvaries ever with the cross that turns not back.'

And not only is Lowell's work tinkered with but abbreviated to suit a supposedly less savage era and one when slavery is no longer of interest; and so we miss in our hymn books his gory blast against slavery and the power of the last stanza of his poem. We need not miss them here.

> 'Slavery, the earth-born Cyclops fellest of the giant brood,
>> Sons of brutish force and darkness, who have drenched the earth with blood.
>> Famished in his self-made desert, blinded by our purer day,
>> Gropes in yet unblasted regions for his miserable prey; –
>> Shall we guide his gory fingers where our helpless children play? . . .'

> 'New occasions teach new duties; Time makes ancient good uncouth;
>> They must upward still, and onward, who would keep abreast of Truth.
>> Lo, before us gleams her camp-fires! we ourselves must Pilgrims be,
>> Launch our Mayflower, and steer boldly through the desperate winter sea,
>> Nor attempt the Future's portal with the Past's blood-rusted key.'

This was not in the least great poetry, but thrilling stuff for the times.

Lowell went from strength to strength. As a political satirist he published the first series of *The Biglow Papers*, a spirited mixture of puns, word twists, bogus notes, a Latin proemium and letters to a newspaper and poems in straight Yankee vernacular, all directly and obliquely attacking the Mexican-American War, and inevitably bringing in slavery. It made him famous. His New England poems have been described by the scholarly modern American critic, Edmund Wilson, as 'the best dialect verse ever written in the United States'. Wilson was less complimentary about Lowell's other poetry, condemning it as 'self-consciously literary and, in consequence, mostly banal', and equally critical of his prose which he described as suffering from 'a rocky angularity of syntax and a gritty collocation of consonants'. Nevertheless, Lowell's contemporaries had a higher view of his talents and his scholarship. His marriage with the reformer Maria was idyllic, despite the fact that of their four children only one survived infancy, and, dejected by these personal tragedies, and the apparently unassailable forces of the pro-slavery lobby, she herself fell into a decline. On the strength of his mint-fresh royalties, payments for contributions and salary as an editor, Lowell took her to Europe for a long holiday. He there broadened his scholarship by studying Italian literature and especially Dante. But she was past recovery. She died in 1853, before his general recognition as a man of letters.

He was to succeed Longfellow as Professor of French and Spanish literature and of Belles-Lettres at Harvard, and marry again, but still remain faithful to his first wife's humane views by publishing a second series of *The Biglow Papers* during the Civil War which castigated slavery even more effectively than the first series had debunked the Mexican War. At the Harvard Commemoration in 1865, after the war, he declaimed an Ode for the occasion which in its final printed form took its place in the front rank of poems proceeding from the war, but which even so mostly served to show the mediocrity of most war poetry.

At the height of his writing and scholarly career he took up other work, going first as Minister to Spain and afterwards as President Hayes's Minister to St. James's. In his time he had written fairly sharply against England, though not as sharply as Mrs. Trollope and Dickens had castigated the States, but age had mellowed his former opinions, and he was forgiven. His second wife died in England and was buried there. The hymn-writer, political satirist, poet, teacher, and diplomat returned to the United States so Anglicized that he always wore a top-hat at Cambridge Massachusetts, until he died at the age of seventy-two in the same house in which he had been born; an unusual and possibly enviable thing to do.

★

Lowell did write other hymns, or, other hymns were plucked from his writings and used in Unitarian hymnaries, but he is best remembered for only one. So is the last subject of this chapter, a lady also of Unitarian stock who wrote but one hymn yet that has been given such universal acclaim she has a firm place in the hierarchy of American hymn-writers.

Julia Ward was privileged by birth and by fortune and therefore, within one definition, belonged to the aristocracy of the United States. This is to touch on a delicate subject to Americans, who claim, sometimes, to be classless. Be that as it may, Julia's father was a very rich banker, descended from one of Cromwell's officers, who discreetly left England at the Restoration of Charles II and settled in Rhode Island. Other ancestors were colonial governors. His own father held a distinguished position in the Revolutionary Army. Samuel Ward's position was thus socially secure. So was that of his wife, born Julia Rush Cutler. In New York, Julia Ward's birthplace, Society was artificially restricted to the number who could be fitted into the ballroom of Mrs. William Astor's mansion for her annual rout, the apogee of the season held on the third Monday of every January. These, 'the Four Hundred,' whose motto was *'nous nous soutenons'*, were selected by the arbiter of taste and protocol, Ward McAllister, who happened to be Julia Ward's first cousin, and included other rich families of colonial ancestry such as the Schermerhorns – pronounced 'Skairmern', the Rhinelanders – pronounced 'Ryelanner' – the Van Rensselaers, the Kings and the Joneses – the last being the very grand and immensely rich Joneses up with whom one kept if one aspired to rise in the social scale.*

Julia Ward had a brother, Sam Ward, who became Mrs. William Astor's brother-in-law, but after the death of his first wife married beneath him, allowed the family bank to fail, and found Astor doors closed on him. He did not mind in the least. Others were open, and he had enormous self-confidence. Indeed it was said that he was the only man in America capable of strutting when sitting down. He had a gamey reputation for lobbying Congressmen for gain, but was highly regarded as the best talker and greatest wit of his day. He was highly intelligent, with a superb library and a connoisseur's gallery of pictures, and he was the gourmet of his day. He knew his wine as no-one else did. His dinners were celebrated as the most perfect ever given in Washington, Boston, or New York, and his was a generation which ate and drank its way through some of the most splendid food and drink the world has known. Indeed a delicious native duck, the canvas-back, was almost eaten into extinction. When Dickens wrote his *American Notes* he mentioned flights of canvas-backs 'blackening the waters'. An article in *Blackwoods Magazine* stated: 'The man who has feasted on canvas-back duck, cannot philosophically be said to have lived in vain.' By the end of Julia Ward's long life (she lived

---

* The Joneses not only set a social target but also an enviable literary one. Quite magically, because she was upper-class, a woman and an expatriate, all of which told against her, Edith Newbold Jones, later to be Edith Wharton, proved to be one of the three, or, perhaps, four major American novelists to the present date. Her book *The Age of Innocence* is a history of New York Society from the 1840s to the 1870s.

from 1819 to 1910), the species had moved from its former wild haunts, and even from the kitchens of the rich, into aviaries of exotic waterfowl.

To be born into such a world of abundance had its other attractions and advantages. Julia Ward from her earliest days showed an interest in aesthetics. It was carefully nourished. Her home contained a gallery of carefully and well-chosen pictures. She was enchanted by them. Her mother, described as 'the author of various occasional poems', indulged and encouraged her urge to express herself in verse and romantic stories and plays. It appears that nothing in her education was left to chance. She attended excellent private schools and excellent private tutors. Her preceptor in German and Latin was the distinguished Dr. Cogswell, a former Professor of Geology and Mineralogy and College Librarian at Harvard, later editor of one of the ablest critical journals of the day, the *New York Review*, a well-travelled man with many languages, acquainted with some of the greatest figures of the century, Goethe, Humboldt, Béranger, Byron, Scott, Jeffrey, and the intellectually audacious circle of Lady Blessington in London. His influence on her was great. He taught her that intellectual enquiry was something to be desired for itself and to think beyond the boundaries of New York Society or even her own country. Being spirited, she chafed at her father's refusal to let her go out in society until she was older than most girls of her class, but from him and from Dr. Cogswell she learnt the epicurean virtue of restraint. She loved music, singing and routs and enjoyed herself in society, doubtless eating her fair share of that doomed species of duck, but when, with her father's approval, she accepted an offer of marriage, it was not from one of her young contemporaries.

Samuel Gridley Howe was nineteen years older than she when he proposed marriage to the clever, delightful and very rich Miss Ward, and she accepted him. We are in no position to be sure whether she married him as a father substitute, or because he was handsome and had a martial bearing, or if indeed the marriage was arranged, or at least suggested, by her prudent parents. At all events it turned out very well. The callow contemporaries faded from her life. In strong relief the Bostonian Dr. Howe stood out; knowledgeable, dependable, a knight-errant for many causes, with a touch of eccentricity which most found endearing though critics found him odious. His good looks he had inherited from his mother; his eccentricity from his father, a highly successful businessman who though rich was 'near' and frugally only sent one of his sons to university, it being fortunate for Samuel that he was the lucky one.

First in Brown and afterwards at Harvard, where he graduated as a medical practitioner, he left straight for the Greek-Turkish war to do battle for the Greeks. For six years he fought, acted as general surgeon and physician, collected and controlled supplies – a whole shipload of food and clothing was sent from America – and helped to reconstruct the devastated country, treating it all as a crusade. Prostrated by swamp-fever in Corinth he was obliged to return home; but he soon refound his enormous vitality, accepted an appointment to look after a newly-founded school for the blind in Massachusetts, left for Paris to learn French methods of teaching the blind and there found himself unable to resist becoming involved in the affairs of the Poles in exile. Although it seems extraordinary, he was made President of the Polish Committee, and found American funds to assist the Poles in their fight against Prussia. Rushing to the scene of action, he was inevitably arrested by the Prussians for aiding their enemy, and held prisoner for six weeks. Afterwards he asserted that prison conditions and interrogation were so harassing that he would be affected all his life. Exaggerated or not, they did not affect his ebullient philanthropy. He returned to his father's house in Boston to open the school for the blind. In order to comprehend their situation better he went about blindfolded at first; but found it scarcely practical. Nor was his old home suitable. He sent out appeals. A mansion was given him by the executors of a Mr. Perkins, endowments were promised, and the Perkins Institute began its career with the resourceful Dr. Howe at the helm. It brought him immense credit. One contemporary declared, 'I would rather have built the Blind Asylum than have written Hamlet'.*

It is doubtful if the doctor's young wife, whom he married in April 1843, would have agreed. She always had a good sense of proportion. But she loyally watched him move from crusade to crusade, and aided him whenever she could. He interested himself in the instruction of the deaf and the care of the mentally deficient, earning the affectionate sobriquet 'Chevalier Howe' for his work at the Massachusetts School for Idiotic and Feeble-Minded Youth; then aided a company for the better treatment of lunatics; became an abolitionist, actively preventing the forcible return of many runaway slaves to the South and co-editing an anti-slavery paper and even went so far as to abet John Brown who, far from being the mythical hero who inspired the Northern armies and about whom they sang,

---

* This was Horace Mann, a consumptive lawyer, turned educator, turned Congressman and college principal, who took an interest in Transcendentalism and phrenology and denounced profanity, intemperance, smoking and ballet dancing with puritan vigour.

was an ignorant, failed businessman and bloodthirsty maniac, whose mother and uncles were in lunatic asylums, who married a mad wife named Dianthe Lusk by whom he had seven children, two of whom were of unsound mind, who saw visions, and conceiving the idea of governing in the mountains a kingdom of liberated negroes, led a vengeance band of followers to massacre five illiterate poor whites who were pulled from their beds at night and literally chopped to bits with old-fashioned two-edged broadswords. Declared an outlaw by the President of the United States and the Governor of Missouri, Brown fixed on Harper's Ferry in Virginia as his headquarters and there he was overpowered by a company of marines, tried and hanged for treason. His behaviour before execution was stoical, but neither that nor the nineteen sworn affidavits by his relatives and others that he was mad could save him. None of these grisly facts appeared to be known by those soldiers who imagined he was a hero and not a monster whose soul was to march on and on and on in the famous song. Dr. Howe did know of them and should have known better than to abet such a man; but he went busily on with his knight-errantry as member of a government Sanitary Commission during the Civil War, and afterwards to work for the liberty and feeding and clothing of Cretans, even taking his wife and family out to Greece to manage the distribution of supplies. There was something obsessive about the doctor's philanthropy. It passed through phases of searching for just causes, so that, in the end, he became a compulsive interferer, a nineteenth-century public protester on a grand scale.

Mrs Howe spent the early years of her marriage travelling in Europe, meeting literary lions and leaders of thought in many countries. She polished her mind, learning to speak fluently in Italian, French and Greek, and was extremely well versed in the works of Kant, Hegel, Spinoza, Comte, and Fichte. She espoused the women's suffrage movement, became an ardent feminist, and, learning about penal reform, she was a delegate to a reform congress held in London. Besides all this she preached from Unitarian pulpits in America as well as in San Domingo, and Rome in Italy, not in the five Romes of her native land in New York, Georgia, Oregon, Pennsylvania or Tennessee. All the time she could spare from her husband's crusades and the five children she bore him, and her social and literary life, she devoted to writing and publishing lyrics and travel sketches and lecturing her friends; but it was the Civil War, and a single hymn, that made her as much a household name as Harriet Beecher Stowe had become on the publication of *Uncle*

Tom's Cabin. Both before and during the war Mrs. Howe's Boston home, Green Peace, was a centre for antislavery activity. In this atrocious war, the bloodiest of its kind in history and which was won simply by those who pounded the others most and for the longest time, it was possible to drive out in a carriage, as though to a picnic, and watch the pounding. Despite the keenness of Mrs. Howe's mind there was no doubt in it that the North was right and the South wrong. She lacked the objectivity of observers who had visited the South, learnt about its doomed economy and written it up. She had the New England puritan certainty, which even Lincoln lacked, that the Union forces were those of righteousness. Whittier's first patron, William Lloyd Garrison, had denounced slavery Biblically as 'a covenant with death and an agreement with hell'. Mrs. Howe possessed the same semi-religious fervour.

One afternoon Dr. and Mrs. Howe, and their particular friend, a former Unitarian minister who had founded his own splinter Church of the Disciples in Boston and had so great a following from remote districts that the congregation came with overnight baggage and it became known as the 'Church of the Carry-alls', joined a battle-viewing party in Washington got up by the Governor of Massachusetts. They were driven out in a carriage to observe the Army of Potomac in bloody action, and live roughly by sleeping under canvas for a night. They saw the men in action, pounding away at each other for all they were worth, and they heard the drums roll and the trumpets sound and the Union soldiers singing as they marched into action. They sang their favourite song 'John Brown's body lies 'a moulding in the grave', set to a popular tune 'Say brothers, will you meet us?'★ According to one tradition the original 'John Brown's body' words had been written in honour of a Scots soldier who lost his life fighting for the North. According to another it had been written by an anonymous humorist in a battalion of Massachusetts soldiers nicknamed The Tigers about a fellow Tiger called John Brown. After the mad John Brown had been hanged at Harper's Ferry, and the propaganda myth began to spread, the song's wording was adapted and speedily spread through the Union Army. Mrs. Howe was greatly moved to hear their singing, so much so that their friend the minister of the 'Church of the Carry-alls' suggested she write new words to the popular tune which could be used as another hymn. There were good precedents for doing such a

---

★ Used by Methodists in South Carolina this hymn, with its catchy tune, had reached Great Britain and been sold in sheets, from the year 1859, for the benefit of the Ragged School Shoe-black Society.

MRS. HOWE, *circa* 1861

Julia Ward Howe, ardent feminist and penal reformer and Unitarian preacher

(top left) Mrs. Howe; (top right) the crusading Samuel 'Chevalier' Howe; (bottom) part of a facsimile of the hymn which earned Mrs. Howe 4 dollars

thing, he said, and that night Julia Ward Howe did as she was asked. Usually quite able to rise to an occasion, on this she rose superbly. Waking early in her military tent, the rhythm and the metre of the song thumping in her mind, she lighted a candle and, as she herself recorded: 'In the dimness (with) an old stump of a pen which I remembered to have used the day before, I scrawled the verses almost without looking at the paper.'

She was a cultured woman who knew literature and a Unitarian who knew Holy Scripture. Inevitably she was influenced by her knowledge. First, without in any way plagiarising, she must have been affected by one of Macaulay's *Songs of the Civil War* entitled *The Battle of Naseby, by Obadiah Bind-their-Kings-in-Chains-and-their-Nobles-with-Links-of-Iron, Serjeant in Ireton's Regiment, 1824*, an hortatory poem lauding the Protestant Commonwealth Parliamentarians and damning royal courts and bishops. Second, while Macaulay's poem had a different metre, it shared the same subject, civil war, and both were inspired by the person or persons who wrote the third part of the Book of Isaiah, and so vividly prophesied the victory of Christ, through sacrifice, over his enemies:

> '. . . Wherefore art thou red in thine apparel, and
> thy garments like him that treadeth in the winefat?
> I have trodden the wine press alone; and of my
> peoples there was none with me: for I will tread
> them in my anger, and trample them in my fury;
> and their blood shall be sprinkled upon my garments,
> and I will stay in all my raiment. For the day
> of vengeance was in mine heart, and the year of my
> redeemed is come.'

Probably Macaulay and Mrs. Howe were less concerned with this sacrifice than with the notion of the unrighteous being punished. From Macaulay:

> 'Oh, evil was the root, and bitter was the fruit,
>   And crimson was the juice of the vintage that we trod;
> For we trampled on the throng of the haughty and the strong,
>   Who sat in the high places, and slew the saints of God . . .'

> 'Down, down, for ever down, with the mitre and the crown,
>   With the Belial of the Court and the Mammon of the Pope;
> There is woe in Oxford Halls; there is wail in Durham's stalls,
>   The Jesuit smites his bosom; and the Bishop rends his cope.'

Unmistakably, an amalgam of Isaiah and Macaulay, with a dash of *Genesis*, 'crush the serpent with his heel', the *Song of Solomon*, 'In the beauty of the lilies Christ was born across the sea', and the Apocalyptic vision of St. John The Divine, peppered up by Mrs.

Howe's vivid experience the previous afternoon of witnessing man killing and being killed by cannon and musketry and bayonet and sword, caused her to write, as if in ecstasy, lines which described the Union Army standing, like Ireton's, to fight for the cause of the Lord of Hosts:

'Mine eyes have seen the glory of the coming of the Lord:
He is trampling out the vintage where the grapes of wrath are stored;
He hath loosed the fateful lightning of his terrible swift sword:
    His truth is marching on.'

This is the first stanza of a hymn which was to sweep the country, and afterwards the world.

Mrs. Howe was to live long after the defeat of the South right into her ninety-second year in the middle of the Great War. She was to give elevated lectures to Washington Society on such complex issues as 'Moral Trigonometry', write a memoir of her knight-errant of a husband, and publish lyrics with telling titles such as *Passion Flowers* and *Words for the Hour* and other works, *Sex in Education, Modern Society*; and collections of essays, the best, possibly, being her astringent piece *Is Polite Society Polite?*; but never for any of them did she achieve the honours, public as well as private, which rained upon her for the hymn she wrote at the suggestion of the Reverend founder of the Church of the Carry-Alls which came to be used by most Christian denominations from Roman Catholic to the strictest Calvinists. However, these other writings probably brought her more royalties. Her indictment of the South, an enlistment propaganda song of inestimable value to the North, was first published in the *Atlantic Monthly* in 1862. For the outright sale of the Battle Hymn of the Republic Mrs. Howe received four dollars.

CHAPTER FIVE

SING HIGH

LAST of the Victorians to come to use hymns in their worship were the High Churchmen. They mistrusted the emotional tug in so many of the Low and Broad Church sacred songs, and had the strongest distaste for fervid and revivalist hymns which they regarded as intellectually dishonest and liturgically impious. Then, like the early fathers who, hearing heretics spread their errors by popular song, contrived to confound them by teaching orthodoxy through even more popular songs, High Churchmen of the early Victorian era began to realise Bishop Heber was probably right to use such a powerful method of teaching his people. However, they were not all of the same opinion. John Keble, for example, revered as a leader of High Churchmen, considered poetry as a kind of prayer, and, following the example of Bishop Heber and Dean Milman, he wrote devotional poems for the Sundays and Holy Days of the Church's year, published as *The Christian Year* with the subtitle 'Thoughts in Verse', and he intended that they should be for private devotional rather than for congregational use. Despite his intentions, several great hymns were plucked from the work; 'The voice that breathed o'er Eden', sung at a myriad of marriages since it was first put to music; 'There is a book who runs may read'; the Rogation hymn, 'Lord, in thy name thy servants plead'; the Whitsun hymn, 'When God of old came down from heaven'; 'Sun of my soul, thou Saviour dear', heard at the end of countless Evensongs; and his masterpieces 'Blest are the pure in heart', 'New every morning is the love'. For these hymns alone Keble has a place in Church history but he also has another greater claim to be there.

He was the oldest of a triumvirate who led the Victorian High Church revival of the Thirties, named the Oxford Movement because all three, Keble, Pusey, and Newman, were then dons at the university. They shared a common longing to raise the Church of England from the deep sleep in which a large part of it slumbered; and to make the country realise their Church was not a mere department of State, or a provider of income for younger sons, but the Catholic Church of the land, with all its catholic rights, privileges and its duties; a Church not created by the Reformation, but in succession with no break to St. Augustine, to the Celtic Church, to the early Fathers, and to the Church in the Upper Room. Keble, one of the most brilliant of his generation, was content to leave Oxford and live quietly as a country parson, for thirteen years as an assistant curate in Gloucestershire, and for thirty-three as vicar of a village near Winchester. Though it was he, in preaching a famous sermon at Oxford on National Apostasy in 1833, who established himself as the founder of the movement, his life was one of prayer, service, and scholarship, writing for the Church, and attending to the needs of his parishioners.

Second of the triumvirate, Edward Bouverie Pusey, grandson of a peer and well connected, Professor of Hebrew at Oxford for sixty-four years, and Canon of Christ Church, also wrote for the Church. He gave his name to the movement, for at one time opponents would speak of 'Puseyites' in a pejorative sense, yet he lived a life very much apart, cut-off not only by the death of a young wife whom he adored and for whom he mourned for fifty-three years, but also by a harsh self-discipline which made him practise unsmiling, silent gravity, keep his eyes down, and live to an old age as austerely as a desert hermit in a corner of a magnificent college. Neither he in his lonely agonising, nor Keble in his cut-off parochial life, could give quite the same leadership to the movement as John Henry Newman. Born in London, the son of a rich Evangelical banker, Newman was a great scholar and theologian, sufferer, and very holy man. His single-minded bold approach to Catholicity held together the Tractarians, as they came to be called after the publication of teaching tracts, which bore intellectual witness to the rightness of the Oxford Movement. To them the Church of England was the middle way. It had nothing to do with Dissent or the Protestant churches of Europe and America, and scarcely anything to do with the Roman Obedience. But the Evangelicals and the 'papist hunters' made trouble from the start.

Newman's life is more familiar than that of most hymn-writers, and can only be given the briefest note. In 1845 he 'poped' or was received into the Roman Catholic Church. Thereafter he was

The selfless John Keble, founder of the Oxford Movement and modest writer of
great hymns (*National Portrait Gallery*)

studiously ignored, left at the Oratory of St. Philip Neri which he founded in a Birmingham suburb, writing a vindication of his decision in the classic *Apologia pro Vita Sua*, rewarded in the end by a Cardinal's hat and the veneration of a great number of English people. No-one would seriously deny the claim made for Newman that 'no-one influenced the Church of England more than he during his lifetime, and few have influenced the Roman Catholic Church more since his death'. More than a century after his death nine international scholars were working on Newman and at least ten thousand separate studies have been published on him as a writer, which makes him only second to Shakespeare and Kant, and a lengthy cause has been started for his canonisation as a saint. To the ordinary churchman he will always be remembered as the author of many prayers: amongst them the evening petition which begins 'O Lord, support us all the day long of this troublous life until the shades lengthen and the evening comes, the busy world is hushed,the fever of life is over, and our work done', and for his *Dream of Gerontius*, written after his reception into Rome, and from which two hymns are taken and sung in churches of all denominations: 'Praise to the Holiest in the height' and 'Firmly I believe and truly'; but his unforgettable contribution to hymnody was written in 1833 when he was still an adored leader of the Tractarian movement at Oxford and Queen Victoria was still a princess with her hair down.

> 'Lead, kindly Light, amid the encircling gloom,
>   Lead thou me on;
> The night is dark, and I am far from home,
>   Lead thou me on.
> Keep thou my feet; I do not ask to see
> The distant scene; one step enough for me.' . . .

Newman had been on holiday in Sicily in June, not the wisest month to choose owing to the great heat. He was out alone walking, presumably deep in thought, when he found himself lost in a heat haze which turned to a dark and heavy thunderstorm. He was quite unnerved and developed a fever. Even after he had recovered he found the experience made such a deep impression on him that he longed to go home. He and his servant took the next packet out from Palermo. She was an orange-boat heading north for Marseilles, a clumsy tub at the best of times which easily spilt and lost wind. In the straits of Bonifacio she became becalmed and remained so for a week, idling on the tepid water, never really cool. It was then that he wrote the hymn for which he is always remembered. He and his servant

John Henry Newman, who wrote his greatest hymn becalmed in an orange-boat
(*National Portrait Gallery*)

reached England and his mother's home on Tuesday July the ninth. The following Sunday in Oxford he heard Keble preach his famous sermon on National Apostasy. The hymn was not actually published until the following year, 1834. Oddly, Newman might never have heard it used as a hymn because he became a Roman Catholic before it reached the Church of England hymnody, and he had died before it reached the Roman Catholic hymnody. But he knew about it, and declared it had become popular because of the tune *Lux benigna* set to it by Dr. John Bacchus Dykes, a musician and a Church of England Divine whose reputation rests on his three hundred hymn tunes. His memorable tune for Newman's hymn came into his head almost as a set-piece in its entirety as he was walking past Charing Cross Station. But another tune, *Sandon*, by G. H. Purday, enjoyed equal popularity, so Newman was probably being over-modest. The poem has been interpreted allegorically in many ways; but however regarded, it always struck a response in the Victorian heart. Mrs. Tait, wife of Dr. Tait, successively Headmaster of Rugby, Dean of Carlisle, Bishop of London, and then at the Queen's firm but very strange request because, as she told Lord Beaconsfield, he had been ill at London 'and the change would be good for him', Archbishop of Canterbury, lost five children in the two spring months at the Deanery in 1856 and beneath a large black framed picture of her dead darlings had Newman's penultimate verse inscribed, 'And with the morn those angel faces smile'. There is no doubt it stands in the first four or five most popular hymns of the Victorian era. Certainly it was the Queen's favourite. She had wanted to invite its author to tea at Windsor, but Prince Albert had advised against the introduction of so controversial a High Church Oxford clergyman at the royal tea table, and she had complied. But she quite understood Mrs. Tait's sentiments, and the feeling of her people of all denominations for the hymn, and it was read to her as she lay dying at Osborne House, supported by the one good arm of her eldest grandchild, the German Emperor, in January 1901. Possibly they were the last words she heard.

> 'So long thy power hath blest me, sure it still
>   Will lead me on,
> O'er moor and fen, o'er crag and torrent, till
>   The night is gone,
> And with the morn those Angel faces smile,
> Which I have loved long since, and lost a while.'

From 1845, when Newman 'poped', the Oxford Movement stood in peril as lesser men, some of them extremists in ritual and doctrine,

(top left) J. B. Dykes and (top right) W. H. Monk, whose music has complemented many great hymns, with hymn-writer and compiler Sir H. W. Baker (bottom left) and (bottom right) Samuel Sebastian Wesley, William Whiting's fellow 'Hoppy' (*Hymns Ancient and Modern*)

tried to seize the reins of leadership. *The Times*, which had recently developed into the 'Great Thunderer' and become the great influence it was to remain, baffled the public by printing leaders friendly to the Puseyites for a period of four years. There was a simple, undisclosed reason. The proprietor, John Walter, though not himself an Anglo Catholic, had a son who had been up at Oxford when Newman's dominance was at its strongest. A plea from young Walter assured the Anglo Catholics of favourable leaders. Meanwhile some kept faith with the Church of England; others, for a variety of reasons, 'poped'.

★

Amongst the latter was the prolific translator of Latin hymns Edward Caswall. Son of a country parson and then one himself, he was swept up in the Tractarian tide and resigned his perpetual curacy in Wiltshire two years after Newman had gone to Rome.* Unlike Newman he had a wife, and had to wait for Mrs. Caswall to die, which conveniently she did of cholera in Torquay in 1850, before he could join the Birmingham Oratory and be ordained. Much of the time between, he and Mrs. Caswall spent in Rome, where he translated an immense number of Latin hymns, publishing two hundred of them in *Lyra Catholica* and many more in other works. Amongst his most familiar were 'Bethlehem, of noblest cities', 'The sun is sinking fast', 'Jesu the very thought of thee' and 'O Jesu, King most wonderful', two centos from a lengthy Latin eleventh century hymn of forty-two stanzas, and he had a share in the hymn known as 'Stabat mater dolorosa' – 'At the Cross her station keeping', translated by several hands from a hymn attributed to many authors including three mediaeval Popes. Caswall led a scholar's somewhat uneventful life as an Oratorian, which could scarcely be said of another English clergyman who 'poped' in the Oxford earthquakes and also became an Oratorian.

Frederick William Faber was the grandson of a Church of England parson, and nephew of an Evangelical theologian, an antiquary famous in his day, George Stanley Faber. Young Faber was born at his grandfather's Yorkshire Vicarage and, from all accounts, was a handful in the nursery and something of a spark amongst the local lads as a boy. There exists a tradition that, caught trespassing with

---

* The living he held had been presented to him by an uncle, the strictly Evangelical Bishop of Salisbury, Dr. Thomas Burgess, first President of the Royal Society of Literature and author of more than a hundred works, and blaster of the supporters of Catholic Emancipation. Fortuitously he had died of apoplexy some time before his nephew went over to Rome.

some other lads by a very irate farmer, he put forward such a strong plea in their defence the farmer was nonplussed and forgave them all. To Frederick's natural talents was added a cocktail of education in various establishments. He moved successively from Bishop Auckland Grammar School to a tutor at Kirkby Stephen, then to Shrewsbury School, and finally to Harrow. This regular change of masters and company affected young Frederick less than the death of his mother when he was fifteen. He was a sensitive, impressionable boy, quick to learn and clever. He was inclined to be something of a dandy, following Beau Brummell's dictation about the niceties of dress when he matriculated at Balliol College, Oxford, in July 1832. Strangely, he did not go into residence at Michaelmas, and not until the following Lent term. There might have been a connection with the death of his father that year. Frederick, still only eighteen, had brothers and sisters but at that time appears to have been a solitary young man. He indulged his liking for rich neckcloths, and bright waistcoats of velvet and silks, sprigged and shot, and cultivated the arts chiefly as a poet. It would seem he was an incipient aesthete of the pre-Pater era at Oxford. At the end of his first year he wrote a long and self-revealing poem entitled *The Cherwell Water-lily* which, rather surprisingly, aroused wide admiration in manuscript, and even more so after it was published in 1840. His educational pilgrimage was not yet done. Within a year he moved from Balliol to University College of which he was elected a scholar; and he took the step taken by many young men of promise, speaking with great distinction at the Union. Two years later he was awarded the Newdigate prize with a poem in English, *The Knights of St. John*, a romantic subject which highly suited him.

He had gone up to Oxford an Evangelical. Like hundreds of others he fell under the spell of John Henry Newman, and, being impulsive, swung as far to Catholicity as he possibly could. He took a respectable second and went abroad for a year with his brother, a clergyman. They toured the Rhine and several German states, which Frederick described in a long series of letters and a journal. On his return to Oxford in 1837 he was elected to a Fellowship of his college, and assisted Newman and the Tractarians by contributing a paper explaining the Donatist schism, and by translating the six treatises of St. Optatus, who was Bishop of Milevis in North Africa towards the end of the fourth century, and a spirited refuter of Donatists. This work established Faber as a scholar. Simultaneously he developed his poetic talent, and, because the Lake District was a Mecca for poets, it was particularly agreeable to him to take undergraduates up there on reading parties. He lost little time in making the acquaintance of Wordsworth, and the sixty-seven year old Poet Laureate quickly took a liking to the young don. They struck up a warm friendship. As Faber was twenty-three he had reached the canonical age for ordination, and, in what today might seem rather a casual fashion, he left his reading party to look after itself for a time, went to Ripon to be made deacon by the bishop there, and returned to read with his undergraduates, write verses for Wordsworth to look over, and help the parson of Ambleside as honorary temporary curate. Doubtless he missed his gorgeous waistcoats, but sober black suited his florid good looks, and a year later he was ordained priest by Bishop Bagot* at Oxford.

It would seem that at this stage of his career Faber was not quite sure what to do with himself. He went twice to the Continent, on the second occasion as tutor to a boy from Ambleside, and wrote up his travels for publication in 1842 as *Sights and Thoughts among Foreign People*, wrote a good deal of poetry and was more often at Ambleside than anywhere else.

Though correctly dressed as a good Tractarian clergyman, he permitted himself the idiosyncrasy of following the current fashion amongst laymen for jewellery, and he wore thin gold chains about his white scarf tie and over his subfusc waistcoat. In the autumn of 1842, he was offered a college living, the Rectory of Elton in Huntingdonshire. He was at last being challenged. His travel book, dedicated to the Poet Laureate 'In affectionate remembrance of much personal kindness, and many thoughtful conversations on the rights, prerogatives and doctrines of the holy church', if studied with care, indicated the way he was moving towards Roman Catholicism. He sought Wordsworth's advice on whether he should tie himself to the responsibilities of a parish. The old crocodile of Rydal gave him an enigmatic reply: 'I do not say you are wrong, but England loses a

---

* Richard Bagot (1782–1854) was always spoken of as 'Poor Bagot', because he was forever in the eye of clerical hurricanes. Being simultaneously Bishop of Oxford, Dean of Canterbury, and Rector of the rich living of Blithfield in Staffordshire, he excited a good deal of hostile criticism when his pluralism was exposed in the newspapers. Then, as Bishop of Oxford when Tractarianism was at its height, he tried to please everyone and almost succeeded in pleasing no-one. The Prime Minister, Robert Peel, offered him a way out; translation to the See of Bath and Wells if he resigned all other benefices. Sixteen years of Oxford had been enough for Bagot and in 1845 he went down to sleepy little Wells. There, in his enchanting Palace, he enjoyed a little peace, but his health began to fail and, appointing a retired colonial bishop as his Auxiliary, he took himself off to invigorating Brighton. Unfortunately the Auxiliary turned out to be a fervent Low Churchman and Bishop Bagot's examining chaplain, Archdeacon Denison of Taunton, was a bellicose Tractarian. A furious quarrel began which was to result in resignations and deprivation and to reach the highest law courts, and 'Poor Bagot', though chiefly down in Brighton, was right at the centre of it until he died in 1854.

poet.' Faber chose to be Rector of Elton, but scarcely had he been put into the living than he left for a lengthy journey on the Continent determined to examine and test the practical results of Roman Catholicism. Dr. Wiseman, later Cardinal of Westminster, was then looking after the Collegio Venerabile Inglese and was only too happy to introduce the Rector of Elton to influential churchmen at the Vatican. The people of Elton must have been bemused when a new and virtually unknown parson returned from foreign parts after twelve months and, hurling himself into parish life with unflagging zeal, preached to them with marvellous eloquence, but also introduced full choral Masses, devotion to the Sacred Heart and auricular confession, and would insist on referring to the Blessed Virgin as 'Mamma'. English country people accommodate themselves with kindliness to most clerical eccentricities, but they detected a whiff of the brimstone about their Rector. He published a book on the life of St. Wilfrid, a seventh century bishop of great force of character who devoted most of his time to substituting Roman for Celtic practices, and this caused a furore far beyond the boundaries of his parish. His poem *The Cherwell Water-Lily* was re-appraised and with some malice. In less than a year he had 'poped'. Together with some of his persuaded parishioners and some old friends, he attended a formal reception into the Roman Catholic Church on the 16th November, 1845, by Bishop Wareing, Vicar-Apostolic of the Eastern District.

Newman had been received the month before by a Passionate Father. The two converts, so different in temperament, had rather similar careers in the Roman Church. Each established a community at Birmingham; Faber, the Brothers of the Will of God, usually called 'Wilfridians', because Faber took the name in religion of Brother Wilfrid; Newman, three years later, the Brotherhood of St. Philip Neri. Brother Wilfrid hurried off to Rome to receive the papal blessing for his community and was well received by Gregory XVI, an ultramontane Pope who died a few months afterwards, when the Risorgimenti he loathed were investing the Papal States.* In 1847, through the generosity of a rich and eccentric Earl of Shrewsbury, the Wilfridians were given a new home, Cotton Hall, a manor house in the Staffordshire hills. In the same year Brother Wilfrid was formally ordained a priest in the Roman Communion and put in

---

* Times were so serious that the conclave to elect the successor of Gregory XVI was one of the shortest in history. To play safe the cardinals elected a liberal sympathiser, Pius IX, destined to be on the throne of St. Peter for thirty-two years, much longer than any other Pope, and see the creation of the modern papacy. He was the first 'Prisoner in the Vatican'.

charge of the mission at Cotton. Newman's return to England after two years abroad, to establish and be Superior of the Oratory of St. Philip Neri in a rich suburb of Birmingham, coincided with the break-up of the community of Cotton. Faber began to serve his novitiate as an Oratorian, but the termination of his novitiate by dispensation indicates that he was at odds with his former hero, Newman.

The two being temperamentally unsuited, it was better for everyone concerned when Faber and another established a branch of the Oratory in King William Street, London. Then, in 1850, a more suitable site was found at Brompton and the Foundation became a community separate and independent from Newman's Oratory in Edgbaston. An Italianate Oratory House with a private chapel and library, and long high corridors 'Well adapted for exercise in wet weather' according to the *Illustrated London News*, was built on the site of a former private school for boys and, though a contemporary artist compared the Oratory House to a 'Giant haystack petrified', the Fathers were well satisfied, and Faber went so far as to say Brompton was 'The Madeira of London'. From Birmingham came a not unexpected different view. Newman considered the place 'essentially in a *suburb* . . . a neighbourhood of second-rate gentry and second-rate shops'. Generous donations made it possible for a public church to be added; a long building with side chapels and a long deep sanctuary, plain without and exotic within, a triumph of polychromy, and constantly being altered and enlarged to meet the needs of the public and the fancies of Father Faber. He was Superior for the rest of his life; an eloquent and persuasive preacher, brilliant scholar and linguist translating from Italian and French, editor of a forty-two volume *Lives of the Saints,* a writer of books on meditation, simple teaching tracts, and a considerable number of hymns. Some of the last have a sugary touch which demonstrates flaws in his taste. But Faber can not be dismissed as a hymn-writer, simply because of his bad verses which vary in sentimentality from the just acceptable to the truly fearful. At his best, Faber was a very good hymn-writer indeed. He wrote the Good Friday hymn 'O come and mourn with me awhile', the Communion hymn 'Jesu, gentlest Saviour', and the evening hymn sung at endless mission services, 'Sweet Saviour, bless us ere we go' which ends with the petition:

> 'For all we love, the poor, the sad,
>   The sinful, – unto thee we call;
> O let thy mercy make us glad;
>   Thou art our Jesus and our All.'

Then there are 'There's a wideness in God's mercy', and 'Holy Ghost, come down upon thy children', and widest-known, perhaps, of all his works, a poem of insight into the love of God, 'My God, how wonderful thou art'. Finally, making clever use of the refrain popularised by revivalists, he wrote the thrilling hymn of the angels:

> 'Hark! hark, my soul! Angelic songs are swelling
> O'er earth's green fields, and ocean's wave-beat shore;
> How sweet the truth those blessed strains are telling
> Of that new life when sin shall be no more!
> Angels of Jesus, Angels of light,
> Singing to welcome the pilgrims of the night!' . . .

That Father Faber had a sincere and passionate love for God can never be doubted. His scholarship was recognised by the Church, for Pope Pius IX made him a Doctor of Divinity. He continued to be a great traveller, collecting church gossip, – often meat and drink to members of religious orders – useful tit-bits of ultramontane theology and endless questing for pieces for the Oratory, a reredos from here, an altar from there, altar rails, candles, paintings, statues, mosaic panels, aids to the priest's comfort in confessionals, hangings and rugs, and a baldacchino. His acquisitions were rare and expensive, but collecting came to a halt when he was taken ill on the main island of Malta. So ill was he that he waited to make the long journey home through Italy. His peregrinations were over. He wrote more hymns, publishing a collection of one hundred and fifteen in 1862, prefacing them with a note: 'It is an immense mercy of God to allow anyone to do the least thing which brings souls closer to him. . . . That our Blessed Lord has permitted these hymns to be of some trifling good to souls, and so in a very humble way to contribute to His glory, is to the author a source of profitable confusion as well as unmerited consolation.' The expression 'profitable confusion' was typical of Faber. He never regained his health, and he had an extravagantly long time 'in the cypress shade', for it was twelve years before he finally died. But, then, so much was extravagant in the life of the former aesthetic poet in vivid silk waistcoats, and former Rector of Elton, with his golden jewellery and his quaint way of addressing the Blessed Virgin as 'Mamma'.

★

Of those Tractarians who kept to the Church of England, none could have been more different from Frederick Faber than the poet, translator, and theological scholar, Isaac Williams, who had an enviable freedom from nervous excitement of any kind, cultivating a sort of stoical indifference. He was the third son of a Welshman from

Llanrhystid in Cardiganshire, who practised at the English chancery bar, and a Welsh lady from Cwmcynfelyn in the same county, where Isaac was born in 1802. He grew up in London and was tutored by a former scholar of Eton and Kings, at first close to his home, then, when his tutor moved, at the Surrey village of Worplesdon. At fifteen he was sent to Harrow – ten years before Faber went there – where he showed up 'mellifluous Latin verses' and had unusually wide interests. When he went up to Oxford in 1822 as a scholar of Trinity, his acquaintance was deliberately chosen and exclusive. He rather avoided his own college and mixed mostly with the best minds in Oxford, then found at Oriel. The best undoubtedly was that of John Keble, who had taken his double-first and been awarded a fellowship at Oriel at the age of eighteen, a distinction only shared by Robert Peel who became Prime Minister. Strangely, William did not meet Keble at Oriel but at his mother's home in Wales during his first vacation from Oxford. Keble was at a crossroads in life; still only twenty-eight, but not ambitious to remain much longer as a tutor of Oriel. For some as yet unrevealed reason he was that summer a guest of Isaac's grandfather Davies at Cwmcynfelyn near Aberystwyth, and had an immediate and profound influence on the young undergraduate.

Under Keble's guidance he determined to dedicate his life to scholarship and poetry, and, in the following year, he delighted everyone by gaining the Chancellor's prize for Latin verse, with a poem called *Ars Geologica*. The choice of subject showed the range of his interests, at a time when natural history and other sciences were beginning to have a wider appeal. That same year Keble left Oxford to take up a Gloucestershire curacy. His pupils went to visit him and read with him. Amongst his first reading party at Southrop were four who were to become leading Tractarians: Isaac Williams, Richard Hurrell Froude, Robert Isaac Wilberforce and Sir George Prevost. They were again down at Southrop the following year. Williams left an account of these reading parties and the impact Keble had upon his undergraduates; 'To find a person always endeavouring to do one good, as it were, unknown to one's self, and in secret, and even avoiding that his kindness should be felt and acknowledged as such, this opened upon me quite a new world. Religion a reality, and a man wholly made of love . . . this broke upon me all at once.' It became the disciple's professed intention to follow as closely as possible in Keble's footsteps as poet, priest, scholar and teacher. He overdid it. Working for lengthy stretches at a time at classics and mathematics he had a breakdown. Far too ill even to attempt a double-first, he had to be content with a doctor's certificate and a pass degree. Keble advised him to offer himself for ordination and take things as easily as possible in a tiny country curacy for as long as was necessary. Everything was arranged so that he could nurse himself back to his former health. The High Church Bishop of Gloucester, Dr. Bethell,* made him deacon and he became curate of Windrush-cum-Sherborne, a small village with two hundred and ninety-one inhabitants and close to Southrop, so that he was within reach of Keble. There he lived two quiet years, cultivating a deep personal piety and studying Hebrew as well as writing poetry. His friends saw him frequently and noted the steady improvement in his health.

In 1831 he felt able to return to Oxford where he was ordained priest by 'Poor Bagot' and obtained a fellowship at Trinity and went into residence as tutor and lecturer in philosophy. This coincided with the unopposed election of Keble as Professor of Poetry at Oxford, an event which caused great satisfaction to his young protégé. A year after, Williams was made Dean of College and ultimately became Vice-President. More important to him was his attachment to Newman as assistant curate of St. Mary's, and he became one of a quartet – Keble, Newman and Froude were the others – who contributed sacred poems to the *British Magazine* which were later collected together and published in 1836 as *Lyra Apostolica*. Williams also wrote celebrated tracts for the Anglo-Catholic cause, one of which on 'Reserve in communicating Religious Knowledge' excited a good deal of hostility, largely because of its title. Anti-Tractarian clergymen preached against him and his work, some of the newspapers following suit in print. Williams's manner, whether natural or acquired, was excessively modest and retiring. He was not so pained by the furore as his friends were on his behalf. When Keble's tenure of office as Professor of Poetry was concluded Williams was chosen by the Oxford Tractarians to stand as the new professor. Known for his amiability and piety, and for his closeness to Keble, it seemed natural that Williams should be Keble's successor. His poetry did not match *The Christian Year* in popularity but his poem *The Cathedral* was much admired.

Unfortunately at this juncture, when all seemed to have been

---

* Christopher Bethell (1773–1859) was Bishop of Gloucester from 1824 until 1830, when the Duke of Wellington translated him to the more lucrative See of Exeter in 1830, from which he was translated six months later to the still more lucrative See of Bangor where he was Bishop for twenty-nine years, his usefulness considerably limited by the fact that he could not speak Welsh and one hundred and ninety-five thousand out of his two hundred thousand people could not speak any English.

safely and sensibly arranged, another candidate was proposed, James Garbett of Brasenose, a finished scholar and expert in exegesis who now held a college living down in Sussex. Described as 'guiltless of poetry', he was, nevertheless, a noted translator of the classical poets, and he might have done had he not been an ardent and vociferous Evangelical. Dr. Pusey at once detected a plot to make the election a test of strength. To the dismay of Newman and Williams and most of the other Tractarians, Pusey send out a circular accusing the Evangelicals of making the election a party issue. It was the worst move he could have made. Scarcely anything could have more roused the Evangelicals than a scolding from Dr. Pusey. That which should have been discussed over the teacups and port at Oxford became a national no-popery crusade, angering everyone who stood in the middle, neutral ground. To the dismay and distaste of Isaac Williams, and the relish of his opponents, supporting committees were set up for each of them in London and Oxford to manage the election. 'Poor Bagot' wrung his hands over the mischief done in the University. Newman foresaw disaster and said so. Gladstone, already with a foot on the ladder of statecraft as Peel's President of the Board of Control, and a strong Tractarian, proposed that both candidates should stand down. But by then both parties felt too committed, and the contest went on. Williams learnt to his chagrin that a handful of his friends were not prepared to support him in so contentious an issue. Then two bishops and two hundred and fifty lesser clergymen signed an address begging each Committee to hold its hand. Garbett's Committee refused. Williams's Committee compromised by taking a straw vote of pledges, and discovered that he stood in danger of losing. Much mortified, Williams withdrew his name exactly a week before the election. Garbett went forward unopposed to take Keble's chair, and, though he was one of the most unpoetic Professors of Poetry ever seen at Oxford, he held on to it for ten long years. It was also Garbett who replaced Manning as Archdeacon of Chichester when Manning exchanged gaiters and Gothic coolness for a Cardinal's crimson and the splendour of the Church of Rome. The Tractarians were dismayed by their rout.

On Isaac Williams it had a more profound effect. He withdrew altogether from Oxford and from public life. He was not simply miffed but deeply wounded. He went down to Keble's brother, Thomas Keble, who was a country Rector in Devonshire, and there remade the acquaintance of the Chapernownes of Dartington House, a family he had known as a young undergraduate. That June he married Caroline Chapernowne and determined to be assistant curate to Thomas Keble. The abandonment of his position as a leading Tractarian, an intimate of Newman at the centre of affairs, as well as an academic life of some distinction, for a simple life deep in the country – and the exchange at the age of forty of celibacy for marriage – signified how traumatic the election combat had been for him. He was Thomas Keble's curate for six years, during which time Mrs. Williams regularly bore him children, and his health, which had never been robust, deteriorated. He was so feeble in 1846 that Dr. Pusey extricated himself from his hermitage in Christchurch and went down to say good-bye to Williams. So did Newman, recently received into the Church of Rome. In the event Williams lived for another nineteen years and Newman had to make a second good-bye visit from the Birmingham Oratory when the time came.

In 1848 he gave up his post and moved to the Gloucestershire village of Stinchcombe, which nestles upon a little hill south of Dursley about the vale of Berkeley and Severn. Very likely Shakespeare was acquainted with the place, because in *Richard II* he makes Percy, Bolingbroke and Northumberland look down from the brow of Stinchcombe Hill to Berkeley – 'the castle by yon tuft of trees'. The parson of the parish was his brother-in-law, the Reverend Sir George Prevost, who was a leading Tractarian, and became Archdeacon of Gloucester, and looked after Stinchcombe from his considerable parsonage for sixty-two years. Until 1630 the village had been part of the parish of Cam, then was hived off as a perpetual curacy, though a notice in the church states that the tower and spire, wrecked by lightning in November 1883, had been restored and rededicated to Prevost by his friends in the parish and the archdeaconry, and he is described as Rector. It was a delightful retreat for a sick man, and Isaac Williams became his brother-in-law's honorary assistant curate, living with his family in a house specially built for them. E. A. Freeman, who had been a scholar and Fellow of Trinity at the same time as Williams, assured him of intellectual company by also settling in Stinchcombe that year.

Sir George appears to have been something of a Doctor Grantley as country parson and Archdeacon; a well-organised, determined man, quite the contrary in temperament to his gentle and debilitated brother-in-law. He tried to jolly Williams along. The small Church dedicated to St. Cyr had a chancel, a nave with a gallery, a porch and a tower with one bell*, and was in a very dilapidated condition.

---

* This bell was inscribed 'John Pinfold, Gent, Churchwarden 1692', and doubtless he gave his name to Evelyn Waugh's peculiar 'Gilbert Pinfold', for Waugh lived and wrote at Piers Court in the village, which he called 'Stinkers', until the Second War.

Prevost proposed that, between them, he and his curate should restore and embellish it as a good Tractarian Church. How much Isaac Williams was able to assist, beyond contributing handsomely to the funds, is not known. Probably it was little. Sir George went at it with a will, levelling and lowering the churchyard, rebuilding a large part of the church with steps leading up to an altar and with a reredos; paving the church with a reproduction by Minton of some old tiles he found in the former church; and heating the sanctuary with an upright cast-iron radiator of twelve columns topped with a flat plate, an extraordinary Victorian tortoise stove resembling a credence table made with organ pipes. He also provided a new and better pulpit and a well equipped vestry behind a screen, and handsomely furnished the whole building. It ended as a Tractarian relic too large for the modest needs of Stinchcombe, but, in its way, both handsome and interesting.

The rebuilt church was consecrated by the Bishop of Gloucester on the 26th July 1855 and it was a great event. John Keble came all the way from Hursley to preach at festal evensong. An attenuated Tractarian, but now Bishop of Oxford, Samuel Wilberforce, overcame his dread of railways, for he always said he could never enter a carriage without reflecting that he might never leave it alive, and travelled down to preach at the morning liturgy. The assistant curate, Mr. Isaac Williams, was made a great deal of by his fellow members of the Oxford Movement, but he lacked the energy or the will to respond with more than pleasantries. More and more he spent a life of retirement at Stinchcombe, seeing only his immediate family and close friends, educating his sons, six of whom survived him, and writing sermons and poetry which, as if reflecting his pulse-rate and weakness, was struck in an increasingly low key. But his influence was large, especially as a writer of hymns. He did not write a great many, but of those that he did several assure him a place in the affections of Christian singers. His translated hymn 'Disposer supreme, and Judge of the earth' seems almost too thunderous for so mild a man with its couplet:

> 'As when the dread trumpets went forth at thy word,
> And one long blast shattered the Canaanites' wall.'

But he also wrote the softer hymns 'O heavenly Jerusalem of everlasting halls', 'Lord, in this thy mercy's day', and most easily remembered, 'Be thou my Guardian and my Guide', with its reflection on penitence and Christian hope in the last two stanzas:

Isaac Williams, a leading Tractarian and academic who withdrew to a country living following a contested election (1859 portrait by W. H. Cubley, reproduced by kind permission of the President and Fellows of Trinity College Oxford – Thomas-Photos, Oxford)

'And if I tempted am to sin,
  And outward things are strong,
Do thou, O Lord keep watch within,
  And save my soul from wrong.

Still let me ever watch and pray,
  And feel that I am frail;
That if the tempter cross my way,
  Yet he may not prevail.'

Isaac Williams faded away entirely, being given the last rites of the Church at the hands of his brother-in-law on May Day in 1865. A stained-glass window was erected to his memory in Trinity College Chapel, and two windows on the north side of the Stinchcombe Church were given stained-glass in his memory; one depicting the Ascension, the other, the Transfiguration. He was buried outside in the south west part of the church, next to the grave of his infant son Richard, which also bore an inscription to his father the Chancery barrister from Llanrhystid in Cardiganshire. His own memorial is simply inscribed 'Isaac Williams, Clerk, B.D.', with the dates of his birth and death, and the prayer *Domine Miserere Mei*.

Stinchcombe is not what it was. With all due respect to a busy incumbent, the village lacks the vitality it must have had when the Tractarian flame burnt brightly. The parish has been rejoined to Cam again; the former Church House and then Curate's House, misnamed the Old Parsonage, is a private house. The Venerable Sir George Prevost's Parsonage, misnamed the Manor House, is now an hotel. The Williams's house, misnamed first the Vicarage and now the Old Vicarage, is in private hands. Less than three hundred and fifty yards down from that former quiet retreat is the motorway from Birmingham to Bristol. Its roar is muted by summer leaves, but it is still a noise. Ichabod!

★

It is of interest to note how many of the Tractarians came from Evangelical backgrounds. Newman himself did, and so did Father Faber and the translator Father Caswall; and so did another translator whose name is familiar wherever hymns are sung, John Mason Neale. His father, Cornelius Neale, was a considerable scholar, Senior Wrangler at Cambridge, and a firm Evangelical, being the son of a rich china merchant who had frequently been visited by 'the old African blasphemer', John Newton, when he was Rector of St. Mary Woolnoth in the City. Cornelius was nervously disposed; and this state was not improved by marriage to a domineering woman who claimed to be delicate but who, in reality, had the strength of a lioness, for she was chronically restless, and moved her family to house after house after house, never putting down one root; nor was the poor man's state improved by his conviction that he might be doomed to follow seven half-brothers and sisters and ten blood-brothers and sisters to an early grave. The tantrums of self-centred Mrs. Neale, and the thought of those seventeen dead relatives, sent him into mild attacks of hysterics, when he would throw books about the place. Though a deeply convinced Low Churchman, he felt uncertain about his own vocation, and took years in deciding whether or not it would be right to be ordained. When, at the age of thirty-one, he finally made the decision, and was made deacon to serve as assistant curate at Mildenhall in Suffolk, Mrs. Neale declared she could not abide the place and made him live thirty miles away in Essex and go to Mildenhall only at weekends. Seven months later he was ordained priest, and, to placate his nomadic spouse, he arranged for a rapid move to a curacy in Hertfordshire; but it was not to be. The carriages, carts, baggage waggons were all ready and they were on the point of moving when he dropped dead – according to one source from phthisis, to another from a heart attack, most probably from a combination of the two.

His young and only son, aged four, was left in a world of women, with three younger sisters, a termagant mother and a grandmother, both of whom were severely Calvinistic. Grandmother Neale called the little boy 'a sacred deposit' and declared they must be sure, 'if he is spared, to train him up for the Lord'. This was commenced by rapid changes of residences to Battersea, thence to Chiswick, thence to Shepperton, thence to Blackheath, though instructed by an old nurse who described him as 'the dearest, dirtiest, lyingest boy' that she had ever loved, a series of tutors at Sherborne School and a school at Farnham in Surrey, where the Bishop of Winchester's butler persuaded him to take his Sunday School classes, and finally as a pupil at a Rectory near Cambridge under the erratic and distant supervision of the Reverend James Challis, Plumerian Professor of Astronomy, who lived not at his Rectory but in the Observatory where he discovered the planet Saturn.

Young Mason, as he was always known as a boy and young man, had by then become a well-read and imaginative boy of great promise. Religion was always of interest to him, and he went out with a friend to sit under the great Evangelical Charles Simeon in Cambridge, but his tutor, the Professor, was not much of an encouragement, closing his church altogether on a Sunday when there happened to be an eclipse of the sun. Neale had no interest in competitive sport, but, though considered frail, he thought nothing of a twenty-mile walk over the heavy clays of Cambridgeshire. He rounded off his 'training up for the Lord' at Trinity College, Cambridge. Old Mrs. Neale would have approved of the 'sacred deposits' attendance at the Sacrament in Trinity College the day after his matriculation where 'one man in three was in tears', and, a few days later, at a grand Sunday School meeting of one thousand four hundred children in the University Church, when the assembly sang a hymn no longer sung:

> 'Holy Bible, book divine,
> Precious treasure, Thou art mine',

to the tune *Sicilian Mariners*, still used for other hymns, among them Bishop Heber's 'O, most merciful! O' most bountiful'. Grandmother Neale would also have understood his naïve interest in phrenology, when he had his bumps read by a Mr. Bunny, but in his second year Mason Neale moved from the Low to the High position, which would have demented her.

By his third year up, he had become an ornament of the University, an exceptional scholar and linguist, and at the core of the Cambridge disciples of the Oxford Movement. He felt a strong vocation to the priesthood and a need not only to clear away the accretions of protestant and deist and Evangelical piety from the Catholic Church of England, but also to turn rubbish out from the parish churches of the land and restore them to their former mediaeval beauty and usefulness. Wise with hindsight we see that mediaevalism was not the pure panacea and that the boxed pews, galleries and three decker pulpits had a great value in their own right. To Neale and his friends at Cambridge they constituted a threat to Order in the Church and the practice of the liturgy. Neale read a good deal about mediaeval architecture and he and two other undergraduates, Webb and Boyce, formed a society with the expressed purpose of studying ecclesiastical architecture and restoring mutilated remains. It was named for an English antiquary, the Camden Society; and with the energy of the young they did remarkable work in studying parish churches up and down the country, reporting on necessary improvements. They also began a periodical entitled *The Ecclesiologist*, which published articles on ritual, symbolism, and church history, music, and furnishings; and these spread, like the Oxford tracts, through the manors and parsonages of the country. A great difference between the

Cambridge Anglo-Catholic Movement and that of Oxford is that it was not inaugurated and carried out by dons as it was at Oxford, but by undergraduates. But despite the callowness of its founders, the Camden Society attracted a large number of members, honorary members and patrons; amongst them, two archbishops, sixteen bishops, thirty-one peers and members of the House of Commons, seven deans and chancellors of dioceses, twenty-one archdeacons and rural deans, sixteen architects, and more than seven hundred others.

Again we hear of an undergraduate of extraordinary promise failing to reach the highest honours. Though he was the son of a Senior Wrangler Neale failed a minor mathematics examination. Perhaps it had been caused by the funeral that same day of the Master's son, or by the presentation a short time before on a fast day of a buttery bill amounting to £91:7s:0d. Whatever the reason, his failure effectively prevented him from going on to take the Classics Tripos*, but again we hear of a way being found around a technicality by a sensible university. Though he only had a pass-degree, Neale was offered the Assistant Tutorship at Downing College, which he at once accepted and took up residence on the 24th September, 1840.

His High Church proclivities had a marked effect upon his three sisters. The youngest was to found a Community in Stepney of which she was Mother Superior for fifty years. The other two, one a semi-invalid, attended the highest of High Brighton churches. But he had no effect upon his mother, who remained a convinced Evangelical and, Brighton being Brighton, found there a church most suitable to her Calvinistic faith.

It was suggested by Downing that he might be College Chaplain, so he began to set about getting himself ordained. This was not as easy to manage as might be thought. As a founder of the Camden Society and a Tractarian with ultramontane leanings, not many bishops would consider him. But his tutor at Trinity also held in plurality an Archdeaconry in the Diocese of Gloucester, and he arranged for the Bishop of Gloucester and Bristol to make Neale deacon on the sixth of June 1841 at St. Margaret's Westminster in London. St. Margaret's was then regarded as a good centre for their ordinations by some country bishops, and it was convenient to Neale. The new deacon promptly took a three-week holiday in

---

* The rule which made this necessary was rescinded by the Senate a year after Neale took his degree.

France, before spending the rest of the summer in his mother's house at Brighton. At Michaelmas, he went up to Downing and made the discovery he ought to have known long before, that most dons and undergraduates would not attend a daily chapel. He protested. Nothing happened. After six weeks he resigned and left the college. Before Christmas he had accepted a temporary assistant curacy at Guildford and began his duties in January 1842. There has seldom been such a hard worker as John Mason Neale, for there can be no doubting his industry, but the Bishop of Winchester heard he was a Tractarian, and let it be known he considered him unsafe. It was this same bishop whose butler had persuaded the young Neale to take his Sunday School class, so virtue was not rewarded.

After a month Neale left and went to take digs in Cambridge while he looked around for another assistant curacy, and there, to the surprise of his family, he became engaged to a daughter of the Rector of St. Botolph's. The young lady was four years older than he but she shared his Tractarian views and her sister had married Edward Boyce, one of his closest friends and co-founder of the Camden Society. By May a living had been found for him in Crawley, Sussex, of which, after being ordained priest, again at St. Margaret's, Westminster, and again by the kindly Bishop of Gloucester and Bristol, he accepted the benefice and, as there was no parsonage attached, took a house for himself. Oddly, though Neale kept a careful journal, there is no reference to the bishop of the diocese, Chichester, before he began duty in his parish. He had great plans. 'Already,' he wrote, 'in my mind's eye I see an incipient choir.' With his real eyes he saw a churchwarden stand on the Altar to open a window. 'Really, the Protestantism of these people . . . is dreadful.' The most important event to a newly ordained priest is his first celebration of the Eucharist, or, as Neale would have considered it, his first Mass. However this was not celebrated on the day after Ordination, which is customary, or even after his arrival in Crawley, but a week afterwards, and then not in his parish but in far away Warwick, and not in a consecrated church, but in a private house, simply because his mother, seeking new ground, had, like Noah's dove, found room for the sole of her foot in that part of England. Crawley was not, though, neglected. Neale already had an assistant. But it proved to be previous. The clime was unsuited to him and he resigned the living after two months, even before he was Instituted and Inducted.

Like his father, Neale never did enjoy good health, but he failed to succumb and did the best he could with it for forty-eight years. For

John Mason Neale, who, in a short, industrious and happy life achieved much, including the founding of an Order and the translation of many great hymns

(top) the chapel of Sackville College, where Neale was Warden; (bottom) St. Margaret's Convent (established by Neale at East Grinstead)

example, on leaving Crawley, he married, and his wife Sally turned out to be a treasure. She supported him in all he did and cared for him in every way. For three years they wintered in Madeira, where the energetic Neale studied the Roman Catholic Church and wrote historical novels. He would like to have assisted the English Chaplain, and did badger him into providing a weekly Eucharist. But the doctors would not let him preach. On their voyages out and back the Neales liked to visit other countries at leisure, Neale being attacked by a brigand in Seville and narrowly escaping being knifed in the back, both of them enjoying a bullfight on Ascension Day in Cadiz – 'saw seven bulls and seventeen horses killed', and inspecting a large number of churches in varying stages of decay. The Newman crisis arose and passed. Neale's position was quite unaffected by it. Always he considered the Church of England as the Catholic Church of the country and he was unperturbed by the fuss over Newman, whom he considered holy but wrong-headed.

That year, 1845, the Neales returned to England permanently. Mrs. Neale had already presented him with the first of their five children, and the doctors declared he could preach again. There were to be no more winters in Madeira. The little family stayed for a short time with his mother who had moved several times since her sojourn in Warwick and was then in London, and then took a cottage in Reigate. Like a clerical Micawber Neale waited for something to turn up. Meanwhile he proved as indefatigable as ever, busy with the affairs of the Camden Society which was renamed The Ecclesiological (late Cambridge Camden) Society, and writing prolifically. He submitted a poem for the Cambridge Seatonian Prize and won it, as he did for the next ten consecutive years. He also revised the Prayer Book edition in Portuguese, translated Bishop Lancelot Andrewes's *Devotions* into Portuguese, and began to collect material for a new edition of a seventeenth century *History and Fate of Sacrilege*, the volume on Portugal for Murray's famous series of continental handbooks, his life of the Saints, and most notable of all, his history of the Eastern Church.

In January 1846 his Micawberism was rewarded. He was offered the Wardenship of Sackville College in East Grinstead by Earl De La Warr on behalf of his Countess, a joint patron with her sister. It was not preferment in the ordinary sense. Indeed Neale was never offered any sort of preferment by the church of his ordination. The Episcopal Church in Scotland offered him the Provostship of St. Ninian's, Perth, which gratified him, but he refused because the climate would have struck him dead; and Harvard conferred on him

the degree of D.D.; and the Metropolitan of Moscow also honoured
him; but the Church on which he had such claims tried to ignore
him. Sackville College was a seventeenth century almshouse founded
for thirty poor and aged householders, with a chapel attached to the
college. The stipend was £24 a year. Neale went down to see the place.
The buildings were in a sad state; the almspeople not much better. It
was the sort of work to bring the light of battle to Neale's eye. He
accepted the offer and Earl De La Warr helped with the repairs. In
fact the college was just the sort of headquarters for Neale's
enormous capacity for work; he could not have done as much as he
did in his short life, nor with the same freedom, in a conventional
parish. He took up his appointment at the age of twenty-eight in May
1846 and things at once began to happen. The buildings were put in
order. The chapel was repaired and to the amazement of the inmates
Daily Services were introduced. They were equally amazed to be
invited to dine with the Warden in the Hall on Sundays and feasts of
the church. Neale thrived upon it all. His Sally gave a good picture of
him, and expressed some of her own difficulties, in a letter to a
friend: 'I never saw my dear husband in better health, or more
thorough enjoyment than of this post and its duties. Our suite of
apartments is made very comfortable, but it is a trying house for
servants, the want of bells, the many evils and difficulties of cooking
by wood fires, and – our Sunday dinners are *I* think pleasanter in
theory than in practice!'

Neale's 'repairs' to the chapel included the setting up of a rood
screen and the construction of a high Altar within a painted and
decorated sanctuary. A bigoted local parson immediately scented
popery, and with the hearty support of the Brighton Protestant
Association laid information with the Bishop of Chichester, Dr.
Gilbert. At Earl De La Warr's request, Neale had not sought the
Bishop's licence to officiate at Sackville College, as it was considered
extra-parochial and confirmed as such in 1814 by a secretary of the
then Bishop of Chichester. Dr. Gilbert, nominally a High
Churchman, was certainly no Tractarian, and he lived in subjection
to the Brighton Protestant Association. Therefore he heard the
objection, and acted on it by inhibiting Neale from conducting
services in the College Chapel. That he had no legal right to do so did
not affect the issue in Neale's eyes, nor did the fact that the parson
who laid information against him was afterwards discredited and
forced to fly the country one step ahead of the authorities, who
wanted him for forgery. To him, a bishop, by his consecration, had a
moral authority which in conscience he could not resist. For sixteen

S. JOHN DAMASCENE. 57

S. THOMAS'S SUNDAY.

The four following Odes are the four first of our Saint's Canon for S. Thomas's Sunday, called also Renewal Sunday : with us Low Sunday. The first Stanzas are marked with inverted commas, as being *Hirmoi*.

ODE I.

ἄσωμεν πάντες λάοι.

" Come, ye faithful, raise the strain
  " Of triumphant gladness !
" GOD hath brought His Israel
  " Into joy from sadness:
" Loosed from Pharaoh's bitter yoke
  " Jacob's sons and daughters ;
" Led them with unmoistened foot
  " Through the Red Sea waters."

'Tis the Spring of souls to-day :
  CHRIST hath burst His prison ;
And from three days' sleep in death,
  As a sun, hath risen.

A hymn by St. John of Damascus (see page 4) from Neale's *Hymns of the Eastern Church*

years, as long as the inhibition lasted, he held no services in the Chapel, using other parts of the College instead, and conducting them much as a layman might, not reading the Absolution nor even wearing a surplice. And until he founded the Society of St. Margaret, an order of nursing-sisters, and there was a convent oratory, he only said a private Mass for family and friends in his own apartment.

The founding of an Order is probably the most contentious of all Neale's innovations. Pusey had begun the first Anglican sisterhood, and caused hysterical wrath amongst extreme Evangelicals. They considered such places 'unhealthy'. Nothing upset the black Protestants more than religious communities. They were disgusted by the vows taken of poverty and chastity and obedience; particularly, for some doubtless Freudian reason, the vow of chastity. Celibacy was regarded by them as quite the most horrid of Romish practices. Neale, blessed as he was by his devoted Sally and their children, found himself constantly abused by the Evangelicals of Brighton for setting up a nest of celibrate sisters. In 1854, the same year Neale invited two sisters to take residence in the College, living under vows to look after the elderly inmates, an anti-papist named Moultrie, who had long smouldered with anger at the advance upon England of the Scarlet Woman of Rome, published an outburst of philippics entitled *Altars, Hearths, & Graves*, including a passionate plea against celibacy –

> 'God give her wavering clergy back that honest heart and true,
> Which once was theirs 'ere Popish fraud its spell around them threw;
> Nor let them barter wife and child, bright hearth and happy home,
> For the drunken bliss of the strumpet kiss of the Jezebel of Rome.'

Hopefully Neale's sense of humour came to his aid when his work was attacked with dotty trash, but it still did not make his work any easier. He was often haled into court by litigious Evangelicals, from which, almost always, he emerged the victor. Moreover his almspeople were not always easy. Naturally there were the usual grumbles, and barrack-room lawyers at work among them, but they even suffered from a partially senile widow named Furminger who allegedly threw things about the College at night time, and could never be caught at it, not even when Earl De La Warr obligingly sent in a private detective disguised as a French-polisher. In the end the detective's incompetence didn't matter, for widow Ferminger died, and the hurling of solid objects by night abruptly ceased.

When more sisters joined the Order in 1855, Neale took a house for them in Rotherfield. It was appropriate because the daughter of the Rector of Rotherfield took her vows and was clothed as the first

Superior. But they were fourteen miles from Grinstead, and Neale waited until a suitable house fell vacant in East Grinstead and the first Community of the Society was established. Some of the sisters were trained in nursing at Westminster Hospital in London before settling in a convent close to Sackville College. Their very correct founder, Father Neale, offered the Rule of his new Community to the Bishop of Chichester, who, unable to do anything else, wisely approved it and merely advised minor alterations in certain articles of dress.

Less wise were Mrs. Neale and the Vicar of East Grinstead. She naturally did her duty by attending Divine Service in the parish, but she wrote to object when the Vicar left out part of the words of Administration at the Holy Communion, and preached a sermon in which he denied any sort of Real Presence at all in the Blessed Sacrament. Clergymen at that time did not hesitate to dehort as well as to exhort, nor to put difficult parishioners in their places. The Vicar wrote Mrs. Neale a withering reply to her protest. It ended, 'And now, Madam, I have only to express my regret that I should have a parishioner so little sensible of her real position, as to presume to write two such letters such as yours, and to assure you that however much I may pity the tenderness of your conscience, I pity your want of humility, delicacy, and information infinitely more'. The Vicar chafed at the Catholic sore which, as he believed, poisoned his parish, and which was beyond his curing. Neale was obeying the bishop's inhibition so far as the College was concerned, but he was also founding an Order of sisters in whose Oratory he would be free to do what he liked. The Vicar preached, and thundered against popery. It made no difference. The Tractarians attracted many followers because they emphasised the need for self-discipline and self-sacrifice, and they were genuinely concerned to help the sick and the old in a practical way. Inspired perhaps by the work of Miss Nightingale, who had leapt to fame as the Lady with the Lamp in 1855, the year after the Community was founded, Father Neale's sisters bravely went out into the wooded countryside round East Grinstead to nurse lonely people sick with fevers whom no-one else dared nurse. They were sustained by their faith and regular prayer from the mother house, where their founder and chaplain introduced Eucharistic Vestments in the sisters' Oratory, said a daily Mass

from 1856, and reserved the Blessed Sacrament two years later.*
Reservation enabled Neale to introduce Benediction of the Blessed
Sacrament which he began in 1859.

The number of sisters increased, but there were also casualties
among them, and two died as a result of the fevers they contracted.
One was buried in the parish churchyard and the Vicar objected to
the Bishop because the coffin had a brick-coloured pall embroidered
with the Roman Cross on it. The funeral of another caused a beery
rabble to go up and stone Neale's apartments, breaking windows
there and almost setting the place on fire. Worst of all was the funeral
of Sister Amy. She had caught scarlet fever from nursing a poor
sufferer in Ashdown Forest and died leaving a will. This was rather
odd considering her vow of poverty, but the Rule was still shaking
down and Sister Amy was in a position to bequeath £400 to her
Community and pass a considerable amount more to her brother.
Her father, a clergyman from Lewes who had strongly objected to
her becoming a nun, was outraged that the Community should have
benefited by his daughter's untimely death. She had asked to be
buried in the family plot at Lewes. Neale and the Superior of the
Sisters, Mother Ann, made the necessary arrangements for the
cortège to go to Lewes. The funeral was interrupted by an anti-
popery demonstration which had been stirred up by the dead Sister's
father, and ended in a riot. It was one of the most extraordinary
episodes in the life of John Mason Neale. His cap and gown were torn
into shreds and he only just managed to take refuge in the King's
Head Inn with four of the sisters. While the sisters made themselves
scarce through the back premises, Neale imprudently tried to bribe
the rioters with beer to go away. It simply inflamed them further. He
escaped only by scaling two nine foot back walls and tramping to the
railway station by back streets dressed in borrowed clothes. There he
was recognised, as were the sisters who bravely turned up at the
station in a fly. Neale was stoned, the Mother Superior was
physically threatened and abuse was heaped upon the other sisters. It
was an ugly day; resulting in highly coloured press reports, a
condemnatory sermon from the dead Sister Amy's father, not of the
rioters but of the Society of St. Margaret; and a temporary cessation

---

* It is claimed he was the first to do so in the Church of England since the Reformation. This is
not quite correct. It was certainly reserved in the reign of Edward VI and his half-sister
Elizabeth I and continued in isolated places for centuries; e.g. in Durham Cathedral at the end
of the eighteenth century. And the majority of Communions were made from the Blessed
Sacrament in Scotland during the eighteenth century because of the Penal Laws against the
Episcopal Church. Moreover Reservation was made at Corfe Castle and in Leeds in England as
early as 1851.

of donations and subscriptions; and the owner of the Convent freehold, a Dissenter, giving them notice to quit. Neale was quite without recrimination. He was consoled by a letter from the Bishop of Brechin: 'Twenty years hence the people of Lewes will kiss the dust off the sisters' feet', a prophecy which turned out to be correct for, in a bad outbreak of fever some time afterwards, the sisters won the open admiration and gratitude of the town. Meanwhile the sisters moved their quarters and carried on working.

If such a thing were possible, Father Neale increased his work load. Considering his physical frailty and that he had to support a tall, angular loose-limbed frame, and put up with indifferent eyesight, his drive and infectious enthusiasm and thoroughness in everything he did were quite astonishing. Somehow every spring or summer he managed a continental holiday away from Sackville College, sometimes with his Sally and one or more of the children, sometimes with friends, occasionally alone. In the College his daily time-table began at 6.30 a.m. on five days of the week and at 4.30 on two of them, and ended at midnight. At the appointed hours he went down to the sisters' Oratory to say Mass and read the Office. He visited and cared for the inmates of the College and the children of an orphanage set up by the sisters, and he saw visitors from beyond. The village barber went up to the College each evening to shave him. For the rest of his time he was said to have worked at a standing desk, lighted when it was dark by candles or by a green shaded student's oil lamp, writing with quill pens and great rapidity and elegance of style a huge number of letters and all manner of other enterprises: learned accounts of church history, commentaries on Scripture, theological criticism, stories and catechisings, contributions to newspapers and periodicals, pamphlets on important questions of the day, biographies and hymns.

His first work was published in 1840 and he turned out at least one book every year for the rest of his life. Though it is as a staunch and loyal High Church priest who restored much of the old faith to the Church of England that he ought to be honoured most, it is as a hymnologist he will be remembered best. He was himself a trenchant critic of the work of other hymn-writers, rejecting many that were and always will be popular if they did not fall within his high standards. For instance he did not like Watts's hymns for children. They had frightened him as a child and he was determined to free others from what he called 'Watts's yoke'. What is more, he considered Watts's theology 'bad', and his views on the Incarnation 'defective'. He was adverse, as well, to Wesley's 'mischievous idea of the necessity of faith only for the forgiveness of sins'. He liked Toplady's 'Rock of ages', but even this he could only accept as a penitential devotion. He was hard on the *Olney Hymns*; 'In some of Cowper's there may be beauty; but Newton's are of the very essence of doggerel'. Even Heber did not satisfy him: 'he brought an elegant mind, but little else to the task.' His own standards were exacting: translation should, if possible, adopt the same metre and arrangement of verses as the original, children's hymns should teach sound doctrine in simple metres.

He was highly successful in meeting these exacting requirements. With a few single exceptions the main body of his translations from Latin hymns was superior to those of any of his contemporaries. A great number are still in regular use, and include 'Creator of the stars of night', 'Ye choirs of new Jerusalem', 'The God whom earth, and sea, and sky', 'Now that the daylight fills the sky', and 'Jerusalem the golden'. His translations from the Greek were both beautiful and apt: among them were 'Fierce was the wild billow', 'O happy band of pilgrims', 'Come, ye faithful, raise the strain' and the ubiquitous martial note of the Lenten Fast, 'Christian, dost thou see them'. His own original hymns were never as famous as his translations, yet they included 'The earth, O Lord, is one great field', 'Around the throne of God a band of glorious Angels always stand', 'With Christ we share a mystic grave', and the carol 'Good King Wenceslas'. Neale loved carols, and had large carol parties at the College, and did not approve of a teetotal, vegetarian enthusiast who had the impertinence to recommend he change the flesh and wine of Wenceslas to:

> 'Bring me milk and bring me bread
> Thou and I will see him fed.'

Father Neale's reply went unrecorded. We may legitimately guess it.

A little more must be said about this polymath and restorer of the old Catholic ways to the Church of England. How he found time to be happy and have a sense of humour and be such radiant company, is an obscure mystery, but we are assured that he did. He also had over-heavenly disregard for some things of the earth. For example, he paid small attention to the condition of his clothes, but he was bothered by change. Therefore, it being important that so busy a priest be not bothered, an identical replacement was put in his dressing room by stealth at night whenever a suit or cassock grew too stained or shabby for further use.

In his middle age he had failures. A home founded by the Sisters at

Aldershot for fallen women did some useful work for a time, but there were vociferous local prejudices against fallen women in Aldershot, and the home was too far away for Neale to supervise. It had to be abandoned. But he had grand successes too. After fifteen years the Bishop of Chichester was at last persuaded to remove his inhibition. It made little difference to Neale himself, but put the College and the Convent and the Orphanage on a firmer footing, and Neale showed a token of his appreciation by having his ten Seatonian poems turned into one volume which he dedicated to the Bishop. By this time his Society of St. Margaret had grown in such numbers it required larger quarters. Neale bought a suitable site, had plans drawn up, and, still correct, invited the Bishop of Chichester to be present at the laying of the foundation stone. The Bishop politely refused, which left Neale free to ask a Greek bishop, the Archimandrite Stratuli, to come and bless the stone after the Eastern Rite. Afterwards the East Grinstead village bells rang out, because the old Vicar had died and his successor was more friendly.

Laying the stone was Father Neale's last public act. He was never to see the completed Convent, nor could he have guessed that one day his Society would have convents in Haiti and Sri Lanka, the United States and Canada, two in London and three more in the English provinces. There was no corresponding mental collapse as his health began to crumble, but it was a sign of increasing strain that, in 1865, and quite uncharacteristically, Father Neale started to worry about the ritual question. He also began to dope himself with opium. This deadened pain but it brought on dropsy, which was only relieved by a small operation. The surgeon's scalpel was assisted by the Sisters who stayed up all night praying for their founder. When he had sufficiently recovered he went down to convalesce at Brighton. Two days of the invigorating air tempted him to take a short sail out to sea; but in his debilitated state he could not stand the chill. He was taken back to Sackville College with bronchitis. This, was his old complaint, exhaustion, and what was diagnosed as 'bilious diarrhoea' caused him extreme discomfort and pain. On the 26th July, 1866, he had a second operation, from which he never rallied. During his last weeks his family read to him and the Sisters sang carols and hymns and, at his special request, *the Messiah*. The last hymn he heard before dying on the Feast of the Transfiguration was his own translation of the eleventh century Latin hymn from The Rosy Sequence: 'Jesu! – the very thought is sweet!'

Neale was only forty-eight years of age at the time of his death, but he left behind a rich contribution to scholarship and Christian worship. His funeral was the sort he himself would have enjoyed enormously. An unexpectedly large congregation turned up, and after the committal, everyone sang Father Neale's translation of a hymn of St. Bernard of Cluny 'Brief life is here our portion', then processed back to the College, singing 'Jerusalem the golden' at the top of their voices.

★

Fifty-five miles west of Sackville College, source of Father Neale's fountain of hymns, lies Winchester. When, in the 1850's, *Hymns Ancient and Modern* was promoted by the Reverend Sir Henry Baker, Baronet, Vicar of Monkland on the Welsh Marches, and a small committee of compilers, they invited contributions which would be distinctly Tractarian, and which they hoped to have in print by 1860.

Sir Henry Baker himself contributed translations and originals and adaptions of high quality such as 'We love the place, O God', 'Lord, thy word abideth', 'The King of love my Shepherd is', as well as a strenuous work of Mariolatry, 'Shall we not love thee, Mother dear', which must have inflamed the Protestant Association. The committee naturally depended greatly upon Father Neale, and, too, upon Keble at Hursley near Winchester. From Winchester College itself they received two offerings; one, an evening hymn, 'O faith who didst all things make', written by W. B. Heathcote, a master at the College, which was accepted but did not last through the many revisions of *Ancient and Modern*; another, 'O thou who bidd'st the ocean deep', by William Whiting, Master of the College Quiristers. The latter hymn, reshaped by Sir Henry, turned out to be one of the most conspicuously successful of all time, and a note on its author is not out of place.

Whiting was born the son of a grocer in 1825 in Kensington, then a village with plenty of trees and streams but beginning to swell at the seams owing to a sharp rise in population and the building of terraced houses. The child had a club foot, a deformity which did not seem to prevent him from taking a great deal of walking exercise. In 1829 the family moved from Kensington to the village of Clapham, noted for its religious leaders, and a fashionable healthy area on gravel soil well away from, and high above, the Thames. It was a good place for a grocery business, and, too, for growing children. William and his young sister Ann explored the countryside, and all through his life he regarded himself as rural rather than urban. Circumstances combined to shape his career. Clapham parish was then in the Diocese of Winchester. The Rector, a Fellow of the Royal Society and a distinguished mathematician, was a Prebendary of Winchester and later Chancellor of the Diocese and co-founder of a Training Institution for Schoolmasters. William did well at school and, when his father died at the early age of forty-seven, the Rector of Clapham recommended that he be accepted by the Winchester Training Institution. Had his background been slightly different, his ability and taste for Tractarianism would almost certainly have sent him to Oxford or Cambridge and on to ordination. As it was, he was elected an Exhibitioner of the Institution in 1841 and went to reside there in the same year.

He was sixteen, a fair classical scholar, and he had aspirations to be a poet. Part of his practical training was to teach the Quiristers of Winchester College, sixteen brown-liveried boys who sporadically attended the Institution as pupils, when they were not running errands or fagging for College Scholars or waiting on them in Hall. The Foundation statutes laid down that they should sing in Chapel as well as wait at Hall, but about fifty years before the practice had fallen into desuetude. As a result, the social standing of Quiristers fell low and, at the time Whiting went to the Institution, the boys were little more than unpaid servants. The Warden of the College was anxious to improve their circumstances and position, and decided to re-impose their singing duties. To make this possible, it was agreed that a Master of the Quiristers be appointed, who would live with them in their lodging, tutor them and make sure that they carried out their duties both in Chapel and Hall. The errand-running and fagging were to cease. William Whiting had been noticed at the Institution as a promising teacher. In spite of his club foot, perhaps even because of it, he was an excellent disciplinarian. There was no sky-larking in his presence. And, although he was young, he had a gravity beyond his years. He was offered the post. Whiting was delighted, he saw it as a splendid opportunity. He would be part of the College of which the Second Master was a Tractarian, and the beloved Mr. Keble was not far away. His work, though tedious, would give him a certain amount of leisure. He had no illusions about that state of Victorian society into which it had pleased God to call him, and would scarcely have considered the post beneath him. And so, at the age of seventeen, not much older than his charges, he became first Master of the Quiristers in the nineteenth century to have charge of their boarding and tuition.

He moved into 5, College Street in 1842 and was to remain there thirty-six years. It was a narrow house comprising, downstairs two living rooms, a wash-house and scullery, three rooms above, and two in the attic, and it was far too small. It took time, but the Quiristers' lodgings were eventually enlarged by leasing an adjacent house in the Cathedral Close. There were sixteen Quiristers, all between nine and fourteen years of age, corresponding in number with the Old Testament major and minor prophets. They wore tailed coats, trousers, and hobnailed boots, and were marshalled twice a day by the Master to march in a crocodile to Hall to serve the College men, and collect their own food and drink in wicker baskets. They were also marshalled to Chapel to carry out their prime function. This was not a success. Most were not musical and none was competently trained in singing. The Organist of both Cathedral and College was too decrepit to teach anyone anything, and nothing was done in this respect until he died in 1849 and Charles Wesley's illegitimate grandson, Samuel Sebastian Wesley, was appointed Organist of the Cathedral and, a year later, Organist of the College. Even then it took a long, long time to achieve the Warden's ideal because, although he had four sons of his own, Wesley heartily disliked boys and hated training them. Choir practices were loathed by both parties. Like his accident-prone father, who had tumbled into a hole in the roadway and damaged his brain, Samuel Sebastian Wesley met with an accident which permanently lamed him. The Quiristers, in the charge of two lame men, naturally nicknamed them 'Hoppy', though Whiting preferred to think he was known in College as 'Tyrtaeus,' from the Greek poet of the seventh century B.C. who was also a lame schoolmaster. The boys, or 'men' as they are quaintly known at that academy of learning, respected Wesley because of his genius as a composer and as an organist, but they merely deferred to Whiting because of his authority as their Master. There was nothing of tinsel about Whiting, certainly nothing heroic, and neither his reserve nor his self-importance were attractive to boys. Sadly, he never won the real affection of any of his charges in all his years of service.

In the first two years of his Mastership, Whiting still taught the Quiristers at the Diocesan Training Institution. Then, with the enlargement of their lodging, he tutored them there. He used his little leisure to explore the countryside round Winchester, absorb Anglo-Catholicism, and write rather indifferent verses. In the late 1840s his reserve lessened and he blossomed a little. In April 1850 he delivered a lecture at the Mechanics' Institute on 'Ghosts and Spectral Apparitions'. He spent the spring and early summer preparing for the press a volume of his poems entitled *Rural Thoughts and Scenes*, in the preface for which he wrote, 'When sanctified by

WILLIAM WHITING.
B. 1825. D. 1878.

William Whiting, a stern schoolmaster and trite poet (from the biography by Patricia Hooper, by kind permission of Paul Cave Publications Limited)

religion, and refined in the pure fire of Holy Church's doctrine and precept, Poetry becomes the most powerful instrument in stirring up the heart for good. . . . Poetry such as this stirs as a war-trumpet'. Regrettably his verses were neither a 'powerful instrument' nor 'a war-trumpet'. To quote at random from a longish poem, polished up that summer, entitled 'The Song of the Butterflies':

> 'When the early spring breeze, through the trembling trees
>   Breathes with the perfumes of May!
> All in the mid-air, its perfume we share,
>   And revel the live-long day.
>
> Its nectar we sip from the bright rose's lip,
>   Whilst tasting its sweets with the bee;
> In the sun's golden ray we wantonly play,
>   And blithesome and glad are we . . .'

– and this has six more stanzas which do not improve. His poem 'The Boy-Poet's Love', about Leonard and Marion along the river-edge in the blushing spring, is wishy-washy beyond belief. Not even its author's commendation to the public in the name of the Holy Trinity saved it from being a very bad book.

It somehow surprises one to discover that this schoolmaster, so busy with his duties, his explorations, his lecturing, and his versifying, had the time and opportunity to woo and win the heart of a butler's daughter who was two years older than he and lived in Salisbury Close, of which her brother was Constable. The distance of twenty miles between the two Cathedral Closes cannot have made the courtship easy; but it was managed, and William Whiting and Fanny Lucas were married in Salisbury Cathedral in July 1850. Not much is known about Fanny. The Quiristers' lodging at Winchester, packed with boys, was a challenge not many ladies could have met. There was also a lodger in the house, a fifteen year old organist's apprentice from Yorkshire called Joe. And the subsequent arrival of her William's maiden aunt, Amy Whiting, as a permanent resident would have added a strain on the nervous system as well as on the accommodation.* But Fanny managed. She bore three children to

---

* It is difficult to see how room was found for everyone. At a later stage William's widowed mother and Fanny's widowed mother also joined the household.

her William, – Mary, Billy and Bertie – and, with a little help from old Aunty Amy, she managed the housekeeping. There was a matron*, and resident servants, and the Quiristers did their share, but with no sewage system and no running water, and coals to be carried to each room, she could have had very little time to herself.

Doubtless she was proud of her husband, a published poet – though his second volume of poetry, a fictional biography entitled *Edgar Thorpe*, was scarcely less trite than its predecessor – a man with intellectual outside interests which took him beyond the Quiristers' lodging into the City, as a member and chairman of the Museum Committee, a lecturer and singer at concerts at the Mechanics' Institute, and a regular giver of Penny Readings; and out to Hursley, where he was appointed Honorary Secretary of the Hursley and Winchester branch of the English Church Union, founded in 1860 to further the aims of the Anglo-Catholic party. He had a place in Winchester society, albeit a fairly humble one and not assured, for he had no tenure of office, and was not on the Foundation like the Quiristers in his charge. Then, he submitted a hymn to the Reverend Sir Henry Baker and it was published, after appropriate tinkering, in the first edition of *Hymns Ancient and Modern*. William Whiting's hymn was eventually to be sung all over the world. His hymn can be treated metaphorically, as in the Sacrament of Baptism the child is said to be launched onto 'the waves of this troublesome world', but seamen and lifeboat crews have very much taken it as *their* hymn, and as a prayer for those at sea. When, in the Second World War, Winston Churchill and President Roosevelt met at a secret rendezvous in the North Atlantic, Churchill chose it for singing at Divisions aboard *H.M.S. Prince of Wales* as the most appropriate of all†:

---

* This functionary was there to care for the boys' clothes, later altered in colour from chocolate brown to grey, and their health. Supposedly she also kept them clean, though how she did it is problematical. In the recollection of Quiristers taught by William Whiting, the boys had clean linen sheets only at the beginning of each half or term, and their daily primitive and probably scanty ablutions were carried out at the crack of dawn in the backyard, where there were three stone sinks filled from a pump, and supplemented on Saturday evenings when the sixteen took it in turn, with infrequent changes of tepid water, to stand in a foot bath and clean themselves 'up to the waist', the other half, presumably, remaining grubby. One of the matron's duties was to oil the boys' hair before they jammed on their top-hats and ran to sing in Chapel on Sundays.

---

† The fate of the *Prince of Wales*, which was sunk with a great loss of life in the following year, emphasised that there was real peril 'on the sea'. The present writer recalls the last stanza of the hymn being always sung in Dover before a company of flat-bottomed landing-craft left the harbour, and, to this day, the tune induces a certain discomfort in some way related to agonies of sea-sickness.

'Eternal Father, strong to save,
   Whose arm doth bind the restless wave,
Who bidd'st the mighty ocean deep
Its own appointed limits keep:
   O hear us when we cry to thee
   For those in peril on the sea.' . . .

Whiting's fame was not instantaneous, but it was enduring. The hymn was even adopted by Britain's old enemy, the French, and a translation appeared in hymnals used in the fleets of France. The continuing refrain was rendered thus:

'Vois nos pleurs, entends nos sanglots,
Pour ceux en péril sur les flots.'

It goes without saying that even this hymn has been mauled by those modern liberal improvers who insist on addressing Almighty God in the plural. In a recently issued Evangelical hymn-book of indifferent quality, *Hymns for Today's Church*, 'thee' is changed to 'you' in every hymn. William Whiting's hymn caused particular trouble because of his persistent refrain 'O hear us when we cry to thee'. This has been altered variously, as follows:

'We cry, O God of majesty'
& 'We cry, O Lord of Galilee'
& 'We cry, O Spirit strong and free'.

And in another even worse modern collection the refrain is totally altered to the banal couplet:

'O hear us when we cry to you
For those who sail the ocean blue'.

What Whiting would have made of these trendy renderings we cannot imagine. He wrote other hymns, but none met with any success. His club foot became more of a handicap as he grew older and heavier, and he became increasingly short-sighted. Frustration and regular pain sent him to the bottle and to laudanum, not sufficient for him to become an addict of either, but it was noticed by his boys. Always severe, he became even more so, and he who had always been so punctual was now late for classes, sometimes failing to turn up altogether. There were compensations. The deaths of the older members of the family left more room for the others. He had

FOR THOSE AT SEA.
"Oh Hear Us When We Cry To Thee,
"For Those In Peril On The Sea."

William Whiting's hymn 'For those in peril on the sea' inspired many a sentimental, best parlour, Victorian oleograph such as this

the pleasure of knowing that his younger son, Bertie, intended to offer himself for Orders. We may be sure that Fanny gave him the respect and attention enjoyed by the heads of Victorian families. In the summer of 1877 he and the Quiristers were the guests of the Headmaster's wife, the Hon. Mrs. Ridding, and taken by steamer on the Solent first to Cowes and then, passing Osborne House where the Queen was in residence, on to Ryde. Soon after he caught an infection and had to take to his bed. He never recovered. Ten months later, exhausted by long illness and pain from an abscess on the hip, he died on the 3rd May, 1878. His widow, Fanny, literally tired to death by all she had to do for him and her family, the Quiristers and the household, died of exhaustion five months later. Their daughter, Mary, taught the Quiristers until alternative arrangements were made. Their son, Billy, emigrated to the States but returned home again to become a Warden of Almshouses. Their son, Bertie, went up to Cambridge and was ordained. A Quirister School was acquired in 1882. The Whitings' old home in College Street was demolished before the First Great War.

★

From the introverted community at Winchester, and that of the undoubtedly stuffy lodgings of the Quiristers, it is a dramatic change to turn to the feudal Devon village of Lew Trenchard with its three hundred odd stone houses, church, and historic manor house, exquisite home of one of the most volatile of Tractarian hymn writers, the Reverend Sabine Baring-Gould, a bouncy, extrovert squarson as different from the solemn William Whiting as a cock bullfinch from a town sparrow. He was born nine years after Whiting and in a very different milieu, grandson of a roaring Admiral, and son of a cavalry officer in India and Devon squire, a man of taste and a Whig, who, unable to abide the Tory port-swilling fox-hunters who were his neighbours, let his beautiful manor house, and set off with his wife and children and a retinue of servants on a perpetual peregrination about the capitals and spas of Europe.

It was against this exotic background that the little Sabine grew up, and he loved it all. By repute he was delicate, and so, beyond assays into a pair of English schools, he had no formal education beyond what his intelligent and roaming parents taught him, until he went up to Clare College, Cambridge, in 1853. Destined, if he survived, to inherit from his father as squire of Lew Trenchard, he filled in his time while waiting for his patrimony by teaching, being ordained, and marrying a gorgeous Yorkshire mill girl half his age

The Reverend Sabine Baring-Gould, squarson, novelist, travel writer and author of 'Widdicombe Fair' and 'Onward Christian soldiers' in the garden of Lew Trenchard Vicarage, 1922 (*Western Morning News*)

who presented him with five sons and nine daughters. He came into his inheritance in 1872, and when his uncle the Rector died, he presented himself to the living of Lew Trenchard and acted thereafter as squarson, an enviable position for an Anglo-Catholic in the days of Parliamentary persecution because he was virtually lord of all he surveyed, spiritual and temporal, and no-one could touch, or attempt to touch, his feudal rights.

He was less Catholic in his practices than Father Neale, but then he was less intellectual in his approach to Catholicity, having a more romantic attraction to mediaevalism and the concept of a continuing Church from the colourful, pre-Reformation days. But he was scarcely less eccentric than the flamboyant Father Faber. His parish visiting, like most things about him, was unusual. He would send advance notice so that his people were never taken unawares, and was driven round by his coachman in a large carriage. Having read to and said prayers with certain parishioners, he returned home to the Manor library to write for the rest of the day at a standing desk. For pleasure he collected, and if necessary bowdlerised, old songs of Devon and Cornwall, taking them down from the lips of the men who sang them, and thus anticipating the folk song 'rescue operation' of Cecil Sharpe and others. His best-loved song was 'Widdicombe Fair', with its glorious chorus, and beyond this he was a compulsive writer with many subjects. An indefatigable hagiographer, he wrote *The Lives of the Saints* in sixteen huge volumes; then *The Lives of the British Saints*. As a critical scholar he wrote *The Origin and Development of Religious Belief*, an history of the Evangelical Revival, which is rather unsatisfactory because he was so essentially a romantic Anglo-Catholic. His many excellent travel books were based on the recollections of his childhood, and later, on fresh progresses round Europe made in state with a large company. His skill at spinning yarns compelled him to write novels with exotic names such as *Mehalah,* and *Cheap Jack Zita;* and he spun several yarns in his non-fiction, too, especially in his biography of Parson Hawker of Morwenstowe, as great an eccentric as himself, who founded the Harvest Festival, fished with his parishioners, and was driven from his parish not by the people who loved him, but by protestant zealots who went to law about his supposed Catholic practices and hired thugs to man-handle him physically out of his church and home.

Baring-Gould is only now remembered for his hymns; sacred songs that, like Whiting's 'Eternal Father, strong to save', stretch right across shades of churchmanship and thus have an abiding appeal. 'Through the night of doubt and sorrow' was his own translation from a Danish hymn, *'Igjennem Nat og Traengsel'*.* His originals were untouched by the didactic purpose of advancing Catholicity or Protestantism. They included for example one evening hymn for which he also composed the tune:

> 'Now the day is over,
> Night is drawing nigh,
> Shadows of the evening
> Steal across the sky.' . . .

which has been sung hundreds of times in thousands of churches and chapels. He also wrote a hymn for use at missions, full of joy and zing and catchy enthusiasm – though some say it is in deplorable taste – 'Daily, daily sing the praises', with a melodious refrain:

> 'O, that I had wings of Angels
> Here to spread and heavenward fly;
> I would seek the gates of Sion,
> Far beyond the starry sky!'

His very best, and of this there is no doubt, is the thumping hymn of the Christian Church in which the tramp of soldiers' feet is heard in the rhythm of the verses, and in the tune specially composed for it by Sir Arthur Sullivan.

> 'Onward, Christian soldiers,
> Marching as to war,
> With the Cross of Jesus
> Going on before.
> Christ the royal Master
> Leads against the foe;
> Forward into battle,
> See, his banners go!
>
> Onward, Christian soldiers,
> Marching as to war,
> With the Cross of Jesus
> Going on before.' . . .
>
> 'Like a mighty army
> Moves the Church of God;
> Brothers, we are treading
> Where the Saints have trod;

---

* The original was written by Bernard Severin Ingemann (1789–1862), a Danish Lutheran poet and teacher who had great influence upon the children of his country, second only to that of Hans Christian Andersen. For his seventieth birthday each child in the land contributed the equivalent of a ha'penny for a special present – an exquisite and huge cornucopia made of gold, ornamented with figures from his poetry familiar to them all.

> We are not divided,
>   All one body we,
>   One in hope and doctrine
>   One in charity.
>
> Onward, Christian soldiers . . .'

Sabine Baring-Gould was inexhaustible. He poured out no fewer than one hundred and fifty-nine books, and as for the doubts held by his family that he was too delicate to withstand any sort of formal education and would not last long enough to inherit, he outlived all his own generation, his wife and many of his children, lasting into his ninety-first year. He lived through the First World War, untouched by it, a nineteenth century fly-in-amber, and a Victorian Anglo-Catholic to the last.

★

Whilst it might be prudent, if a little lacking in charity, to be wary of an aggressive golf-player who grows champion dahlias, there can surely be not a trace of harm in a man who loves trouting, and has a fondness for ferns. Such a guileless man was a later Victorian Tractarian, William Walsham How (1825–1897). The Hows were an old Cumberland family, though William's father practised as a solicitor in Shrewsbury, and it was in Shrewsbury that he grew up and was born and was educated at the School under the headmastership of the great Dr. Butler. William's mother died when he was two and a half and his brother even younger. Happily for them their father re-married a lady who turned out to be an endearing stepmother and who presented them with a stepsister.

It was their practice as children to hold church services of their own for which William wrote the hymns. The first of which there is any record was written before he was thirteen and was about the transformation of a butterfly from egg to caterpillar to pupa to imago, being a type of Resurrection. From the beginning he loved fishing, proceeding from bent-pin angling in the Severn, to casting a wet-fly for trout in Welsh streams. He also liked botany. The urban side of him made him take an interest in florists' flowers; that is not the showy cut blooms sold in shops, but the treasure of poorer men, mostly of the artisan class, who formed clubs and societies for the development of chosen specialities, and nurtured them in back yards, on window sills, in boxes, and on scraps of land, raising new cultivars to show in competitions. These florists were poor but eager, and had a strict idea of what they called the 'properties' of a flower. Amongst them were carnations, pinks, provins roses, the hyacinth, tulip, auricula, ranunculus, polyanthus, striped antirrhinum, candytuft, anemone, and pansy. William was a pansy-fancier, being especially fond of the clearly-marked forms, and he and his fellows at school had a small horticultural society which had regular shows. The country side of William made him especially fond of ferns. In the Victorian era fern-growing was ubiquitous, and 'botany bens', as they were called, went from door to door selling one or other of what became a great treasury of fern forms, a treasure which was lost when the fashion changed and scores of Victorian fern forms disappeared. William always had a fernery, but the ferns he liked best were those he found out in the wild and collected for himself.

Both as a fisherman and as a botanist he was rarely without a dog or two to keep him company, usually spaniels. His boyhood was happy. He was as short as Isaac Watts, barely five feet, but better 'graced with advantages of appearance', had a sense of fun and great charm, and easily made friends. He loved hunting and dancing and did both well. He was also well-schooled and showed promise of being a scholar when in 1841 he went up to Wadham College in Oxford to read law. The Tractarian wind was just blowing up to gale force. Inevitably he succumbed to its attractions, and was far more interested in divinity than law.

In the summer of 1842 he joined a reading-party in Ireland led by Arthur Hugh Clough, a don from the Tractarian nerve-centre, Oriel College, though it is questionable whether or not he was influenced by the twenty-three year old tutor, himself a vacillator between the pounding of the Broad Church Dr. Arnold – his former headmaster at Rugby – and the battering of the Puseyite W. G. 'Ideal' Ward.* Clough was young enough not to take life too seriously. He dealt with one member of the party who was over-fancy about the food and drink provided and incessantly complained, by driving a flock of geese from the roadway into the young man's bedroom. As William Walsham How noted in his diary: 'They made a TERRIBLE mess.' He also noted finding drifts of *Pteris Aquilina* on the hillsides, ferns

---

* Ward was a passionate persuader and, apparently, was 'emotionally attached' to Clough, which might account for the fact that he did wean him from Arnold's liberalism but not quite into Roman Catholicism, which he himself embraced soon after Newman and, for publishing a Romanist treatise, was deprived of his Oxford degree. Clough wrote poetry, being remembered as the author of an hexameter poem, described as 'A Long-vacation Pastoral', which told of the hopeless love of an Oxford radical on a reading-party for the daughter of a farmer in the Scottish Highlands, with the Gothick title of *The Bothie of Tober-na-Vuolich*, and of a number of passable lyrics, amongst them 'Say not, the struggle naught availeth'. He remained a Fellow of Oriel until 1848, when he went abroad for a time, then took up a teaching post in London, and died at the early age of forty-two, on holiday in Florence. His sister, Jemima Clough, was a feminist who founded Newnham College for Women in Cambridge.

'considerably taller than I am!'

The young undergraduate took home to Shrewsbury a good collection of botanical specimens and the news that he was going to seek ordination. His practical father at once set about finding a suitable living for him in the area, and bought the next presentation to a rectory, so that, when it next fell vacant, his son could be approached and provided for. Clough continued to dither in his religion, but How was far more definite. In doctrine he was always a firm Tractarian. After further reading-parties in Dresden, where the beauty of the city proved a distraction, and at Talyllyn in North Wales, where trouting and fern collecting were equally distracting, he took his degree as a 'petty compounder', having an income of more than £5 a year but less than £300. He was twenty-one. Aware that he could scarcely spend his whole winters hunting and dancing and his whole summers fishing and botanising, he decided to fill in part of his two years before he could be made deacon on a tour of Belgium and Germany; then, with his brother, on a botanical exploration and fishing holiday in Cumberland. He also read divinity for a period at Durham.

In December 1846 he was made deacon and licensed as one of a band of curates at Kidderminster, not far from Shrewsbury. He was deeply affronted by the coarse and sneering attacks on High Churchmen by people like the renegade to the Church of his country, birth, Christening and education, the appropriately-named Baptist Wriothesley Noel, who, according to William How and his fellow curates, had no business at all to write impertinent verses addressed 'To a Youthful Anglo-Catholic' and published in the *Guardian*. Part of this offensive diatribe ran:

> 'By the prayer which in thy heart
> Ne'er consents to take a part:
> By the heaven thou canst not gain;
> By the hell of endless pain:
> Turn thee from thy follies, quick,
> Youthful Anglo-Catholic.'

It was in this climate of inter-party high feeling that How was ordained priest in 1847. Not long afterwards he was offered a curacy in Shrewsbury which would put him in charge of a daughter church. He sought the Bishop of Worcester's permission, for he had not served his full two years' title at Kidderminster, and was licensed by the Bishop of Lichfield to the work in Shrewsbury. He lived at home with his family for three years, attending to his part of the parish, and, as opportunity offered, riding to hounds, botanising, and enjoying the social life of Shrewsbury. For his last year there he had the companionship of Frances Ann Douglas, a clergyman's daughter whom he married in November, 1849. Eighteen months later the living of which his father had bought the presentation fell vacant. It was the parish of Whittington, seventeen miles to the north of Shrewsbury, in the diocese of St. Asaph and in lovely countryside. It was worth £1,000 a year, which was no small figure half-way through the last century.

The young couple went up to examine their future home. The previous Rector had been a strong Evangelical, as was made evident by texts from Scripture painted in huge white letters on the red outer walls of the church and on some of the village cottage walls. A hymn book was in use which had been compiled by the Rector. An unusual couplet met How's eye as he opened the book:

> 'Earth's axis thou placed in position inclined,
> Thus the seasons contrived with benevolent mind.'

The church was unexciting: 'a curiously ugly brick building', the pulpit a square platform on poles, the organ a barrel-organ, the seating hard benches. The Rectory was also unremarkable, save for a fox chained to a kennel beside the front door which, How was told, was carefully shut up when hounds met in the neighbourhood. 'It was very odorous,' he noted, which seemed to set the fox's fate. The house needed extensive repairs to make it tolerably comfortable, and the grounds were a hotchpotch of shrubberies, paths, arbours and grottos, 'more of a thicket than anything', and 'and apparently made for hide-and-seek', but How saw possibilities in the damp wilderness. Five small streams ran through the garden, with an old-fashioned sizeable bath inconveniently situated right outside the dining-room windows. The garden would be excellent for growing ferns.

On September the twenty-third, 1851, William How was Instituted and Inducted as Rector of Whittington by the Bishop of St. Asaph, and the builders moved into the Rectory, while the Rector and his lady and their servants and spaniels went into lodgings to oversee the repairs, and the work required to put the garden in order, and acquaint themselves with the parish. It was fairly large, seven miles across, with outlying farms and cottages and several hamlets. Rector How rode out visiting on a cob, a dog or two at foot. He found his people disposed to be friendly, though there were some oddities among them. One garrulous old woman told him staccato-fashion: 'The old man and me, Sir, never go to bed without saying the

Evening Hymn. Not that I've got any voice left, for I haven't, and as for him, he's like a bee in a bottle, and then he don't humour the tune, for he don't know one from another, and can't remember the words either; so, when he leaves out a word, I puts it in, and when I can't sing I dances, and so we gets through it somehow.' Another irregular worshipper at the Parish Church was the wife of the local Primitive Methodist lay preacher, who explained her sporadic attendance by admitting to the parson she could not abide the Chapel when her husband was preaching, confiding 'I can't abide he!'

William Walsham How found the life of a Shropshire Rector very much to his taste. After a year the barrel-organ was replaced by a choir of seven little boys, clothed by the Rector in Eton collars and blue ties, and sometimes accompanied by the Rector on his flute. He introduced regular and more frequent services and took great care in preparing candidates for Confirmation. His people grew to love him, as they did Mrs. How. She presented him with children, and both were desolated when, on a holiday on the Welsh coast, their elder child, Maynard aged three, had heat-stroke and died. Hard work and play were their anodyne. The Rector gradually gave up riding to hounds, though he brought his sons up to go hunting and encouraged them to do so. There was gardening and cricket and botanising and fishing as well as pastoral visiting and daily services and study and writing devotional books, in addition to preparing sermons. He had only been three years at Whittington when, helped by a colleague, he brought out a compilation of Psalms and Hymns. His own original contributions were very popular. He was also used by his bishop, who appointed him as inspector of schools in 1852, and Rural Dean of Oswestry in 1854. Later he was given an honorary canonry of St. Asaph and after that admitted to the prebendal stall of a place he had never himself pronounced correctly, Llanefydd. He was also Chancellor of St. Asaph Cathedral. All these posts were honorary but How never lacked for money; in fact, after the death of his father in 1862, he could rightly be described as a rich man.

Even beyond the diocese, How became well-known as a Tractarian conductor of retreats and quiet days, and parish missions. At a Church Congress held at Wolverhampton he established himself as Catholic in doctrine and practice, urging more frequent church services and that they be more reverently celebrated, emphasising that ceremonial was desirable but not essential. He had quite sufficient work to do to justify employing curates, sometimes two or even three simultaneously, and even then he could only fit in his commitments by being methodical★ and orderly. His huge pigeon-hole filing system in the Rectory library was a marvel of efficiency. One of the very few things that could vex this normally gentle clergyman into great vexation was the misplacing of a piece of furniture or a book or paper by one of his children or a servant.

In the 1860s and 1870s the Rector of Whittington achieved fame as a hymn-writer. He was one of the three editors of a S.P.C.K. hymn-book for general use entitled *Church Hymns*, which came out in 1871. A second was Shropshire Rector John Ellerton of Hinstock, and the musical editor was Sir Arthur Sullivan. It contained six hundred hymns. Of How's own, the widest known is the grand processional hymn for All Saints' Day, four stanzas of which must find a place in this book:

'For all the Saints who from their labours rest,
Who thee by faith before the world confest,
Thy name, O Jesu, be for ever blest.
        Alleluya!

Thou wast their Rock, their Fortress, and their Might;
Thou, Lord, their Captain in the well-fought fight;
Thou in the darkness drear their one true Light.
        Alleluya!

O may thy soldiers, faithful, true, and bold,
Fight as the Saints who nobly fought of old,
And win, with them, the victor's crown of gold.
        Alleluya!

O blest communion! fellowship divine!
We feebly struggle, they in glory shine;
Yet all are one in thee, for all are thine.
        Alleluya!'

His other great contributions to hymnody include 'We give thee but thine own', 'O Jesu, thou art standing', its theme influenced both by a poem of Jean Ingelow's and by Holman Hunt's picture 'The Light of the World', 'Behold a little Child', and a hymn superb in theology and sentiment written supposedly for children but ideal for

---

★ He was not quite so careful and methodical about his fishing. As long as it was not in Lent, few things gave him greater pleasure than to go to close or distant streams for the evening rise, and he excelled at casting flies round and under obstacles on to tiny pools and narrow runs, and was a very rapid striker, but all too often he lost a hooked fish because he had hurriedly wrapped an old, dry made-up cast or two round his wide-awake hat on leaving home, and the gut snapped.

everyone*:

> 'It is a thing most wonderful,
>   Almost too wonderful to be,
> That God's own Son should come from heaven,
>   And die to save a child like me.'

Besides his hymn and devotional writing, How had a large number of correspondents. Letter writing required such application and diligence that on one occasion he actually found himself on a steamer passing sublime scenery off the west coast of Scotland, and in the ludicrous position of feeling obliged to go down below and write a long description of the grandeur of the scenery, most of which he was missing because he was writing about it. Occasionally the family enjoyed Continental holidays. He also took temporary chaplaincies, once in Rome for four months, later in Cannes. He took Cannes because the cold of Shropshire winters was beginning to affect the health of Mrs. How. For years she had worked very hard as a parochial visitor and gave constant and loyal support to her busy husband, but her chest was not strong and as time passed she found herself less able to withstand the climate at Whittington.

How kept a diary for twenty-six out of his twenty-eight years as a Shropshire Rector. He dutifully recorded work accomplished, the dates of planting out the flower beds, choir and cricket practices, trouting expeditions, botanical finds, and the birth and death of horses and dogs. Occasionally he described exceptional events, such as the death of his son and his own nearness to death by drowning when bathing from the Isle of Man, and his anxieties about Mrs. How's health. But not once did he mention the many offers of preferment he received after 1867, and which he politely refused one by one; the major High Church livings of Brighton and All Saints', Margaret Street, and the important living of Windsor which carried with it appointment as Reader to Queen Victoria; a canonry at Winchester; and no fewer than five colonial bishoprics – Natal, New Zealand, Montreal, Cape Town, and Jamaica. And we may suppose that had it not been for his wife's health he would have happily lived and died Rector of Whittington. He and Mrs. How had made the Rectory the favourite meeting place of a large circle of friends. They had created a beautiful and interesting plantsman's garden from the 'damp wilderness apparently made for hide-and-seek'. Their family had grown up there, the boys hunting with the local hounds, the girls

---

* The tune most usually sung to this excellent hymn is *Herongate*, a clever adaption by R. Vaughan Williams of an English melody used traditionally as the setting for a song about a deserted village and a mad girl, entitled 'Died for Love'.

William Walsham How, the fern-collecting, fishing Children's Bishop

frequently riding out with their father on his parochial visiting, both sons and daughters accompanying him when he went trouting and fern collecting. Whittington was more of a home than any other place could ever be, and it is significant, perhaps, that he chose to be buried there, not in or near his Cathedral, nor in the Cumberland vault of former Hows.

Whatever his private wishes in the matter, Mrs. How's health was of prime importance, and when it was hinted he might be asked to assist as a suffragan to Bishop Jackson, a kindly, hardworking Tractarian Bishop of London, who did nothing to dissuade doubters in the Creeds from leaving the Church, and who vetoed prosecution by Low Churchmen of the ritualists in the diocese,* the work unofficially proposed, which was general episcopal superintendence of the slums of London's East End, was exactly right for William Walsham How. When Lord Beaconsfield, as Disraeli had become, fresh from the glories of negotiation at the Congress of European Plenipotentiaries in Berlin, formally offered him the appointment, it was accepted. He was consecrated bishop in St. Paul's on St. James's Day, 1879 and returned to Whittington for six weeks for the fearsome task of packing up and saying good-bye to all his people and the family's many friends. As a testimonial of their affection, he and Mrs. How were presented with that favourite dining-room centre-piece of all Victorians, a huge épergne, but this was in excellent taste, having been made in 1775. Moreover, it was of solid silver.

Leaving his people and his favourite trout streams and fern garden, the Rector of Whittington went off to become incumbent of a city living, with a population of four-hundred souls, and a substantial income of £2,500 a year, and begin his work as bishop. He was a little consoled by a gift of a greenhouse stocked with ferns in the garden of his new home. Because of an Act of Henry VIII which had not yet been repealed, he had to take one of a number of see titles in abeyance and the nearest to the East End was Bedford. His successor was to be Bishop of Stepney, but it was as Bishop of Bedford that

---

* Not as many priests were prosecuted under the Act as the Evangelical Church Association wished. But a few cases went through, and five clergymen went to prison for their convictions. Evangelical extremists, such as members of the Anti-Puseyite League, did their own cause no good by eventually arousing public sympathy for the priests they persecuted and whom they handled roughly, and at a later period even the Kensitites, followers of John Kensit of the Protestant Truth Society, eventually lost public support by their irreverent policy of interrupting church services and attacking the clergy. The present writer recalls serving a private Mass said by an old hero of the ritualists, Father Lester Pinchard, who had had several rocks hurled at him in dockland, and who, with his eyes raised to heaven, would declare ecstatically; 'Oh, to have been stoned for the Lord, my boy. Oh, to have been stoned for the Lord!'

How plunged into what has been called 'a sort of ecclesiastical Botany Bay' in the autumn of 1879. The slums appalled him. The parochial clergy were overworked and he did all he could to assist them. Wearing a shovel hat, and apron and gaiters, a pectoral cross about his neck, and carrying his robes and broken down pastoral staff in a bag, he walked through the East End, or frequently caught a tram or omnibus. People would enquire who on earth the little gent was. He was gratified when the answer slowly changed from 'That's a bishop' to 'That's *the* Bishop' and finally, to 'That's *our* Bishop'. He was also known as the Children's Bishop because they loved him so. The East Enders took him to their hearts. He was too little to preach comfortably from many pulpits and churchwardens passed from church to church a specially made pulpit dais on which he could stand. His famous hymns, especially 'For all the Saints', were sung repeatedly, in and out of season.

There was a moment of panic amongst the people when the Bishop of London died in 1885, and, to clear the way for a new Bishop, the new prime minister, Lord Salisbury*, correctly offered How a diocese of his own, unprepossessing Manchester. The clergy and churchpeople of the East End were aghast. They need not have been apprehensive. Once he heard that Frederick Temple was to be the new Bishop of London, How, believing all would be well, refused the offer of Manchester. Temple had never held a parish, having been a schoolmaster, and there had been objections to his appointment to the see of Exeter sixteen years before because he was a liberal theologian, but How was confident they would get on and that all would continue as before.

Temple had scarcely arrived in London before he sent a list of confirmations for his suffragan to take in all parts of the diocese. How wrote a mild reply to say he would, of course, do all he could to help his new diocesan, but he hoped it would not be necessary to go outside his East End again. He wrote: 'The strength and happiness of my position has been its concentration upon a manageable area.' He had made a horrid miscalculation. By return of post came a schoolmasterly rebuke: 'The main business of a suffragan is, and must be, to aid the principal bishop. It is no doubt far pleasanter to have work all to oneself, but it is not consistent with the due working of the whole. . . . I am bishop of the diocese, and cannot divest myself of what belongs to my office.' How was greatly hurt. An

---

* The third Marquis of Salisbury K.G., as Lord Robert Cecil, had been tutored at Brixham by the writer of 'Abide with me; fast falls the eventide', the Reverend Francis Lyte (*q.v.*).

interview with Bishop Temple did no good. He noted afterwards:
'He never would have consented to my remaining suffragan on such
terms'; and he wrote candidly to a niece: 'It is very hard to bear
patiently, but I must try to do so, it is especially hard just after telling
Lord Salisbury that I have given my heart and life to East London,
and could never leave it.' This unhappy contretemps took place in
March. By bitter irony, Bishop How was presented that Easter with a
huge illuminated address from the clergy of East London in which
they expressed their joy and deep thanksgiving that he had not left
London for Manchester. The address was framed in massive oak
with ivy leaves carved round it, emblematic of the affection with
which they clung to the Bishop.

Though put down, the Bishop did not remain dejected for long.
Through her daughter, Princess Christian of Schleswig-Holstein,
Queen Victoria was interested in the Bishop of Bedford. In her
Golden Jubilee year she had tickets sent to the Hows for a special
service in Westminster Abbey. The tickets being numbered, they
believed seats would be reserved. It turned out they were not.
Somehow a chair was found for the still ailing Mrs. How. The little
Bishop quite happily sat on a step in the gangway. During the further
celebrations in London he went to a fair in the People's Palace and
found himself near enough to the 'Vanishing Lady' to observe her
disappear by 'plopping down through a trap-door'. Only two
months afterwards, when he was enjoying a weekend's fishing as
guest of the new Rector of Whittington, he was brought news that
Mrs. How had unexpectedly died of bronchial asthma at Barmouth,
the very place where their first child had died and been buried. He
dashed to Barmouth. The family slowly assembled there. It was
decided she should be buried at Whittington, their home for so long.

Alone except for a little dog, a black Schipperke, which he often
carried about with him, and still unhappy about his relationship with
Bishop Temple, How returned to London. But neither the Queen
nor Lord Salisbury had forgotten his difficult position. A new
diocese was to be made in Yorkshire, part country, mostly industrial,
based on Wakefield. Bishop How was offered the see. He did not
want to go, writing confidentially to one of his sons about the smoke
and coal-pits and mill chimneys: 'It is dreadful, about the most
unattractive post on the bench, but one must not choose for oneself.'
It is just permissible to believe that How was most strongly
persuaded by Bishop Temple's strong advice that he should accept.
It underlined that his diocesan felt no qualms about losing him.

And so How left his beloved dockland and went off to his northern see. His many thousands of books and his ample pigeonhole file, and even some of his collection of ferns, went with him, and he hoped life would not be too uncongenial. In this he was disappointed. The Yorkshire people were no less warm-hearted en masse than his East Enders, but by disposition most were obstinate, and some were proud. He wished to have his new Palace at Mirfield, partly so that he could be away from the Cathedral city and up on the smoky moors, and also so that he could be near his son who was a parish priest up there. But the city fathers were not having that. They rudely made it plain they considered he ought to live in Wakefield. He agreed. He went south by royal request to baptise the second daughter of Prince and Princess Christian, and returned to be informed his people did not care to have what they called a traipsing bishop, one who was forever away. He designed a house so that it could be partly Bishop's Palace, partly retreat house for ordinands, and an architect who was a friend drew up plans for him, but there were complaints about him employing an architect from a distance and not a good Wakefield man; and when the see house which he called Bishopsgarth was built, he was told plainly by his people that they liked neither the name nor the house. This was two years after he had been enthroned as Bishop of Wakefield.

He found them very trying, and he loathed the dirt which could foul his hands and his bishop's lawn sleeves and wrist bands in the course of a single service, but he worked hard and wrote a great number of pastoral and devotional books and hymns for special occasions; and his help as a spiritual director and confessor was regularly sought by many of both the laity and the clergy of the diocese. His charges to ordinands and his mission sermons were deeply appreciated, as was his pastoral work with the mill-hands and especially the younger ones. He founded a boys' home and invited Princess Christian to open it. She accepted and stayed at Bishopsgarth, and his obstinate and complaining people, thrilled by the royal visit, promptly ceased their complaining. Characteristically their bishop at once forgave and forgot their surly treatment, and gradually the people of Wakefield came to have a grudging admiration for the little bishop who so often walked the dirty streets. Occasionally he was treated 'as a favour' to a rendering of one of his own hymns. He accepted the compliment in his usual courteous way.

He had been only a short time at Wakefield when the Prime Minister offered him something infinitely more attractive; the prince-bishopric of Durham. It would have taken him back to a place he knew, where he had read divinity, where, in fact, he had met his wife, and the life of a Bishop of Durham at Auckland Castle with a seat in the House of Lords was as different from plodding in smoky Wakefield as anyone could have imagined. Yet, only two days after he received Lord Salisbury's offer, he politely refused it. Few could understand why. The move would have cut him off from what he admitted in writing were 'the disagreeables and difficulties' with which he had been surrounded, but he was determined not to leave for the wrong reasons, which he considered running away, and determined, too, to do what he could for Wakefield. He entered into correspondence with the Community of the Resurrection, which had been founded by Bishop Gore at Pusey House and which planned to move into the north country, assuring them of a welcome in his diocese, and though he did not live to see them arrive, he arranged for them to go to Mirfield and the very site where he had personally wished to live as Bishop.

His last few years were a running down. From 1892, when he painfully sprained his ankle and instep on a trouting holiday, had to leap from a carriage when the horse bolted and scoured his knees and sprained his wrist, and tumbled down a flight of steps at the Deanery in Edinburgh, he was never quite the same. The irregular hours at which he ate in Yorkshire began to impair his digestion. High tea with a country parson one day, and waiting up for dinner at ten o'clock after a Confirmation on the day following, was not good for an ageing man. He began to suffer palpitations and giddiness.

1897 was the year of the Queen's Diamond Jubilee. Sir Arthur Sullivan, all collaboration with W. S. Gilbert behind him, with a first revival of *The Yeomen of the Guard* being played at the Savoy Theatre that summer, was asked to compose a hymn for singing in St. George's Windsor on Accession Day itself, 20th June, and to be sung at 11 o'clock in the morning in all places of worship throughout the Empire. 'My career Sir is nearer its end than its commencement', Sullivan wrote to the Prince of Wales, and he dreamed of producing a second national anthem to be sung 'by solo, by chorus, played by military bands, at theatres, at music halls, meetings of every description, and on the march'. Alfred Austin, the most awful of Poets Laureate, failed to come up to scratch, and his hymn was refused. The Queen proposed that the Bishop of Wakefield be asked and the Prince of Wales wrote to him.

Within three days of receiving the request, Bishop How returned the completed manuscript to the Prince and it was set to music by Sullivan. On the 20th June the Queen noted in her Journal that the hymn had been sung before her and her family and household at a special Service, and that Sullivan's tune was 'pretty and appropriate'*. She liked the Bishop's words, but despite his scrupulous care to differentiate the two, people found it difficult to separate the Deity from the monarchy when they sang the hymn, and, though it far outclassed the offering of the Poet Laureate, it was not up to Bishop How's usual standard. He offended touchy Scots by referring to 'England's flag' instead of 'Britain's flag', and received abusive letters from Scotland, though none from Wales or Ireland or any other part of the huge British Empire. He was invited to go to stand on the steps of St. Paul's with the other bishops on the 22nd June, the day of the Queen's Jubilee drive through London, but he declined. He also failed to put in an appearance at the Lambeth Conference of Bishops and the reception given them by the Queen two days after the drive to St. Paul's, an occasion which caused her to confide in one of her ladies; 'A very ugly party. I do not like bishops.' The Queen had a robust view and she preferred the man to the office and described the absent Bishop How in her Journal as 'a most charming and excellent man'. Unaware of his monarch's high opinion, and feeling the heat as never in his life before, the Bishop remained in his diocese to join in the celebrations there.

Exactly a month later, on the 22nd July, he was in London preparing for a family holiday in Ireland. The heat had quite bowled him over, he wrote from the Athenaeum, and one sheet as a bed covering was more than sufficient. He had taken a large fishing lodge in co. Mayo not far from Killary Harbour near the Mountains of Connemara, which, in rain or less common shine, was exquisite countryside and conveniently close to the Dhulough. There he planned to meet as many of his large family as were able to join him and fish the waters of the lough. Trouting had taken him to many places beyond the streams he fished as a boy, twice to Norway†, and once to the Ardennes, and to Scotland where his skill as a sharp striker told against him in salmon fishing, but in his declining years he liked nowhere better than Connemara, that most drenched part of the rain-soaked West of Ireland.

The Bishop went from London by train and took ship to Dublin where he slept and continued his journey by express to Galway and

---

* The 'second national anthem' at which Sullivan had aimed was to be published three years afterwards, 'Land of Hope and Glory', written by A. C. Benson and set to music by Edward Elgar.

---

† On one of these two expeditions he caught a huge basket of fish and simultaneously found ferns. 'Fancy,' he wrote, 'my accidentally leaning my rod against a rock and then finding it almost touching a beautiful clump of the rare Woodsia fern.'

thence by the light railway that ran to Clifden, leaving the train at the closest point to Killary Harbour. For the remaining 14½ miles he took an Irish car through Joyce's Country to the head of one of those many dog's tooth inlets which jag the western coast, a superb creek of deep seawater, nine miles long and a mile wide, with precipitous mountains on either side. Killary Harbour, on the north side, is in a setting of grandeur as sublime as any in the British Isles. The Bishop safely arrived there with Skipper, his latest black Schipperke, and abundant valises, trunks, creels, baskets, rods and walking sticks; the symbolic trouting cast wrapped round his wide-awake hat. Quite a number of his family met him. They were concerned by his pallid, worn-out countenance, but though tired he was obviously determined to enjoy himself as much as ever. It proved to be impossible. He had only one day's trouting on the lough. Then he remained in bed, listless and in such a state of collapse that a doctor was summoned. Choleraic attack was diagnosed, the long lowering illness which carried off so many Victorians, and the doctor tried to revive his strength by stimulants and massage. He did not succeed. The family, aware that he was dying, decided to hold a Eucharist. His son Celebrated in the sickroom. Everyone received Communion. After a bout of restless convulsions, the Bishop slowly calmed; and he gave one sigh and died.

In a triumph of organisation considering the distance involved and the eccentricities of Irish transport, the Bishop was buried at Whittington only two days later. At the Convocation of York which met that autumn William Walsham How was described as 'a living voice of sacred song', and it was said 'he could be placed beside Bishop Ken'. Memorials were erected, an addition to Wakefield Cathedral and, at Whittington, a tall cross with a figure of the Good Shepherd carved in relief in the centre and a staff and mitre on the shaft. The Queen sent her Prime Minister's brother, Lord William Cecil, as her representative to the funeral with an exotic wreath, but apart from that, it was an ordinary village affair save for the fact that everyone in the parish was there in addition to a throng of friends. Like John Mason Neale, William Walsham How was honoured by the singing of hymns he himself had written. He would have been the last to claim a place in the Church Triumphant, but it seemed appropriate that they should sing his finest hymn:

'And when the strife is fierce, the warfare long,
Steals on the ear the distant triumph-song,
And hearts are brave again, and arms are strong.
Alleluya!

The golden evening brightens in the west;
Soon, soon to faithful warriors cometh rest:
Sweet is the calm of Paradise the blest.
          Alleluya!'

CHAPTER SIX

SING LOW

DURING the middle and late Victorian era there was a superabundance of hymn-books. One inquiry, conducted by people concerned for the quality of the words and music, revealed that in one small English market town no fewer than thirteen different books were being used in places of worship. Hymns were also published in periodicals and newspapers. They were written in parsonages all over the world and tacked on to the front or the back of sermons. Eventually each Christian denomination thinned out the number of hymn-books and made compilations, subject to revision, which were more or less acceptable to a majority within a group of worshippers, but it was a long, laborious, endless, and thus never wholly successful, enterprise. While it went on, as if to confuse the process of selection, more and more hymns were written. Church and chapel going were fashionable; so was the singing of Services. By the end of the nineteenth century settings had been composed for most parts of the prayer-book. There was a choral version for sailors, not only for use at their Sunday Services, which they called Divisions in the Royal Navy, but also 'During Storms' and 'Before Engaging the Enemy'. There was even a choral version for that small and somewhat intimate Service 'The Churching of Women'. From the large number of hymn writers who were neither Anglo nor Roman Catholic it is difficult to make a representative selection, but it is the aim, in this chapter, to attempt it, because their work was thus more readily accepted by the Broad and Low Church within the Establishment, and within great Chapels of Dissent both in Europe and North America and the mission field, as well as in the splinter chapels, the Bethesdas, Siloams, and Ebenezers of South Wales, and the tambourine and cornet tantara hymnody of the Salvation Army.

Well-finished renderings of German hymns had always been appreciated, particularly since John Wesley's work in that field. Two Victorian ladies were especially skilled at making translations which were accurate in content as well as catching the style of the originals, and at adapting the English to suit the German musical setting. They were almost exact contemporaries, but one, Jane Montgomery Campbell (1817–1878), concentrated chiefly on children's hymns. Born in Paddington, where her father was the Rector of St. James's Parish, Miss Campbell early gave herself to song and to children, teaching singing in her father's parish school. Later she went to live as a maiden lady in the Devon village of Bovey Tracey, on the little river Bovey which runs from Dartmoor to join the river Teign. There she assisted a clergyman in the compilation of two hymnals for children; a *Garland of Songs, or an English Leiderkranz*, and a *Children's Chorale Book*, contributing many translations, among them a shortened version of a peasants' chorus 'Im Anfang war's auf Erden', from a short play by Matthias Claudius written in 1782 about a Harvest Festival in a north German farmhouse. This is the famous harvest hymn:

> 'We plough the fields, and scatter
>   The good seed on the land,★
> But it is fed and watered
>   By God's almighty hand;
> He sends the snow in winter,
>   The warmth to swell the grain,
> The breezes and the sunshine,
>   And soft refreshing rain:
>
> All good gifts around us
>   Are sent from heaven above,
> Then thank the Lord, O thank the Lord,
>   For all his love.'

Miss Campbell's life was evidently uneventful, though its end was far from ordinary. At the age of sixty-one, driving over Dartmoor, her carriage met with an accident in which she was crushed to death.

★

The other Victorian lady translator from the German, who produced more hymns for general use and whose life was very full,

---

★ Even this hymn, by now part of the fabric of rural society in Britain, has been 'improved' by an Archdeacon in the exceedingly rural diocese of Hereford in order to make it 'relevant'. Some unfortunate country celebrants of the Harvest Festival have found themselves obliged to sing, instead of the old familiar lines, the following couplet

> 'The tractors and the combines,
>   They cultivate the land.'

was Miss Catherine Winkworth (1827–1878). She was one of four sisters, the eldest Susanna, always called Sukie, seven years older, having a great influence on her intellectual development. On their father's side they were the grand-daughters of a Low Church parson who had attended the very desperate Colonel Despard to his death on the scaffold for making an attempt on the life of George III; on their mother's side, they were the grand-daughters of a man of Kent who was cut out of his father's will for becoming a Dissenter, but who had the enterprise to start and develop a village school which he sold to buy a parcel of waste woodland and then cleared it, and planted a hop garden. So there was Evangelical piety on both sides of the family. There was also a great deal of money in the background. The Kentish grandpapa had so deep a love for the countryside, with a corresponding deep mistrust of London, that he gave his daughter who became Mrs. Winkworth a far larger dowry than any of her sisters, to enable her to face what he called 'that big black ant-hill'.

To begin with, Mr. Winkworth worked as a Civil Servant, for the very good reason that this would give him sufficient leisure to do what he really wanted, that is, draw and paint and tramp for miles all over London. It hardly seemed in character with his decision to bring up his daughters as Calvinistic Evangelicals with their noses profitably in the Bible and Prayer Book and at the grindstone of learning, with no story book or any sort of worldly treats, and no ordinary pleasure beyond what they dreamt up for themselves; yet, when required to lay aside sketch pad and palette and take over a family business, he too obeyed his Puritan conscience. Quite soon he was a well-to-do silk merchant, who decided in 1829 to do even better up in the north, and moved his family from London to sooty Manchester. He and Mrs. Winkworth went to make a home while their children were left in London under supervision, regarding the move with apprehension. They need not have done so. Mrs. Winkworth agreed with her husband that their daughters needed the best teachers in the schoolroom, so that they could quickly come to enjoy learning for learning's sake. Mr. Winkworth attempted to supervise their drawing and painting and appreciation of art, but he lacked sufficient time. As to his personal supervision of their exercise, they could neither keep up with their energetic papa on his walks nor go so far, and the actual supervision was left to a puffing governess. Mrs. Winkworth took charge of their sewing, music, deportment, and other lady-like accomplishments.

In the schoolroom they were exceedingly fortunate in the composition of their curriculum and in the quality of their tutors. A

Mr. Wallis came in to teach them mathematics, astronomy, geography and geology, and general scientific studies. Their preceptor in history, composition, German and chemistry, who was also prepared to assist Mrs. Winkworth with music, was a youngish Unitarian minister, Mr. William Gaskell, who had part charge of the Cross Street Chapel in Manchester and was a distinguished teacher. Few girls of their class and generation were so fortunate. Their fortune increased in 1832 when their adored Mr. Gaskell married a very beautiful and very talented young lady, who had French and Italian as well as Latin and a taste for literature, Elizabeth Cleghorn Stevenson. When Miss Stevenson became Mrs. Gaskell, Catherine Winkworth was just into the schoolroom. The disparity in their ages did not prevent them from becoming literary confidantes and enjoying a lifelong friendship.

In 1841 disaster struck the Winkworths' home. Mrs. Winkworth, preparing for an evening reception, in some way strained herself. She collapsed with pain. Physicians diagnosed internal injury, but they could not save her. Within four days she was dead. The Gaskells came in to give what comfort they could. The bereaved Mr. Winkworth agreed that his eldest daughter, Sukie, should superintend the schoolroom under the Reverend Mr. Gaskell and that the next eldest daughter should rule as housekeeper. Four years passed. Italian had been added to the German and French learnt by all the girls. Sukie and Catherine were accomplished linguists, especially in German. A lady of their acquaintance who had an admiration for Lord Byron's works, buying and memorising by heart everything that he wrote, surprised but pleased them by becoming their stepmother in 1845. After the wedding it was arranged that Sukie and Catherine should go to Dresden, the exquisite capital of Saxony, staying with an aunt who temporarily resided there attempting to educate her daughters. With aunt as chaperone, the twenty-five year old Sukie and her eighteen year old sister would have opportunities of meeting personable Germans and of reading and talking the language, and of visiting the famous porcelain and picture galleries and the theatre.

Letters passed between Dresden and Manchester. Poor Mrs. Gaskell lost her only son through scarlet fever. Her husband begged her write away her grief and she began work on *Mary Barton, a tale of Manchester Life*. She was in the process of composition and already feeling better for it, when Sukie and Catherine Winkworth returned from Dresden, and there was an excited reunion. Both young women had an excellent command of German. The family and the Gaskells and another Unitarian friend, James Martineau, professor of Mental and Moral Philosophy at Manchester New College, discussed how best their talents could be employed. Sukie, especially, declared she had entered the *Sturm und Drang Periode* and was determined to be useful.

Deep in her social novel, Mrs. Gaskell suggested they visit Mr. Martineau's famous sister, Harriet Martineau, another social novelist who had recently settled in Ambleside. The two Miss Winkworths set off for a long visit to the Lake District, where Catherine had the fortune to meet Wordsworth, though for some reason Sukie did not. The sisters were both fascinated but a little overawed by the famous Miss Martineau, who had had a wretched childhood, believing herself ugly and unloved, and dogged with ill health which deprived her of her faculty of taste and smell – she claimed that only once in her life did she sense the taste of roast mutton and found it delicious – and with increasing deafness; and in her twenties, was battered by misfortunes, the early death of her father and dearly loved brother; engagement to a man named Worthington who went off his head and died; and the collapse of the family business, which obliged all her sisters to go out and work as governesses. By this time she was obliged to make use of a tortoise-shell ear-trumpet and teaching was out of the question. And so she wrote – poetry, translations, essays, stories, history, and, through her blending of fiction with economics, became a literary celebrity. She continued to enjoy indifferent health but travelled in Ireland, Egypt, Palestine, North America, and Italy before collapsing into bed and writing *Life in a Sickroom*. She then took up and practised mesmerism, accepted a pension, gave up religion altogether, became an ardent feminist, and resolved to live in the north. When the Winkworth sisters made her acquaintance she had been incapable of any exertion for three years, and yet, in addition to writing and entertaining, she ran a small Lakeland farm 'with the help of a labourer imported from Norfolk'. Though she had abandoned formal religion, and they could not fail to marvel at her ardent feminism, Miss Martineau greatly attracted Sukie and Catherine because of her acquaintance with so many interesting literary people; Hallam, Sydney Smith, Milman, Malthus, Sam Rogers, Monckton Milnes, Bulwer, Carlyle, and Lord Chancellor Brougham. Their holiday in the Lakes further stimulated their need to use their command of German and write.

The amount of exercise they took – walking great distances and riding – eventually affected Catherine who was less strong than her

𝕷𝖞𝖗𝖆 𝕲𝖊𝖗𝖒𝖆𝖓𝖎𝖈𝖆.　　145

PRAISE AND THANKSGIVING.

I.

𝕿𝖍𝖊 𝕮𝖍𝖔𝖗𝖚𝖘 𝖔𝖋 𝕲𝖔𝖉'𝖘 𝕿𝖍𝖆𝖓𝖐𝖋𝖚𝖑 𝕮𝖍𝖎𝖑𝖉𝖗𝖊𝖓.

OW thank we all our God,
　With heart and hands and voices,
　　Who wondrous things hath done,
　In Whom His world rejoices;
Who from our mother's arms
Hath blefs'd us on our way
.With countlefs gifts of love,
And ftill is ours to-day.

Oh may this bounteous God
Through all our life be near us,
　With ever joyful hearts
And blefsed peace to cheer us;
　And keep us in His grace,
　　And guide us when perplex'd,
　And free us from all ills
　　In this world and the next.

All praife and thanks to God
The Father, now be given,
　The Son, and Him who reigns
With them in higheft heaven,
　The One eternal God,
　　Whom earth and heaven adore,
　For thus it was, is now,
　　And fhall be evermore!
　　　　MARTIN RINCKART. 1636.

(top left) Catherine Winkworth, a bluestocking 'of a *heavenly* blue'; (top right) her sister Susanna; (bottom) an extract from *Lyra Germanica*

elder sister. At the end of 1847 she began to suffer an undiagnosed malaise which, while it did nothing to upset her intellectual power, seemed to aggravate every pain in her body to an acute pitch. She was informed it might well have been caused through over-exertion. Energetic walking was prohibited.

Her greatest comfort at this time and for long afterwards was Mrs. Gaskell. Her novel *Mary Barton* was published anonymously, but it raised such an electric storm from admirers, led by Carlyle, Dickens and Thackeray, and from traducers who resented her attack on the vested interests of cotton manufacturers, led by the *Manchester Guardian*, that she acknowledged authorship. Generously she involved the young Miss Winkworths in her success by introducing them to a variety of interesting and stimulating people. Their sister Emily became engaged to a Mr. Shaen, an intimate of Mazzini and his compatriots, and they became involved in Italian politics. Though never well, Catherine was always on the edge of Emily's exciting circle of Italian patriots in London.

Through Mrs. Gaskell Sukie was introduced to Christian Bunsen, a Prussian Ambassador to the Court of St. James's at the difficult time of the 1848 troubles, formerly secretary of Barthold Georg Niebuhr, diplomat and inaugurator of the method of source criticism in history, and state historiographer of Prussia. She so impressed him that the Baron, as he was to become later, made her his supernumerary secretary in Bonn, and later persuaded her to translate the life of Niebuhr. Her life's work was planned and assured and she did it very well, but though she was to outlive her delicate young sister and protégée Catherine, she never outclassed her as a translator. Through Mrs. Gaskell Catherine also met Bunsen, who urged her to translate the great German *chorales*, and, too, a large number of distinguished writers.

Their father, Mr. Winkworth, took one summer a cottage at Alderley Edge, in lovely country about fifteen miles from Manchester, with a superb view over the Cheshire Plain. He decided to build a house there and part of his grown family moved into a new house in 1850. Catherine found the place greatly to her liking and her health somewhat improved. She read widely; Mill and the Christian

Socialist Canon Charles Kingsley*, and worked, at Baron Bunsen's suggestion, translating Perthe's *Leben*, only to find she was just beaten at the post by another translator who was working with Perthe's sanction.

In December 1853 Sukie returned from translating in Germany and waltzing with the Crown Prince Frederick† and busied herself at sister Emily's house in London with a concourse of eminent writers and divines. Emily left her temporarily in charge and went to Alderley Edge where Catherine and Mrs. Gaskell were hobnobbing with Charlotte Brontë, at that time trembling on the edge of marriage with her father's curate. Miss Brontë confided in Catherine that 'I cannot conceal from myself that he is *not* intellectual; there are many places into which he will not follow me intellectually'. She also confided that she wondered how much her intended would 'take his share of small economies and appreciate her self-denial'. It did not seem a very promising marriage. Catherine concluded that she guessed Miss Brontë's love for the Belgian schoolmaster had been her only one; but she was not sure, and nor was Mrs. Gaskell. Only a month after her marriage to the curate, Charlotte Brontë, or Nicholls as she had become, wrote to Catherine Winkworth from Ireland: 'My husband is not a poet or a poetical man. . . . So far he is good in his way. . . . I will try with God's help to be indulgent to him whenever indulgence is needed.' She did not need to try for long as she died in childbirth nine months afterwards.

Possibly the influence of Miss Martineau and Charlotte Brontë, the literary milieu in which she lived, and her own feeble health, disinclined Catherine Winkworth from matrimony herself, though she was flattered when, in Heidelberg, a young man of thirtyish, Baron von Ruggenbach, who was Prime Minister of Baden and had dark hair and flashing eyes, took a great fancy to her. She decided marriage was not for her. The surrounding German matrons,

---

* A rebel from early youth, when he described his clergyman father's lady district visitors as 'splay-footed . . . with voices like love-sick parrots', Kingsley became a robust undergraduate who was taught to box by a black prize-fighter, then a country parson who fished and hunted and smoked great quantities of tobacco, and, like Mrs. Gaskell, Miss Martineau, and Disraeli, wrote social novels as well as a study of the seashore, *Glaucus or the Wonders of the Shore*. Appointed Professor of Modern History at Cambridge, where he supervised the Prince of Wales, later Edward VII, and afterwards Canon of Chester, then at Westminster he quarrelled with Newman and admired the controversial Darwin, and wished to emancipate women. A competent poet and author, with a social conscience, he is now best remembered for, perhaps, *Westward Ho*, and *Hereward the Wake*, and certainly for *The Water Babies*.

---

† Afterwards the German Emperor Frederick III, father of Kaiser Bill.

'dressed like untidy servants that quite puzzles one as to their age and condition', must have assisted her decision. She was already known in Germany as a populariser of their great hymns. It was her particular forte to render the solemn, inspiring cadences of German hymnody into memorable, almost unforgettable, translations. She worked on her verse translations with all the craft and attention to detail of Carl Fabergé devising his bibelots from gold and pearls, enamel and precious stones. Two collections were published, *Lyra Germanica* in 1855, most of the translation having been made at a critical and disastrous period of the Crimean War, in which all Winkworths, with their associations, were deeply interested; and in 1858, a *Second Series*. The work was dedicated to Bunsen and excited the admiration of a great number of sapient critics. The Christian Socialist, F. D. Maurice, and Charles Kingsley greatly liked it. So did Mr. Martineau, who had returned to London, and even his increasingly eccentric sister in the Lakes, although, having no religion, her appreciation for the collection was solely literary. Mrs. Gaskell was delighted for her great friend. Bunsen, through Sukie, persuaded 'dear Kate' to think of introducing German tunes, and he urged her to produce *The Chorale Book for England*, a complete hymn book of *Kirkenlied*, hymns for public worship, and *Andachtslied*, hymns for private devotion. She worked on the idea sporadically, as her health permitted, for a long time.

Many of Catherine Winkworth's hymns are sung today. Her greatest, 'Now thank we all our God', was a translation of what might be called the second German national anthem. Another, 'Praise to the Lord, the Almighty, the King of creation', was a translation of the favourite hymn of Baron Bunsen's sovereign, the unbalanced Frederick Wilhelm III of Prussia. Yet another, a translation of the hymn of a Silesian monk Michael Weisse, who followed Luther and edited the first German hymn book, has a firm place as an Easter hymn in more than fourteen major hymn books, and is a majestic paean of joy:

'Christ the Lord is risen again!
Christ hath broken every chain!
Hark, the angels shout for joy,
Singing evermore on high,
    Alleluya!

He who gave for us his life,
Who for us endured the strife,
Is our Paschal Lamb to-day!
We too sing for joy, and say
    Alleluya!'

Catherine Winkworth was suffering from an undiagnosed illness when she rendered these German hymns into fine English. Short in stature, but holding herself well, she had an impressive dignity which made her seem taller and larger. She was much loved, partly because she put on no airs and was at pains to put other people at ease, giving each one the impression that he, and he alone, was the centre of her interest for that moment. She also invited confidences, which increased her own wisdom and thus made her that much more helpful to many different kinds of people who went to her in need. She was considered an out and out bluestocking, but a friend took any possible sting from that by saying it was 'such a *heavenly* blue'. Her sense of humour, though sometimes astringent, was never clouded by sarcasm. She could joke with Sukie about the Academy and Landseer's latest of 'The Queen and Prince Albert looking at some dead game . . . which I liked the least of any I ever saw of his', and comment on her relations resident at Alderley Edge, 'Aunt Selina is always making a servant and Aunt Eliza a doctor of herself –', but there was always a twinkle in her eye. Mrs. Gaskell, faced with a truly extraordinary task of writing the life of the unhappy Charlotte Brontë, which turned out to be her masterpiece, leant much upon her younger friend.

The delicate Catherine suddenly found herself needing a complete rest from literary and political associations, and when Sukie was taken ill and moved to Malvern to recuperate, her sister went with her. Unhappily their roles were quickly reversed and a train of disasters began. Sukie became the nurse, Catherine the patient. They stayed in one set of lodgings for several months, but were obliged to move in May 1860. The new lodgings were damp. Catherine went down with pleurisy, an inflammation of the lungs. It was four months before she had the strength to walk across her sickroom. On the 28th November they heard of the death of their friend Baron Bunsen. Catherine tried to re-settle to the *Chorale Book* but made little progress. Trying to reach Alderley Edge for Christmas, more than a year after they had left home, they were snowed up in Worcester, Catherine developed yet another fever, fell down a stair-case, sprained her ankle, and broke some foot tendons. Eventually they reached home, to find their father deeply anxious about his silk business. In less than two months he was brought home, having had a seizure in a railway carriage. He never recovered.

The slump in the silk industry obliged the family to move to less expensive quarters in Clifton beside Bristol. It meant losing many literary friends. Sickness rampaged through the family. Most of the letters of that period were health bulletins. Despite increasing weakness Catherine took on more and more work. She expressed her philosophy in a letter to a friend: 'You say you suppose that people with weak spines must be content to remain in a mist. The world would be quite out of joint indeed if it was so.' The book made at Bunsen's suggestion, *The Chorale Book for England*, was published with éclat in 1862. Catherine interested herself in promoting higher education for women, being elected on to the council of two girls' schools, and after her father's death in 1865, going with Sukie to Darmstadt, the capital of the Grand Duchy of Hesse, where Queen Victoria's daughter, the Grand Duchess Alice, convened a meeting on Women's Work. They dined at the grand ducal palace and were outraged when an English newspaper misrepresented the conference by saying they supported Women's Rights. Miss Martineau and Miss Brontë might have done; Miss Winkworth and Queen Victoria's daughter did not.

Gradually the sisters ran down. So did their step-mother. Old Mrs. Winkworth was too ill to be left and so they took it in turns to travel abroad. Catherine went to Switzerland in the summer of 1878, ostensibly to assist in looking after yet another ill member of the family, a nephew, who was staying in a villa not far from Geneva. She looked forward to a change if not to the rest she needed. She had neither. On the 1st July, barely a fortnight later, she descended for breakfast, talked as usual and read her letters. Afterwards she walked towards the door, when, without warning, she collapsed, clutching her heart. Half an hour later she was dead.

Besides being ailing martyrs to chronic disorders and illnesses – and, one by one, after Catherine's death, they dropped like autumn leaves from the family tree – the Winkworths were representative of a scholarly and consciously literary and musical world of middle-class piety and a generous open-mindedness about religious controversies.

★

Portraits, some thumb-nail, some more elaborate, must be drawn of other Protestant hymn-writers of the period whose original work enjoyed popularity in its day, and, in some cases, still does.

Adelaide Procter (1825–1864) was a much-read poetess, the demand for her poems thirteen years after her death being in excess of any living writer's except Poet Laureate Lord Tennyson. As a hymn-writer she apparently bridged the unbridgeable; becoming a convert to Roman Catholicism and yet remaining truly catholic in that it is virtually impossible to tell her denomination from the content of her hymns. Indeed her most enduring hymn, 'My God, I thank Thee, who hast made', was written seven years after her conversion to Rome, but appears only in the hymn-books of the Presbyterians and Methodists. She was the daughter of an amiable poet with fairly extravagant tastes, who kept a hunter in London in his youth and took lessons in pugilism from the champion Tom Cribb, and met the cost of them by practising first as a solicitor, then as a barrister and Metropolitan Commissioner in Lunacy, but whose real interests lay in literature. His plays were acted, his songs, described as 'not effluences of potent inspiration', published, and he wrote literary criticism; but it was mingling with the literati – Browning, Swinburne, Carlyle, Byron, Hazlitt, Dickens and company – which gave him the greatest satisfaction.

Of his three sons and three daughters Adelaide was the eldest child and the most like him. Her talents were superior to his and poems flooded from the schoolroom and drawing-room as she grew older. She was first published, pseudonymously and unknown to her family, in 1843. In 1853 she began to contribute to Dickens's *Household Words*, using the pseudonym 'Mary Berwick', because she did not want to curry favour and Dickens was a family friend. Her work appeared regularly and, after more than a year, she had the pleasure of hearing Mr. Dickens recommend to her parents that they read and appreciate Miss Berwick. A day later she confessed all. Her literary career was assured. She published two volumes of verse, and, as single intellectual Victorian ladies often did, she risked her Sovereign's disapproval and interested herself in 'Women's Rights'. In 1861 she edited, and had set up in type entirely by female compositors, a miscellany of prose and verse entitled *Victoria Regia*, receiving contributions from, amongst others, Tennyson, Thackeray, Matthew Arnold, and, up in Ambleside, old Miss Harriet Martineau who was as lively and valetudinarian as ever, but losing her teeth 'at a great rate & shall lose more' – and though no-one took any notice, had decided she was ancient enough to be addressed as 'Mrs' – as well as a poem from Lowell in Civil War-torn America.

Miss Procter had the good fortune to write exactly the songs the public wanted and have them set to exactly the tunes the public wanted. 'Cleansing Fires', 'The Requital', 'The Message', and, above all, 'The Lost Chord' which, put to music by Sir Arthur Sullivan in the anguish of hearing his brother had died, became the best-known ballad of the century. It was whistled by urchins, played on B flat cornets at every street corner, honoured by a special place at the Leeds Festival of Music in 1877 – 'with organ *obligato*' – and even sung to high Society by Mrs. Ronalds, a demi-mondaine whose favours were shared, amongst others, by Queen Victoria's second son, the Duke of Edinburgh; the American millionaire, Leonard Jerome; and the song's composer, Sir Arthur Sullivan. Momentarily forgetting his mother sitting firmly on the throne, the Prince of Wales swore 'I would travel the length of my kingdom to hear Mrs. Ronalds sing "The Lost Chord" '. Society was the more affected when it was heard that their songster, and the writer of sensible, plain hymns, was infected with phthisis. The malady eventually killed her, but, the Victorians being lusty in woe, it increased her sales and her fame. A Low Church bishop commended her hymn 'My God, I thank thee' over fulsomely: 'This most beautiful hymn touches the chord of thankfulness in trial, as perhaps no other hymn does, and is thus most useful for the visitation of the sick.' Such praise of her writing may be exaggerated. Perhaps praise of the beauty of her nature was not. Dickens, who knew her very well, described her as 'Perfectly unselfish, swift to sympathise, and eager to relieve, she wrought at such designs with a flushed earnestness that disregarded season, weather, time of day or night, food, rest'. She tried the cure at Malvern. It was of no help. She took to her bed and, within fifteen months, had succumbed to the tubercle bacillus, and been buried in that Victorian Valhalla Kensal Green cemetery.

★

The same sacrifice of sickness was demanded of other English lady hymn-writers. Eliza Sibbald Alderson (1813–1889) was the sister of Dr. John Bacchus Dykes, the musician and divine who composed a great number of well-known anthems, settings for canticles, and more than three hundred hymn tunes, many remaining in popular use.* It was claimed that Mrs. Alderson had the accomplishment of versifying and that she completed a dozen hymns. One survived. It was asked for by her brother, the Reverend Dr. J. B. Dykes. He wanted to compose a solemn setting for a Good Friday hymn. His sister provided 'And now, beloved Lord, thy soul resigning'. Sung without sentimentality, or used as private devotion, it has considerable merit. It underscored the Victorian pietistic attitude to suffering, and from all accounts Mrs. Alderson suffered enough herself. It would seem her clergyman husband never achieved any

---

* They include *Lux benigna* for Newman's 'Lead kindly light', *Nicaea* for Heber's 'Holy, Holy, Holy!', *Hollingside* for Charles Wesley's 'Jesu, Lover of my soul', and *Melita* for Whiting's 'Eternal Father, strong to save'.

Adelaide Procter, an unselfish poetess, friend of Dickens and author of 'The Lost Chord' (*National Portrait Gallery*)

comfortable preferment. He acted as *locum tenens* when incumbents were absent, until he was appointed Chaplain of the West Riding House of Correction. The grim Chaplain's House in grimy Wakefield was their home for forty-four years, and Mrs. Alderson survived for another thirteen years. It is reported that she passed them in much suffering. It was on the anvil of her personal affliction that she forged her hymn which rings so truly:

> 'O Love! o'er mortal agony victorious,
>   Now is thy triumph! now that Cross shall shine
> To earth's remotest age revered and glorious,
>   Of suffering's deepest mystery the sign.
>
> My Saviour, in mine hour of mortal anguish,
>   When earth grows dim, and round me falls the night,
> O breathe thy peace, as flesh and spirit languish;
>   At that dread eventide let there be light.'

★

Another unfortunate lady hymn writer was also from the north, but from the other side of the Pennine Chain. Jeannette Threlfall (1821–1880) was the daughter of a vintner who married above his station and thus declassed his progeny at a time when such things mattered. But both parents died while Jeanette was still a child and the declassed orphan was taken in by an uncle and aunt. She enjoyed writing poetry, which was just as well for she met with an accident which lamed her, and another accident soon afterwards which made her quite helpless. In this fearful condition she managed to remain cheerful enough to produce poems which were published in periodicals and made up into small collections, with such significant titles as *Leaves from a Retired Home* and *Sunshine and Shadow*. Her life ended in the shade of Westminster Abbey where she was known to the dean and the canons and much admired for her gentle forbearance and her robust faith. Dean Stanley, Canon Farrar, and Bishop Christopher Wordsworth, all men of stature, not only in the close but in the nation, spoke highly of Miss Threlfall, and were moved by her Palm Sunday hymn for children, 'Hosanna, loud hosanna', which, though a trifle sentimental, had, and has, a wide appeal, particularly to Chapel-goers. The fourth stanza gives its measure:

> 'Hosanna in the highest!
>   That ancient song we sing;
> For Christ is our Redeemer,
>   The Lord of heaven our King:

O may we ever praise Him
With heart and life and voice,
And in His blissful presence
Eternally rejoice.'

*

Inevitably clergymen contributed their share, and possibly more than their fair share, of Evangelically inclined hymns. The Reverend Mr. William Bathurst (1796–1877), son of a Bristol M.P., heir to an uncle's estate of Lydney Park, Gloucestershire, and kin to Earl Bathurst at Cirencester, took Holy Orders and was presented by the noble Earl to the valuable Rectory of Barwick-in-Elmet near Leeds. He was a cultured gentleman and published a translation of Virgil's four *Georgics*. He also published *Psalms and Hymns for Public and Private Use*. It included 'O for a faith that will not shrink', which is particularly enjoyed by some hymn-singers, but evidently was an unconscious cri-de-coeur of its unhappy author, who increasingly found himself pressed with doubts, especially about Baptism and the burial of the dead, and whose faith shrank and shrank. Scrupulously he resigned his living, retiring with his doubts to a beautiful house in Darley Dale in Derbyshire, until he succeeded to his estate in Gloucestershire.

*

Another priest-author was the Reverend George Hunt Smyttan, (1822–1870), son of a physician on the Bombay Medical Board, and author of *Thoughts in Verse for the Afflicted, Mission Songs and Ballads* and *Florum Sacra*, and part author of one of the most evocative Lenten hymns:

'Forty days and forty nights
Thou wast fasting in the wild;
Forty days and forty nights
Tempted, and yet undefiled:'

For undisclosed reasons, he also resigned his living in 1859 and travelled for some years. In fact, he was travelling in Europe during the Franco-Prussian War when, as a non-belligerent in that more civilised era of campaigns and battles between professional soldiers, he was perfectly safe, but he died unexpectedly in Frankfurt and, being unidentified, was given a pauper's funeral in a cheap grave. So strange an end could not have gone unmarked. Yet there is no record of the feelings of his friends and family when the facts of his fate eventually became known.

*

The other part-author of Mr. Smyttan's famous hymn was also a clergyman, the Reverend Mr. Francis Pott (1832–1909). He tinkered with the original, pruning here and there, and adding and subtracting for his own publication *Hymns Fitted to the Order of Common Prayer*, and, later, for *Hymns Ancient & Modern*. Where Smyttan stops and Pott starts in 'Forty days and forty nights' is now an academic and rather dull question. The point is, we have the hymn. Mr. Pott published other hymns, rendering a translation of a mediaeval Latin hymn as the familiar Easter hymn 'The strife is o'er, the battle done' and 'Angel voices, ever singing', both of which also appeared in *Hymns Ancient & Modern*. He lived to an old age; but he, too, resigned his living. It was deafness which drove him from Bedfordshire to the draughty village of Speldhurst, near Tunbridge Wells, where he lived in silence for eighteen long years. The fate of poor Mr. Pott, earless in Speldhurst, seems less hard when Beethoven is recalled composing in total silence whilst fighting malignant diseases and terrors of the mind. In any case, as has been clearly shown in the preceding sketches, a great many hymn writers have had to contend with affliction.

★

Here is another, George Matheson (1842–1906), a man blind from the age of eighteen, but who had the will and ability to succeed as scholar, theologian and scientist, Doctor of Divinity and Laws, a Fellow of the Royal Society of Edinburgh, author of learned volumes and one volume of verse entitled *Sacred Songs*. His affliction appeared to make little difference to his career as a minister of a Scots Kirk but there is evidence of a bruised heart when, on a June evening in 1881, only a few hours after the marriage of his sister, a lady for whom he greatly cared and to whom he was engaged told him that she could not marry a blind man. Alone in his manse at Inellan in Argyllshire, and unable to see the paper on which he scribbled, the minister wrote out a hymn which guarantees him a place amongst hymn writers of stature; an unforgettable lament for a lost earthly love, a recognition of the human predicament of sightlessness, and an acknowledgement that divine love is a soothing salve;

> 'O Love that wilt not let me go,
>   I rest my weary soul in thee:
> I give thee back the life I owe,
> That in thine ocean depths its flow
>   May richer, fuller be.

O Light that followest all my way,
   I yield my flickering torch to thee:
My heart restores its borrowed ray,
That in thy sunshine's blaze its day
   May brighter, fairer be.

O Joy that seekest me through pain,
   I cannot close my heart to thee:
I trace the rainbow through the rain,
And feel the promise is not vain
   That morn shall tearless be.

O Cross that liftest up my head,
   I dare not ask to fly from thee:
I lay in dust life's glory dead,
And from the ground there blossoms red
   Life that shall endless be.'

Later, he gave an account of how he came to write the hymn. 'Something had happened to me which was known only to myself, and which caused me the most severe mental suffering. The hymn was the fruit of that suffering. . . . I am quite sure that the whole work was completed in five minutes, and equally sure it never received at my hands any retouching or correction.' This extraordinary feat bred another from the composer, Dr. Albert Lister Peace, who three years later was invited by a committee compiling *The Scottish Hymnal* to set a tune to Matheson's work. Peace recalled that he was in Brodick Manse, Arran, and read through the four stanzas very carefully several times, then 'I wrote the music straight off, and I may say that the ink of the first note was hardly dry when I had finished the tune'.

★

America being America and the land of phenomena, there should be no surprise in discovering that the most prolific hymn writer ever known was a citizen of Southeast, Putnam County New York, nor that she, too, suffered a grave infirmity, being blinded by an incompetent physician at the age of six weeks, thereafter seeing next to nothing and only dimly perceiving any shape or colour, for the rest of her long life; nor that her early predilection for composing verses was actually discouraged by her teachers at the New York Institute for the Blind until a travelling phrenologist read her bumps and declared writing poetry would do her no harm. From that moment the reservoir dam of rhyming burst out in little Fanny Crosby and she gushed a torrent of verses until she died at the age of ninety-four. The Institute for the Blind where she had been a pupil readily accepted her as a teacher. How she found time to produce so many

songs, and teach, and lecture, and attend literary salons, and address
political and army and church notables, as well as both Houses of
Congress not once but several times, and fall in love with one of her
blind pupils and marry him and settle down as a married poetess in
Brooklyn, is past fathoming. But she did it. Correctly we should
speak of her as Mrs. Alexander van Alstyne, but as, later, the
Methodist Episcopal Church honoured her by having, in their
annual calendar of religious events, a 'Fanny Crosby Day', it seems
more appropriate to stick to her maiden name. This prodigy turned
out hundreds of songs, some put together in collections, others
printed on single sheets. She was the authoress of 'The Hazel Dell',
'There's Music in the Air' and 'Rosalie the Prairie Flower', which
were sung all over the world.

Born in 1820, it was not until her middle age and towards the end
of the Civil War, in 1864, that she turned her attention to hymns,
moved either by the fearfulness of the carnage, or, more likely, by
her husband, for Mr. van Alstyne was a musician and a church
organist. Once started, there was no holding her. Music publishers
commissioned her to produce a certain number of hymns a week.
There were days when, as she said, she could not write one hymn.
They were very few, and usually she managed seven or eight a day.
So large was the torrent that her publishers feared the public would
not credit Fanny Crosby with all that she produced. Pseudonyms
were found and used. At the end of her immensely long and eventful
life she had penned between seven and eight thousand hymns,
published under no fewer than two hundred and sixteen
pseudonyms. Her popularity was huge, most probably on account
of the tunes to which her hymns were set, but some have lasted.
About sixty are still sung in American Evangelical churches, and
quite a few in Britain. The Methodists have not lost their relish for
Fanny Crosby's emotional heart-tuggers with refrains such as 'Jesus
keep me near the Cross', 'I am Thine, O Lord', 'I have heard Thy
voice', 'Behold Me standing at the door', and one which was used by
the Evangelists Moody and Sankey to make boozers tremble and
turn them to temperance: 'Rescue the perishing, care for the dying,
snatch them in pity from sin and the grave.' Her famous hymn, 'Safe
in the arms of Jesus', was written in precisely fifteen minutes,
sandwiched between other compositions on the same day, and as it
seems to have an appeal to both High Church and Low is thus unique
and thus possibly worth quoting:

> 'Safe in the arms of Jesus,
>   Safe on his gentle breast,

> There, by his love o'ershadowed,
>   Sweetly my soul shall rest.
> Hark! 'tis the voice of Angels
>   Borne in a song to me,
> Over the fields of glory,
>   Over the jasper sea,
>   *Safe in the arms, &c.'*

But the remainder are undisputedly Evangelical. Her most frequently used hymn today is 'To God be the Glory! great things he hath done!', the strains of which, heard booming out from church, chapel or tabernacle, are as much an Evangelical-detector as 'I'll sing a song to Mary' or 'Faith of our fathers, living still' denote the presence of Catholics. It is the most durable of her millennia of hymns:

> 'To God be the glory! great things He hath done!
> So loved He the world that He gave us His Son;
> Who yielded His life an atonement for sin,
> And opened the Life gate that all may go in.
>
> *Praise the Lord! praise the Lord!*
>   *Let the earth hear His voice!*
> *Praise the Lord! praise the Lord!*
>   *Let the people rejoice!*
> *O, come to the Father, through Jesus the Son:*
> *And give Him the glory! great things He hath done!'*

Exhilarating Fanny Crosby!

★

The Reverend John Ellerton (1826–1893) would undoubtedly have heard of Fanny Crosby. Indeed as a hymn writer himself, as well as a compiler of hymn-books and general expert in hymnody, he could scarcely have missed such a phenomenon, but it is doubtful if he cared for her work. Ellerton was of Yorkshire stock though born in London. He had one brother, eleven years younger than he, which, according to a contemporary commentator, made him 'virtually an only child – a fact which must have materially tended to foster the peculiar shyness and sensitiveness of his temperament', a generalisation about only children so breath-taking it must be suspect. He was educated at several private academies before being sent at the age of twelve to King William's College on the Isle of Man, where he had to live down the fact that his mother aspired to a literary life and had published improving stories, one under the title *How Little Fanny Learned to be Useful*. He probably kept it to himself that he liked poetry and was something of a rhymester, though an older contemporary at the school, Thomas Brown, a Manxman in speech and ways, was also a poet and not a bad one at that. The latter's narrative poems *Betsy Lee* and *Fo'c'sle Yarns* were admired by George Eliot and Browning, which is some testimony of their worth, and he made an excellent parson-schoolmaster, though his career ended dramatically, perishing in the pulpit while preaching to a congregation of petrified public schoolboys. Another, almost exact, contemporary, was Frederick William Farrar, destined to become Master of Marlborough, Chaplain to the Queen, Canon and Archdeacon of Westminster, and Dean of Canterbury, author of the best-selling *Life of Christ* and equally popular story of life at King William's College *Eric, or Little by Little*, a pearl amongst the genre of Victorian school stories to which he added *Julian Home: a Tale of College Life* and *St. Winifred's, or the World of School*.

John Ellerton's genius was to be less heavily rewarded. He left school in 1844 when both his father and his young brother died, and he and his mother moved from London to Ulverston on the Lancashire coast. It was a great and good change. The Lakes were to hand, indeed Coniston Lake and Coniston Old Man were in the parish, which is really a long strip of many miles running south from some of the highest peaks in the Fells to Ulverston, called Ooston by the natives, at the bottom end. In the middle of the nineteenth century it was a handsome market town, used as a winter residence by the local gentry. Lakeland was to be Ellerton's base until he went down from Cambridge and was ordained. At the university he came under the influence of the Christian Socialists F. D. Maurice and Charles Kingsley yet would commit himself to no party within the Church. He was ordained and he and his mother moved to Easebourne in Sussex, then a village, now a suburb and nursery of English polo. In his three years as assistant curate there Ellerton maintained a middle course of churchmanship and took a particular interest in hymns. Later he was a curate at Brighton and involved in a conflict between his Vicar, a rich clergyman of the old school,* and the bigoted and excitable Evangelical incumbent of Trinity Chapel. Life in Brighton was never dull. Ellerton published his first hymnal there, *Hymns for Schools and Bible Classes*.

Nine years after ordination he was offered an incumbency in Cheshire by the Marquis of Crewe; the village of Crewe Green, with a brand new church designed by Sir Gilbert Scott – the only one he designed in brick – and not only care of the farmers and workers on the

---

* His son, the highly eccentric Anglo-Catholic Father Arthur Wagner, dissipated the family fortunes by peppering Brighton with vast churches.

Crewe Estate, but care of the men and boys at the London North-Western Railway works, and also of Lord Crewe himself to whom he was appointed Chaplain. Before he left Brighton he married a young lady from his congregation and, together with his mother, they moved to the industrial north. His mother was to die and be buried at Crewe Green. He himself was to gain a place close to the top of the ranks of hymn-writers during his busy time as parson there.

John Wesley once remarked that the emergence of a new first-class hymn was as rare as that of a comet appearing. John Ellerton was an obvious exception. In 1866, for a festival of parish choirs held at the huge and beautiful church at Nantwich only a few miles away, he wrote the evening hymn 'Saviour again to thy dear name we raise'. Only two years later, and again especially for a choir festival at Nantwich, he wrote a second evening hymn, 'Our day of praise is done'. The years 1870 and 1871 saw a sunburst of hymns all written in Crewe Green, no fewer than twenty-six hymns, originals and translations, all good, some excellent. Amongst them were 'Now the labourer's toils are o'er', sung at most funerals for fifty years; the Passiontide hymn 'Throned upon the awful Tree'; a translation from the Latin Mozarabic rite, 'Sing Alleluia forth in duteous praise'; a translation of the Christian hymn by Caelius Sedulius, 'From east to west, from shore to shore'; and there was the apogee of his work, 'The day thou gavest, Lord, is ended', the favourite of millions of hymn singers, with its associations of the end of a day, of a life, of the immutability of the Church, and the impermanence of earthly

'The day thou gavest, Lord, is ended,
    The darkness falls at thy behest;
To thee our morning hymns ascended,
    Thy praise shall sanctify our rest.

We thank thee that thy Church unsleeping,
    While earth rolls onward into light,
Through all the world her watch is keeping,
    And rests not now by day or night. . . .

The sun that bids us rest is waking
    Our brethren 'neath the western sky,
And hour by hour fresh lips are making
    Thy wondrous doings heard on high.

So be it, Lord; thy throne shall never,
    Like earth's proud empires, pass away;
Thy kingdom stands, and grows for ever,
    Till all thy creatures own thy sway.'

After such an amazing effusion it might be considered reasonable for John Ellerton to have slowed down his hymn-writing. To the contrary. He contributed many to the revised version of *Hymns Ancient and Modern* of 1875 and was invited by the S.P.C.K. to be an editor, with William Walsham How (*q.v.*) and another clergyman, of *Church Hymns*, published in 1871. Compiling information about the hymns and their writers and the composers of the tunes, and selecting hymns which fell within his own rather strict standards, was a laborious task and done in addition to his work as a parish priest.

His busy work at Crewe Green came to an end when he was offered the Rectory of Hinstock in Shropshire in 1872. He did not much like it there. The church was very plain and at that time without a chancel. The Rectory was red-brick and modern and full of pitch-pine. There are stories of him not getting on with his parishioners.

But all the time he was establishing his reputation as a hymnologist, and enjoyed a degree of peace denied him four years later when the Dean and Chapter of St. Paul's offered him the important and busy parish of St. Mary's, Barnes, bordered on three sides by a loop of the Thames, and thus an unhealthy place. Three of his children died there. Toiling with his parochial duties by day and his hymnology by night he was more and more overworked. Appeals for help from clergymen compiling their own hymnals and for information from other hymnologists such as the Reverend John Julian were seldom refused. For example, he gave immense care and attention to a request from the Reverend Prebendary Godfrey Thring, Rector of Hornblotton in Somerset, who put together the *Church of England Hymn-Book*. As a follower, though uncommitted, of Maurice and Kingsley, he interested himself in the poverty of his people, in sewage disposal, water supplies, derelict buildings. It all proved too much. A bout of pleurisy in 1884 almost carried him off; but in effect it saved him. Realising he could not carry on, he resigned the living and took continental chaplaincies and a holiday in Florence until much of his strength returned. By this time William Walsham How was the beloved bishop of the East Londoners. He knew Ellerton's worth, and, hearing of a vacant living in the Essex countryside, he commended him to the patron as 'the best living hymn-writer'.

Ellerton was appointed and took up residence in his new parish of White Roding. Described as 'amid scenery totally devoid of any special interest' and 'difficult for a literary man to tolerate', he and what remained of his family settled in the moated Rectory with a wilderness of a garden, and began the last phase of his life. He was intrigued by his predecessors at White Roding: Rector Budd who

John Ellerton, an overworked hymn-writer and compiler who always had time for others

Evening
[after Service, Sundays or Festivals]

Saviour, again to Thy dear name we raise
With one accord our parting hymn of praise.
We stand to bless Thee ere our worship cease
Then, lowly kneeling, wait Thy word of peace.

Grant us Thy peace through this approaching night;
Turn Thou for us its darkness into light;
From harm and danger keep Thy children free,
For dark and light are both alike to Thee.

Grant us Thy peace upon our homeward way;
With Thee began, with Thee shall end the day:
Guard Thou the lips from sin, the hearts from shame
That in this house have called upon Thy name.

Grant us Thy peace throughout our earthly life,
Our balm in sorrow, and our stay in strife;
Then, when Thy voice shall bid our conflict cease,
Call us, O Lord, to Thine eternal peace.

Amen.

Nantwich Church
1866.

FACSIMILE OF THE MS. OF J. ELLERTON

Facsimile of an 1866 M.S. of Ellerton (*Hymns Ancient and Modern*)

wrote elegant epitaphs of successive wives, and whose eccentricities were still talking points in the parish, and Rector North who, though deprived of sight, had ruled the village through his wife and daughters and had been deeply loved. The village church had a good organ and Rector Ellerton soon organised a choir of men and boys in surplices and girls in white dresses. His hymn writing continued, though at a much slower rate, and he concentrated on his researches into hymnology. He had many correspondents. A citizen from Iowa, claiming to be 'an authority upon hymn matters', invited Ellerton to give information about himself, and received a civil reply. A man called Smith sent from St. Albans a Latin translation of 'The day thou gavest, Lord, is ended':

> 'Jam, Deus, accepit lux a Te praebite finem
> Processit jussa nox tenebrosa Tuo'

– and received courteous thanks. He wrote often to former curates, to Bishop How, to old friends, to the Reverend Dr. Julian, busy on the last stages of compiling his huge *Dictionary of Hymnology* in his Yorkshire vicarage.

In December 1891 he had a slight paralytic stroke. Advised to take a change of air, he left a curate at White Roding and went down to Torquay. That May he had a second stroke, which greatly handicapped him, and he made arrangements to resign his living. Rather tardily, the Church of which he was such an ornament bestowed on him an Honorary Canonry of St. Albans. He did not live to be installed but lay there in his bedroom in Torquay, growing weaker and less conscious each day. That, at any rate, is what his family presumed. The thoughts of a dying man are generally hidden. We know that in his latter years he had taken to referring to his youth, and it is not overfanciful to believe that he might have been doing the same in his illness: recalling the musk roses in the garden at Ulverston (or Ooston) and the cry of the birds on the mud-flats; thinking of his school days with the author of *Eric or Little by Little*; remembering, perhaps the impious battles between High and Low in Brighton, the lads at the Mechanics' Institute of the London North-Western Railway at Crewe, the ugly Rectory at Hinstock, and the crushing overburden of work in Barnes.

Less than half-conscious on his death-bed, he quoted hymn after hymn and not only his own; but when he did die and was buried at Torquay, they gave him a fine funeral set within a Eucharist, which was a little High for someone so determinedly in the middle, and sang six of his own hymns.

Though earnest, sincere, immensely hardworking, loved by his family and few intimate friends, and as a hymn-writer and hymnological scholar close to the top of the tree, there is not much to suggest in what is known of his life that Ellerton ever really enjoyed it. We can but hope that he did.

These few may be accepted as representative of the hymn-writers whose work was acceptable to Victorian Evangelicals from all denominations, and whose hymns have long outlived them. And there remains one, so eminent a hymnist, so precise a theologian, and so diversified in her talents, that she merits a chapter all to herself. And she shall have it.

CHAPTER SEVEN

THE DOYENNE

A HAPPY husband may be indulged if he exaggerates about the qualities of his wife, but the Right Honourable and Most Reverend Primate Archbishop Alexander of Armagh, did not, in fact, exaggerate, when he wrote of his wife, in February 1896, that she was 'in a singular degree the hymnist of the whole English-speaking communion'. Pugnacious disciples of women's liberation will be angered to learn that the good Archbishop did not attribute his wife's powers entirely to herself but to the 'sane and masculine influence' of a certain Dr. Hook.

Of Hook it may be said that he was one of *the* Hooks, all talented progeny of John Hook, Minister of the Tabernacle in Norwich, a conventicle Meeting House, still affectionately known as 'The Cucumber Frame', and from whose loins sprang James, organist at Vauxhall Gardens in its raffish heyday, a dramatist and composer of songs, 'Come, kiss me, dear Dolly' and 'The Lass of Richmond Hill'; then a second James, who wrote the libretto of two of his father's Drury Lane pieces *Jack of Newbury* and *Diamond cut Diamond*, took Holy Orders and married a great friend of the debauched 'Prinny', thereby gathering to himself rich livings in six counties and ending as Dean of Worcester. His son, Walter Hook, contrived to be both angular and plump – the horrid result of turning teetotal – and was another no less successful, but much more deserving, gleaner of preferment, becoming Dean of Chichester in his later years, and refusing the offer of further deaneries of Rochester, Canterbury, St. Paul's, and Winchester. He was the Dr. Hook to whom the Archbishop referred, and Vicar of Leeds at the time his 'sane and masculine influence' enabled Mrs. Alexander to be what her husband claimed. We may judge from a prospect of the doyenne of hymn-writers how much she and how much Dr. Hook may take the credit for her position.

Mrs. Alexander was the second daughter of a Major John Humphreys, a Norfolk gentleman and landed proprietor in Ireland, who had served in the Royal Marines, fought at the Battle of Copenhagen when Nelson's affected blindness saved the day, was wounded in action in the West Indies and was invalided home to Ireland, where he became Brigade Major of the co. Tyrone Yeomanry. The Registry of Deeds in Dublin tells us that he took a house in the then fashionable area of Dublin, Eccles Street. In 1816 he married a Miss Elizabeth Reed, belonging to that strata of society called 'The Gintry' by the original Irish, the Picts and their conquerors with whom they intermarried, the Celts. The old song had it that 'St. Patrick was a gentleman who came of county family'. As wave after wave of invaders or settlers voluntarily or involuntarily came to Ireland, chiefly from England and Scotland, they became known as 'The Anglo-Irish' or 'The Protestant Ascendancy', a caste set apart from the native Irish, very British, but certainly no longer English or Scots. Elizabeth Reed's grandfather had sat in the Irish parliament; her uncle was a soldier and first in the breach at the storming of Savannah in the Revolution; and her brother, Thomas, fought at the Battle of Waterloo in the 12th Lancers and later, as a general, was a force in suppressing the Indian Mutiny.

One of Major Humphreys's principal friends was Lord Aberdeen ('Athenian' Aberdeen, *q.v.*), later Foreign Secretary and Prime Minister. Aberdeen happened to be brother-in-law of the fourth Earl of Wicklow, a considerable land owner; and he recommended his friend Humphreys without reserve, as a most suitable gentleman to look after the Wicklow properties and affairs. Major Humphreys was offered the post of Agent and he accepted. The principal seat of the Earls of Wicklow, Shelton Abbey, in the wooded Vale of Avoca, was then an unpretentious rather isolated house which the Earl was determined to do up in the Gothic manner. The Countess was already acquainted with Mrs. Humphreys and they had many friends and interests in common. The chief, after their respective marriages, both in the year 1816, was the regular delivery of children; Lady Wicklow bearing seven daughters, and Mrs. Humphreys two sons and three daughters.

When her second daughter, and the subject of this sketch, was born in Dublin in 1818, Mrs. Humphreys asked her friend to stand as sponsor. Lady Wicklow gladly agreed and the child received her own Christian names, Cecil Frances; the first a baffling masculine-feminine name, and the second almost so, a curious and perverse practice adopted by many of the Irish. Both sides of her family were military, which probably accounts for Fanny growing into a methodical and painstaking child, generally obedient but certainly with a will of her own. She early developed a passion for words. She would fondle them as many other girls fondled dolls and kittens, amassing them like treasure from the stories told her by her nurse, her mother, and her godmother, and, of course, by the servants, the Irish always liking a tale and desperate to pass it on; and through a great deal of reading. The grown-ups declared she read far too much and tried to ration her literary diet. It made small difference. Authors will out. At a very early age Fanny wrote stories and verses and issued a weekly periodical written in small sewn cahiers in a neat but unformed hand. Mrs. Humphreys had Scots connections whom Fanny visited by sailing packet at a very tender age. She never forgot that first visit. It was a considerable voyage from Dublin to Leith and, on arriving to stay with Drummond and Buchanan relatives, she met the great Sir Walter Scott, who took her on his knee, and spoke kindly to her. It was a memory she treasured for ever.

When Fanny was eleven there was an important change of surroundings. Major Humphreys conceived it would be more convenient to be nearer Shelton Abbey and the family moved south from Dublin to Ballykeane, a fine Georgian house in beautiful countryside of meadows and woods, only six miles from a seaside cove. By this time Shelton Abbey had been 'gothicked'; the front adorned with buttresses and pinnacles, the parapet battlemented, a new wing thrown out, and a 'Prayer Hall' made with stained-glass windows to give it exactly the sort of mediaeval abbey look so much admired by certain of the Protestant Ascendancy. Lord Wicklow's liking for bogus monastic surroundings led, in the end, to trouble, for the unmarried daughters of the house all became Roman Catholic nuns. But this is to anticipate.

The little Humphreyses and the little Howard girls from Shelton Abbey enjoyed an idyllic childhood in the soft countryside of co. Wicklow. There were the Actons, too, at Westaston, two girls and a boy, but they were a non-surviving lot, all the children dying in their 'teens. Fanny made a particular friend of Lady Harriet Howard. They liked the same things, especially reading and writing; though while Harriet was happier with prose composition, Fanny preferred poetry.

As she grew into adolescence Fanny's interests in literature were quickened even more by further visits to Scotland. Her Aunt Anne, a sister of her mother, was married to Thomas Thomson, an eminent advocate in Edinburgh who belonged to a select circle of contributors to the *Edinburgh Review*. He liked Fanny, whom he saw on her regular visits to Edinburgh, having a good opinion of her versifying talent, and introduced her to many of the literati of the time: among them, the old gossip Samuel Rogers, the poetess Agnes Strickland and her sister the historian. The advocate's elder brother was the Reverend John Thomson, a Kirk Minister and a famous landscape painter of the day, whom Fanny often visited. She liked to recall Turner's visit to his fellow artist, examining each canvas with care in complete silence, and making the single comment when he left: 'Very fine frames, Mr. Thomson.' She also recalled a visit of Landseer, who was then on the edge of immense fame as an animal-painter. Her life at home was strictly supervised, Mrs. Humphreys realising the value of learning early the necessity of application, and she insisted her daughters had all the intellectual advantages of her sons. Being herself well-read and of an inquiring mind, she encouraged Fanny's writing skills.

In 1833 Major Humphreys was offered another post, again at the instigation of his friend Lord Aberdeen. The second Marquis of Abercorn, Lord Aberdeen's stepson, had just reached his majority and needed a steward to look after his immense properties. It was a big step to take, but the family took it. Lord Abercorn was nephew of Lady Wicklow and thus cousin of her seven daughters. There was every hope there would be exchanged visits between the Humphreys' family and the Howards of Shelton Abbey. Fanny Humphreys and Lady Harriet were determined to keep in touch and managed to remain close and intimate friends despite the distance between them. Barons Court, the Marquis of Abercorn's seat up in co. Tyrone, was a twice enlarged and altered grand mansion, neo-Classical outside and sumptuous within. The Humphreys's new home, Miltown House, was in an attractive Elizabethan style and not far from Strabane; oak-panelled walls hung with heavy tapestry, well laid out gardens, and several fine fruit trees. As there were fields and woods beyond, and, at the end of the flower garden, a dell where there ran something between a brook and a river, working a flour-mill, before it joined the slow-running River Mourne on its way to the River Foyle, Lough Foyle and the North Channel, there could have been no sense of being anywhere near a town. It was there that Fanny established the firm foundation of her religion, wrote some of her finest hymns, and found the man she married.

Both she and her friend Lady Harriet were greatly impressed by the Catholic revival at Oxford. They were tract readers and had most of Keble's *The Christian Year* off by heart. They found it a richer religion than Irish Protestantism, and more substantial meat for the inquiring appetite. Keble's Assize Sermon which formally began the Oxford Movement was preached in the year the Humphreyses moved north to co. Tyrone. Under this strong influence they did the good works expected of Christian ladies with rather more enthusiasm than some, and they also planned to become tract writers themselves and they successfully collaborated their talents, Lady Harriet writing the prose and Fanny Humphreys the poems, on themes intended to spread High Church principles. They began writing in 1842. By 1848 there were sufficient tracts to make up a book which was published. Before that date Fanny Humphreys had visited her uncle in Winchester, Sir Thomas Reed, and through him had actually met the famous Doctors Keble, Pusey and Manning, besides other leaders of the Movement.

She had also met through her older sister Annie, who was now married, the famous Vicar of Leeds, Dr. Hook. Hook was not considered a sound Catholic by ultramontane Tractarians, but to a certain extent he supported ceremonial, and he certainly supported the setting up of the first nunnery, and was the very first to preach the unbroken continuity from the Upper Room to the nineteenth century Church of England. He certainly impressed Miss Fanny Humphreys, though it is hardly to be wondered at, considering he was so forceful a preacher that he rebuilt his parish church for a congregation of four thousand and held them spellbound with his orations. She begged him to glance over her verses and suggest alterations. The result was her first book of sacred poems, *Verses for Holy Seasons*, edited and with a preface written by Dr. Hook. Published in 1846, like the first offerings of most poets there were veins of gold in the general dross. Dr. Hook's steadying influence protected Fanny from the more flamboyant side of Anglo-Catholicism, though her own reserve would have protected her just as much.

Then there was the restraining influence of the Rector of Camus-Juxta-Mourne, the official title of the incumbent of the rich living of Strabane, whom she could not help herself admiring despite his deep Calvinism. The Reverend James Smith was romantically appealing, a man who had chosen the pulpit rather than the boards, though his longings to have been a tragedy actor were never quite stifled and gave a thespian quality to some of his thunderous denunciations. His flocks were fascinated as he lambasted sinners with devastating eloquence. Fanny later told one of her children that the Rector's orations had been so thrilling his son was asked: 'Will ye no set your Reverend Da to give the hearers a tarin' before Christmas?'

When Harriet Howard of Shelton Abbey died, Fanny lost the first love of her youth. Not long after, and there may have been a connecting link, it is believed she lost her heart to a young clergyman in the Church of Ireland, four years older than she, who was a religious and philosophical writer of great force, and already called the Burke of Anglican theology. Appointed first Professor in Moral Theology in Trinity College Dublin, the Reverend William Archer Butler was nominated by the University to a living in co. Donegal, in 1837 when Fanny was eighteen. His Rectory was not far from Strabane and he found it convenient to call often at Milton House. At this distance in time, and after such a shattering of the old society, it is not easy to see the lives of the Victorian leisured classes at all clearly. We know how they dressed. We know what they ate. We know that they were comfortably cared for. We know about their manners. We know that they visited each other with great regularity and for long periods of time. We know that, somehow, they managed to find the energy and the occasion to achieve an astonishing amount; far more than seems possible today. Yet, in many ways, they remain inscrutable. All that is known of the affection Fanny had for William Archer Butler is that it was ardent, though decently restrained, most probably returned, and that it was cut off by his untimely death from fever in 1848.

That broken-hearted year saw the publication of her greatest literary triumph: *Hymns for Little Children*, with a kindly Preface written by no less a figure than John Keble. It rightly caused a storm, because no hymn-writer before or since has included between the covers of a single volume such extraordinary successes. Dr. Julian in his *Dictionary of Hymnology* commented on the contents of the book: 'They remain unequalled and unapproachable.' Inspired, perhaps, by her lost loves, certainly by her deep personal piety born from the teaching of Dr. Keble and Dr. Hook and the Gospel message of the local Rector, and by her feeling for a place and the lessons it can teach, she produced verses of high quality which are such models of Christian teaching that they are like crystallised sermons of simplicity. She had a habit of writing a hymn for a particular person, or a particular event, with a particular idea in mind. She was probably astonished by the ready acceptance of her verses by the broad stream of Christians everywhere, who used them constantly. It was an astonishing feat, especially considering the fierce antagonisms of Christians at the time; well demonstrated by the prayer of a Nonconformist minister who hated Disraeli because of his opposition to the claims of Dissent, and uttered with passion in his chapel: 'Kill this man, O Lord, kill him. *We* cannot kill without being hanged ourselves, but thou canst kill him.' Fanny's hymns were binding rather than divisive. Fourteen of the poems were written with the express purpose of explaining parts of the Apostles' Creed. Three of them are ageless. The amazing fact of the Incarnation through the Blessed Virgin is taught perfectly adequately by 'Once in royal David's city'. The doctrine of the Atonement is taught equally clearly by 'There is a green hill far away', a tour de force in compressed theology. And the marvels of creation, 'Maker of heaven and earth', are memorably illustrated by –

> 'All things bright and beautiful,
> All creatures great and small,
> All things wise and wonderful,
> The Lord God made them all.'

There has been much speculation as to the places Fanny had in mind when she wrote about the 'green hill'. Most probably it was Derry, the cathedral city of the diocese. Less likely is the suggestion that it was one of the two conical mountains, Bessy Bell or Mary Gray, which are to the south of Strabane, and are named for 'two bonnie sisters' of a Scotch ballad who caught the plague from their lover and died in 1645.

The site where 'All things bright and beautiful' was written is undoubtedly Markree Castle, a gigantic house 'gothicked' in 1802 by the architect Francis Johnston by the addition of a tower, battlements, and other features, and enlarged to twice its original size. The seat then and now of the Coopers of Markree, it is situated on the Ushwin River at Collooney in Sligo. It is only a short distance from Ballysadare Bay and the open Atlantic on the west coast, and has always been an astonishment even in a land of astonishing buildings. Fanny Humphreys stayed there on the first occasion in the 1840's, by which time her host, Colonel Edward Joshua Cooper, who sat as a Member of Parliament, and was famed for travel and astronomy, had caused an ornately furnished private observatory to be built at Markree. And by then some of Johnston's alterations had been altered and his interior decorations redecorated in a lavish, gilded Louis XIV style, and huge castellated entrances to the demesne built, the chief one, with turrets and posterns and curtain walls, described as 'one of the most spectacular in Ireland'. Markree had everything; immensity of size and grandeur, a place beside a winding river with rushy water-meadows, and, beyond, heather-covered mountains on all sides. Moved to write her hymn about creation by her surroundings, Fanny must have written it on the terrace by the entrance front of the Castle, looking out to the river and the mountain:

'The rich man in his castle,
    The poor man at his gate,
GOD made them high or lowly,
    And order'd their estate.

The purple-headed mountain,
    The river running by,
The sunset and the morning,
    That brightens up the sky;

The tall trees in the greenwood,
    The meadows for our play,
The rushes by the water,
    To gather every day; –

He gave us eyes to see them,
    And lips that we might tell
How great is God Almighty,
    Who has made all things well.'

Everything changes. By the time she returned to Markree as Mrs. Alexander in the 1870's, Colonel Cooper had had it yet again altered and enlarged by a Scotch architect. It had a new entrance, the dining-room was more immense than ever, a Gothick chapel attached as well as a galleried hall with timbered roof, and the whole massive work was topped by a newly built battlemented and machicolated tower.

The rich man was indeed in his castle, and, perhaps, the poor man at his gate. That stanza of the hymn is no longer sung save by those loyal to the old *Hymns Ancient and Modern,* usually for reasons that, in egalitarian days, such contrasts are somehow unseemly, though it is difficult to see why. The best reason for omitting it has been given to the present writer by the last chatelaine of Markree, whose cherished home it was for forty-five years; that no riches today could keep such a castle intact and usable.

Mrs. Francis Cooper herself now lives in the observatory, the telescope having been sent first to Hong Kong and the surviving parts on to Manila, where the lens remains in use. Her oldest son, and the present owner of Markree, lives comfortably in a small part of the former stables. Her second son has emigrated to Australia. His twin brother had a restaurant not far from the Castle known over a large area for the high quality of its food. The Castle itself is no longer

(top left) a Junoesque portrait of Mrs. Alexander by Kennedy which hangs in Derry Palace; (top right) Archbishop 'Willy' Alexander; (bottom) Markree Castle (Mrs. Francis Cooper)

habitable. Like a great dying Titan it is gradually falling to pieces and one far distant day it will be no more. The stripped interior exudes damp and, in rare bouts of drought, stucco falls in flakes and in powder and dried cement drops from between the masonry. The double staircase of oak and the roof timbers feed insects and fungi. The turrets, ramparts, battlements and machicolations slowly erode in wind and rain but eventually must tumble down. The porte-cochère which has sheltered so many notables, and its flight of stone steps, will inevitably crash to the ground. Even the mullions and transoms of the oriels and the vaulting, keyed together by their own weight, will become skeletal before they, too, crumble and decay. The memorial of Markree, however, in Fanny Humphreys's hymn, will last, we may believe, for ever.

'C.F.H.' as she called herself as an authoress, became 'C.F.A.' in 1850. Her bridegroom was a young clergyman, William Alexander, called Willy by his friends and family. He was a near neighbour, living a few miles to the south-west of Strabane, where he was Rector of the wild and remote parish of Termonamongan, no less than forty-five thousand, four hundred and one acres of undulating heath moors, peat hags, streams and a few meadows and patches of arable land; containing, then, about four thousand inhabitants, the greater part, of course, being Roman Catholics. It is said they had not known each other for very long. Fanny Humphreys was six years older than he and a sketch should be given here of Willie Alexander and his accomplishments.

The Alexanders were also of 'the Gintry' and that part of the family from which Willy came had the strikingly percussionate patronymic of the Alexanders of Boom. This derived from Boom Hall, their home, so named because it was close to the Boom of Derry placed there during the Siege. Willy's father had served in the Army, first as Ensign in his own father's regiment, then as a Lieutenant in the 49th Regiment on active service in the war with America (1812–1815), but, disliking peacetime soldiering, he read for Holy Orders, took a living in the Derry diocese and was a Prebendary of Derry. He and his wife had four daughters and three sons. Both Willy's brothers served in the armed forces, the elder as an Admiral in the Royal Navy, the younger boy being killed in action by frenzied sepoys at Delhi in the Indian Mutiny. After an emotional upheaval, Willy's sister Matilda was married to an old school friend,

Maximilian Dallison, a squire of Kent;* and, again after a surprising tempestuous passage, with no less a person than Otto von Bismarck, his sister, Mary, had married an Irish clergyman. His other two sisters were to marry equally well; one to a landowner in co. Tyrone, the other to the Very Reverend Dr. Andrew Smyly, Dean of Derry, for there is nothing quite like keeping such things in the family.

Some of the Alexanders had been to Tonbridge school in far away Kent and Willy was sent there too. He had then gone on to Oxford where he came under the influence of the Tractarians and went through a very bad time of doubting when Newman 'poped', but he emerged stronger in the end, and with a clear and kindly understanding of, if not a total sympathy with, what Anglo-Catholicism stood for. He took prizes and might have been a don, or, having decided to be ordained, he might have offered himself to the richer Church of England. He felt it his duty to return to Ulster and was a curate in Derry until his appointment in Termonamongan.

There was no doubt in anyone's mind, except, probably, in his, that Willy Alexander was destined for the highest preferment. He was quite guileless, a natural innocent, with a modest opinion of himself and would never have dreamed of such a thing. As it was, he could scarcely believe his good fortune when the talented Miss Fanny Humphreys of Milltown House showed she was not indifferent to him. He knew and admired her poetry. To a limited degree he was a poet himself. But, though they had many friends in common, they were scarcely acquainted. Yet he was sure he was right to ask for her hand. Neither was starry-eyed. Fanny had admirers but, at thirty-two, she was fortunate to have an offer from so attractive a young man as Willy Alexander. She still felt the loss of her friend Harriet, indeed she never did get over it, and the death of Archer Butler had been almost as bitter a blow. Moreover there were long periods when she was given to melancholy; not, fortunately, to the doomed, damned *toska* of the Slavs, but to the fatalistic sadness of so many of the Irish in both castle and cabin which might have had something to do with the climate. She had a certain languor, a lack of that vitality which is the gift of some women. In appearance she was unexceptional. Even her doting Willy wrote after her death; 'Her face had no pretension whatever to regular beauty.' He then listed her special attractions and attributes, but he might have left out that

---

* This excellent man sent his clerical father-in-law the handsome present of a pack of beagles which were joyfully received and loved and regularly hunted through co. Tyrone until, one Lent, old Prebendary Alexander 'gave up beagles', which seems a trifle excessive as a piece of self-denial.

one word 'whatever'. Kennedy, in his painting of her done years afterwards, and printed as an illustration on page 255, shows a certain Junoseque quality. But a contemporary *carte-de-visite* photograph taken by the ubiquitous Messrs. Elliott & Fry, who seem to have photographed absolutely everyone of any consequence, shows a thickening and hardening above her fichu which, with her eyes and general mien, suggests a certain firmness of character. To steal something worth stealing from the riches of American idiom, Fanny might well have been a tough cookie.

Lacking a parsonage, they were lent Berg House, a hunting lodge which lay in the parish, by a relative of Willy's. It cannot have been easy for Fanny to sever herself from the comforts and society of Milltown House and move to the loneliness of wild Termonamongan; but a protracted and very happy honeymoon at Barons Court, by invitation of the Abercorns, was helpful in shoehorning her into a life very different from the one she left. Having accepted Willy at the Altar, she did so with her whole heart; undertaking the duties of a Rector's lady with a stern earnestness. She would walk out in teeming rain and through squelchy bogs and over miry roads to do her duty to the sick and housebound. If it killed her, she would not neglect her duty of regularly going out to meet her husband on his way home from an exceptionally long parochial visit made by foot. Each of them knew what it was to be soaked, quite literally, to the skin; all their wraps and clothes drenched by the teeming Irish rain. Each of them rather dreaded the scarcely visible enemy which in fine weather droned out from the heather, hordes of gnats. But each shared an acceptance of the very best teachings of the original Oxford Movement and had a genuine concern for the wretchedness of some of the parishioners, and each was prepared to do what they could for them whatever their denomination. In 1852 their first child, a boy, was born. With the usual perversity of 'the Gintry', they gave him, besides Robert, the muddling masculine-feminine name of Jocelyn, and then always called him Joe. Their second son* was also given, besides John, his mother's masculine-feminine name of Cecil; but he did not begin life in the loneliness of Termonamongan.

In 1855 Willy was preferred to the parish of Upper Fahan. It was a beautiful place to live, only nine miles from Derry though in co. Donegal; quiet on the shore of Lough Swilly – translated as the Lake

---

* They also had two daughters, Eleanor who remained unmarried, born in 1857, and Dorothea who married in 1893.

of Shadows – and of infinite interest to the Alexanders, who shared a liking for the plants and shells and birds of the waterside as well as admiring the cragginess of mysterious Donegal, disagreeing profoundly with the fourth Earl of Bristol and Bishop of Derry, who described the area as 'presenting nothing curious to engage admiration, and nothing horrid enough to stare at'. It was at last possible for them to receive visitors, and, both loving hospitality, they began to give it freely. Fanny planted a rose garden which thrived and was the delight of them both – later ploughed up by a 'utilitarian' Rector – and made fast friends with the Jones family who lived at Fahan House, on the other side of the lane from the Rectory. Miss Agnes Jones, though a strict Evangelical, became one of Fanny's particular friends. Agnes Jones had enormous vitality and was a strider through life. Fanny, with three little children and less strong than she had been in their wild and lonely first parish, rather envied her friend's energy. When Miss Jones went to Kaiserworth to train as a nurse, the Alexanders gave her every encouragement. They applauded her courage in going to Miss Nightingale to ask for work and her brave decision to accept the advice of the Lady of the Lamp and go to train nurses to look after the inmates of the colossal workhouse in Liverpool. When, after only three years, she died of overwork and typhus, a Liverpool heroine, they arranged for her body to be brought back for burial at Fahan, and Willy composed lines for a memorial plaque for her in his church.

The Alexanders were very content at Fahan. Willy was not overburdened with parochial affairs, and Fanny wrote a good deal of poetry there. The best known hymn of this period, perhaps, was 'The golden gates are lifted up' – a great favourite of Mark Twain, who learnt it by heart and would recite it often, a cigar drooping from the corner of his mouth. The general belief that Willy Alexander would attain great eminence proved to be true. From their comfortable home beside the Lake of Shadows, they moved to Camus-Juxta-Mourne and an ugly barrack of a Rectory set, as is the frequent Irish habit, at least three inconvenient miles from the parish church in Strabane. It was the richest living in the diocese and demanded more from its parson than Fahan had done. Willy gave up his long walks and took to a jaunting car, which made him gain weight, 'a problem which grew with the years', as his daughter and memorialist was to put it. Fanny's pleasure at being so close to her parents at Milltown House was not to last long. Willy was appointed Dean of Emily, which gave him extra work and income but did not force him to move house, and he began to make a considerable reputation as a contributor to newspapers and learned and social periodicals and magazines, and as a preacher – in England quite as much as in Ireland. In 1867, the Queen, at the instigation of her Prime Minister, Lord Derby, through her Lord Lieutenant of Ireland, the Marquis of Abercorn, offered Willy the richest see in Ireland, Derry and Raphoe*.

Willy was forty-three and Fanny forty-nine when they moved to the Palace in Bishop Street, Derry, and into the freehold of what he himself described as 'an opulent prelacy with extensive patronage'. Both became extremely busy, Fanny doing what she could, especially for the poor and sick in the streets beyond the city walls, though she still had not regained her strength and was more often employed looking after the needs of her husband and children and their servants, and their many visitors. She was respected by all, and loved by a large number, though her natural reserve and steely will made some people afraid of her, and she had a numbing shortness with flatterers. One visitor asked her breathlessly: 'Don't you yearn on starlit nights to be up in the Alps, high above the earth, on the line of the eternal snow?' Fanny fixed her with a look. 'No!' she said sharply. Like many reserved people she adored dogs and the Palace seemed full of them. They were all over the drawing-room when she entertained informally, peering short-sightedly at her guests and meeting their needs from a tea urn.

The Bishop frequently had to be away. Sometimes Fanny accompanied him, especially to the houses of friends, but she refrained from going abroad if possible. The spirit of adventure which had made her so much enjoy the voyages by sailing packet to and from Scotland in her childhood and youth had altogether gone. When Willy went to the United States and then to South Africa for the marriage of their daughter Dorothea, it was their daughter Eleanor who accompanied him. Fanny lacked the vitality. She led a regular life, austere, loving her dogs and her family, accepting her duties as a Bishop's wife with as good a grace as she could manage, and still writing verse.

In all, her collection of hymns made a noble contribution to hymnody. Apart from the immortal trio already mentioned, she wrote, besides many others, 'Forsaken once, and thrice denied' for St. Peter's Day, 'Forgive them, O my Father' and 'His are the

---

* One newspaper, commenting on the appointment, noted that the new Bishop many years before had won a prize at Oxford for a contratulatory *Ode to the Earl of Derby* which had concluded: 'He will remember God, and this day, and me.' Indeed Lord Derby had remembered him.

thousand sparkling rills' for Good Friday, 'Jesus calls us! – o'er the tumult' for St. Andrew's Day, and, of great importance to her compatriots, the glorious stirring hymn for St. Patrick's Day, 'I bind unto myself today'. Allegedly a translation from a hymn by St. Patrick himself, the poetry is essentially that of 'C.F.A.'. Part of it runs:

'I bind unto myself to-day
  The power of God to hold and lead,
His eye to watch, his might to stay,
  His ear to hearken to my need.
The wisdom of my God to teach,
  His hand to guide, his shield to ward;
The word of God to give me speech,
  His heavenly host to be my guard.

Christ be with me, Christ within me,
  Christ behind me, Christ before me,
Christ beside me, Christ to win me,
  Christ to comfort and restore me,
Christ beneath me, Christ above me,
  Christ in quiet, Christ in danger,
Christ in hearts of all that love me,
  Christ in mouth of friend and stranger.

I bind unto myself the name,
  The strong name of the Trinity;
By invocation of the same,
  The Three in One, and One in Three,
Of whom all nature hath creation;
  Eternal Father, Spirit, Word:
Praise to the Lord of my salvation,
  Salvation is of Christ the Lord.'

When she came to die in 1895 she did it with all the Victorian sense of occasion; not quite so theatrically as Tennyson, who died on a sofa with a copy of Shakespeare open in his hand and the setting sunbeams shining on his face; but after a lengthy, silent illness, when a sudden change in her condition made the doctors send for the Bishop, who was at a Confirmation in a distant part of the diocese. He came as soon as he could and arrived, trembling and ashen, to find her still alive. As well as he could he prayed with her. She smiled, sighed, and died.

The death of Mrs. Alexander when announced in *The Times* was bracketed with news that the Alexanders' friend Lord Elgin had been appointed Viceroy of India; that thirty thousand, eight hundred and seventy-five paying visitors had entered the Chicago World's Fair where Swaine and Adeney of Piccadilly, then as now excellent leather manufacturers, won a prize for whips; that the Lord

Mayor of London had presided over a special meeting of seventeen temperance mayors; that Madam Albani had entertained the Queen at Balmoral with classical arias concluding with a rendering of 'The Blue Bells of Scotland'; and that an eccentric bride and bridegroom had set off from Rome by balloon to enjoy a honeymoon across the Alps, and plunged to earth outside Turin, killing the bridegroom and seriously injuring his bride and the balloon aeronaut. It all seemed tosh beside the news that the best of all hymn writers had died. Bishop Alexander, soon to be Primate and Archbishop of Armagh, was stricken with grief but consoled by the expressions of the grief of so many besides. Her funeral was the occasion of a display of so much love and affection and respect that he was astonished. He wrote to a close friend that 'our hard northerners' had behaved as if a great soul had left them. 'They packed the streets in thousands,' he wrote, 'hushed and awestruck. The hearse was much laden with hundreds of flowers sent by kind hands. The autumn day was of genial softness. . . . Surely she rests well.'

She lies in a grave, marked by a white cross, on a green hill outside the city wall, a fitting place. And fitting words were said by Bishop Montgomery, who followed Willy Alexander in the see of Derry and Raphoe, when he unveiled a window in the cathedral put there in Fanny's memory:'So Ulster and the Diocese of Derry in particular, claim one of the great hymn writers. It is a unique gift. I am not aware that it can be acquired. I have never heard of anyone who could sit down and say "I will, here and now, write a hymn that will live." Ecclesiastics, statesmen, historians, poets, have their day, and a noble day; then pass, forgotten in great part; but the hymn writer, if taken to the heart of the race, lives through the centuries.'

SOME SOURCES CONSULTED

Unpublished Manuscript material

Memoranda on the Alexander Family by Major Travers King dated 23rd March and 18th November, 1984.

Memoranda on the family of Major John Humphreys, R.M., and on Lady Harriet Howard and her family by Michael Maclagan Esq., F.S.A., Richmond Herald, dated 15th November and 11th December, 1984.

Memorandum of Mrs Leslie Mackay after examining the letters of Francis Lyte and the second Marquis of Salisbury at Hatfield House dated October, 1984.

Memoranda about Markree Castle by Mrs Francis Cooper of Markree dated 20th November, 1984 and 9th June, 1985.

Published works

Ackroyd, Peter: *T. S. Eliot* (London, 1984)

Alexander, C. F. (Ed. &c.): *The Sunday Book of Poetry* (London, 1865)

Alexander, Cecil Frances (Ed. Alexander, William): *Poems* (London, 1896)

Alexander, Eleanor: *Primate Alexander* (London, 1913)

Alexander, Robert: *The Alexander Family of Boom Hall* (pb. privately, Londonderry, n.d.)

Baily, Leslie: *The Gilbert & Sullivan Book* (London, 1952)

Barkley, J. M. (Ed.): *Handbook to the Church Hymnary, Third Edition* (Oxford, 1979)

Barrow, John: *A Tour Round Ireland* (London, 1835)

Battiscombe, Georgina: *John Keble* (London, 1963)

Bell, Alan: *Sydney Smith* (Oxford, 1980)

Boston, Noel T.: *Norwich Note Book of Hymns and Hymn Tunes* (Norwich, 1940)

Boulter, B. C.: *The Anglican Reformers* (London, 1933)

Bowden, Fr. J. E.: *Life and Letters of Frederick William Faber* (2nd. ed. London, 1888)

Briggs, L. C.: *Annotated Hymns Ancient and Modern* (London, 1867)

Brooke, C. W. A.: *Companion to Hymns Ancient and Modern, Old Edition* (London, 1914)

Bull, Josiah: *Memorials of the Rev. W. Bull* (London, 1764)

Burton, Elizabeth: *The Early Victorians at Home* (London, 1972)

Cecil, David: *The Stricken Deer or The Life of Cowper*(New ed. reprinted, 1944)

Cecil, Lady Gwendolen: *Life of Robert, Marquis of Salisbury*, 2 vols. (London, n.d.)

Chadwick, Owen: *The Victorian Church*, 2 vols. (London, 1971–2)

Christ-Janer, A.; Hughes, Charles W.; and Smith, Charles Sprague (Ed.): *American Hymns Old and New Volume One* (New York, 1980)

Colloms Brenda: *Victorian Country Parsons* (London, 1977)

Cowper, Wm.: *A Memoir of the Early Life of W. Cowper* (London, 1816)

Cunnington, C. Willett and Phillis: *Handbook of English Costume in the Nineteenth-century* (London, 1959)

Dearmer, Percy (Compiler): *Songs of Praise Discussed, A Handbook to the best-known hymns and others recently introduced* (London, 1933)

Edwards, David: *Christian England Volume 3* (London, 1984)

Faber, Geoffrey: *Oxford Apostles* (London, 1933)

Fox, Adam: *English Hymns and Hymn Writers* (London, 1947)

Frost, Maurice (Ed.): *Historical Companion to Hymns Ancient and Modern* (London, 1962)

Hacker, Louis M. and Kendrick, B.: *The United States since 1865* (New York, 1949)

Hare, Augustus J. C.: *Shropshire* (London, 1898)

Hare, Augustus J. C.: *The Story of my Life*, 6 vols. (London, 1896–1900)

Hayns, David: *Poet and Parish Priest, Reginald Heber's Life in Malpas and Hodnet* (pb. privately; Malpas, 1983)

Heber, Amelia: *Some Account of the Life, &c. Reginald Heber, D.D., Lord Bishop of Calcutta*, 2 vols. (London, 1830)

Heber, Reginald: *The Poetical Works of Reginald Heber, D.D. Lord Bishop of Calcutta with steel portrait and illustrations and a Life* in Warne's Lansdowne Poets (London, n.d.)

Hennell, M.: *John Venn and the Clapham Sect* (London, 1958)

Hinde, Thomas: *A Field Guide to the English Country Parson* (London, 1984)

Holland, John and Everett, James: *The Life of James Montgomery*, 7 vols. (London, 1854–6)

Hooper, Patricia: *William Whiting* (Southampton, 1978)

How, P. D.: *Bishop Walsham How* (London, 1898)

Housman, H.: *John Ellerton* (London, 1896)

Howe, M. A. De Wolfe (Ed.): *New Letters of James Russell Howe* (New York, 1932)

Hughes, Charles W. (Ed.): *American Hymns Old and New, Volume Two* (New York, 1980)

Julian, John: *Dictionary of Hymnology* (Rev. ed. London, 1925)

Johnson, Samuel: *Lives of the Poets* (London)

Keble, John: *The Christian Year* (1st Ed. London, 1826)

Lightwood, James T.: *Hymn-tunes and their Story* (London, 1905)

Longford, Elizabeth (Countess of Longford): *Eminent Victorian Women* (London, 1981)

Lough, A. G.: *John Mason Neale* (London, 1983)

Lough, Arthur G.: *John Mason Neale – Priest Extraordinary* (Newton Abbot, Devon, 1975)

Lovell, E. W.: *A Green Hill Far Away* (Dublin & London, 1970)

Lowell, James Russell: *The Complete Poetical Works* Authorised copyright edition (London, n.d.)

Mable, Norman: *Popular Hymns and their Writers* (2nd Ed. Rochester, Kent, 1951)

Magan, W.: *Umma-More* (Salisbury, 1983)

Martin, Bernard: *Life of John Newton* (London, 1950)

Martin, Hugh (Ed.): *A Companion to the Baptists' Hymn Book* (London, 1953)

Moorson, R. M.: *Historical Companion to Hymns Ancient and Modern* (London, 1889)

Martineau, Harriet: *Autobiography* 2 vols. (London, 1983)

Milford, H. S. (Ed.): *The Complete Poetical Works of William Cowper* The Oxford Edition (London, 1905)

Moore, Kathrine: *Victorian Lives* (London, 1974)

Nelle, Wilhelm: *Schlüssel zum Evangelischen Gesangbuch für Rheinland und Westfalen* (1924)

Newton, John: *An Authentic Narrative of some. . . . Particulars in the Life of. . . .* (1st Ed. London, 1764)

Northcott, William Cecil: *Hymns in Christian Worship; the use of Hymns in the Life of the Church* (London, 1964)

Norton, C. E. (Ed.): *Letters of James Russell Lowell* 2 vols. (New

York, 1894)

Parry, K. L. (Ed.): *Companion to Congregational Praise* (London, 1953)

Parry, D. W. (Compiler): *Hymns and Tunes Indexed* (Croydon, 1980)

Phillips, Charles Stanley: *Hymnody, Past and Present* (London, 1937)

Rear, Michael: *John Henry Newman* (London, 1983)

Richards, L. E. & Elliott, M. H.: *Julia Ward Howe* 2 vols. (New York, 1915)

Routley, Erik: *I'll Praise my Maker* (London, 1952)

Routley, Erik: *Hymns and Human Life* (London, 1952)

Routley, Erik: *Hymns and The Faith* (London, 1955)

Row, W. (Ed.): *The Works of A. Toplady, with Memoir* (2nd Ed. London, 1825)

Rowell, Geoffrey: *John Keble* (London, 1983)

Shaen, Margaret, J.: *Memorial of Two Sisters, Susanna and Catherine Winkworth* (London, 1908)

Southey, Robert Ed.: *The Works of William Cowper with a Memoir* 15 vols. (London, 1834–7)

St. Cyr's Church, Stinchcombe: A Brief History (privately printed; no location, n.d.)

Stevenson, G. J.: *The Methodist Hymn-Book, illustrated with Biography, Incident and Anecdote* (London, 1883)

Telford, John: *The Methodist Hymn-Book Illustrated in History and Experience* (6th Ed. London, 1952)

Walton, Isaac: *The Life of Mr George Herbert* (1st Ed. London, 1670)

Watkin, John: *A Biographical Dictionary of the Living Authors of Great Britain and Ireland* (London, 1816)

Whale, John: *One Church, One Lord* (London, 1979)

White, T. E.: *The Age of Scandal* (London, 1950)

Whiting, William: *Edgar Thorpe or The Warfare of Life* (Winchester, 1867)

Whiting, William: *Rural Thoughts and Scenes* (Winchester, 1851)

Whittier, J. G.: *The Panorama and other Poems* (New York, 1856)

Whittier, J. G.: *Snow-bound* (New York, 1866)

Wilks, Brian: *The Brontës* (London, 1975)

Williams, Isaac (Ed. Prevost, Ven. Sir George): *Autobiography* (London, 1892)

Wilson, Edmund: *Patriotic Gore* (New York, 1962)

Winkworth, Catherine: *Lyra Germanica; Hymns for the Sundays and Chief Festivals of the Church's Year* New Ed. (London, 1860)

Winkworth, Susanna (Ed.): *Letters and Memorials of Catherine Winkworth* (London, 1883)

Winkworth, Catherine (Trs.): *Lyra Germanica: Second Series, The Christian Life* New Edition with Illustrations (London, 1867)
Winkworth, Catherine (Trs.): *The Chorale Book for England* (London, 1862)

Hymnals
American Hymns Old and New 2 vols. (New York, 1980)
Anglican Hymn Book (London, 1966)
Congregational Praise (London, 1951)
Hymns Ancient and Modern Standard Edition (London, 1916)
Hymns Ancient and Modern New Standard Edition (London, 1983)
Hymns Ancient and Modern Revised (London, 1950)
Olney Hymns (1st Ed. London, 1779)
Hymns for Today's Church (London, 1982)
100 Hymns for Today; a supplement to Hymns Ancient and Modern (14th impression, London, 1979)
The Baptist Hymn Book (London, 1962)
The BBC Hymn Book (London, 1951)
The Church Hymnary, Third Edition (London, 1973)
The English Hymnal 21st impression of a new Edition (London, 1983)
The Methodist Hymn-Book (London, revised text to 1954)
The Oxford Book of Carols Twelfth Impression (Oxford, 1943)
The Redemption Hymnal (London, 1955)
The Westminster Hymnal (London, 1966)
Fellowship Hymn Book (London, 1926)

Standard Reference Books
American Dictionary of Biography
Bartholomew's Survey Gazeteer of the British Isles
Burke's Landed Gentry 18th Ed. in 2 vols. (London, 1965)
Burke's Peerage, Baronetage and Knightage 105th Ed. (London, 1970)
Burke's Irish Family Records (London, 1976)
Burke's Guide to Country Houses, vol. 1. Ireland (London, 1978)
Crockford's Clerical Directory
Dictionary of National Biography
Encyclopaedia Britannica
Grove's Dictionary of Music and Musicians
Murray's Handbook for Travellers in Ireland (London, 1912)
The Concise Cambridge History of English Literature (Cambridge, 1944)

Newspapers & periodicals

Athenaeum
Gentlemen's Magazine
Irish Times
Londonderry Sentinel
Quarterly Review
St. Margaret's Magazine (pb. in East Grinstead from July, 1887)
Sussex Advertiser
Sussex Express
The Observer
The Sunday Times
The Times

INDEX OF HYMNS

INDEX